Ancestors

The Origins of the People and Countries of Europe

STAFFORDSHIRE LIBRARIES, ARTS AND ARCHIVES
Please return or renew by last date shown

PERTON LIBRARY			
10. DEC			
01. FEB 97			
19. DEC 98			
19. JAN 99			
06. FEB 99			
17. APR 99			

572.94

BERG, M.

Ancestors

18.1.95

If not required by other readers this item may be renewed, in person, by post or by telephone. Please quote details opposite and date due for return, If issued by computer, the numbers on the barcode label on your ticket and on each item, together with date of return are required.

2/1/003/89   100% recycled paper.

STAFFORDSHIRE LIBRARIES

3 8014 00765 7841

Ancestors

The Origins of the People and Countries of Europe

Martin Berg
and
Miles Litvinoff

The Authors
Martin Berg is a writer and lecturer who has written widely on European peoples and their past. He has travelled in Europe, the Middle East and North Africa over thirty years, and carried out research in Germany, Italy and France. He has also lectured in a number of European countries and in the United States of America. His main interests are the early peoples of Europe, their culture and art. A northcountryman, he now lives in the West Country, from where he makes forays into Europe for its museums and into the Mediterranean for its sun.

Miles Litvinoff, the author of the section 'The Beginnings of Europe', is a freelance writer and editor specializing in historical and environmental subjects. He is an Open University tutor.

Index by Frank T Dunn
Maps by Edward Ripley

Copyright © 1992
by Eurobook Limited
All rights reserved throughout the world
No part of this publication may be reproduced, stored in a retrieval system or transmitted by any means, electronic, mechanical, photocopying, recording or otherwise without the prior written permission of Eurobook Limited

ISBN 0 85654 661 5

Printed in Portugal

Contents

9 Foreword
10 Map: The Countries of Europe

The Beginnings of Europe

14 The Time Scale

16 The Continent of Europe
The land
The changing climate
Soils and vegetation

19 The Old Stone Age
The first Europeans
The Neanderthals
Hunter-gatherers of the Ice Age
Cro-Magnon culture

22 The Later Stone Age
The end of the Ice Age
Communities of the Middle Stone Age
From foraging to farming
Village life in the New Stone Age

26 The Bronze Age
Battle axes and beakers
Warrior society
Agriculture and trade in the Bronze Age
Early Mediterranean civilization

30 The Iron Age
Iron-workers and iron warriors
The Greek city-states
Alexander's Macedonian empire
The Iron Age north of the Alps
Celtic tribal kingdoms

34 The Roman Empire
Rome's beginnings
Political troubles
The Roman achievement
Byzantium and the fall of Rome

37 The Great Migrations
The northern barbarians
The Huns
Migrants from the east
The barbarian kingdoms

40 A Time of Change

41 Languages and Races of Europe
Europe's language families
European races

The People of Europe

48 Alamanni	82 Gauls	122 Sabines
49 Alans	84 Gepids	123 Samnites
50 Angles	85 Germans	123 Sarmatians
51 Arabs	88 Goths	124 Saxons
53 Avars	91 Greeks	127 Scotti
54 Balts	95 Gypsies	128 Scythians
55 Basques	97 Huns	129 Serbs
56 Bavarians	98 Iberians	130 Sicels
57 Belgae	100 Illyrians	130 Slavs
58 Bretons	101 Irish	133 Slovaks
59 Britons	102 Jews	134 Slovenes
60 Bulgars	104 Jutes	134 Suevi
62 Burgundians	105 Lapps	135 Swedes
63 Celts	106 Ligurians	137 Thracians
67 Croats	106 Lombards	138 Thuringians
68 Czechs	108 Magyars	138 Turks
70 Dacians	109 Minoans	140 Ukrainians
71 Danes	111 Mongols	141 Vandals
73 Etruscans	112 Normans	142 Vikings
76 Finns	113 Phoenicians	146 Vlachs
77 Franks	115 Picts	146 Welsh
81 Frisians	116 Romans	

The Countries of Europe

148 The Foundations of Modern Europe

152 Albania	245 Luxembourg
156 Austria	248 Norway
161 The Baltic States:	253 Poland
162 Estonia	257 Portugal
164 Latvia	261 Romania
165 Lithuania	266 Russia
168 Belgium	273 Spain
173 Bulgaria	279 Sweden
178 Czechoslovakia	284 Switzerland
183 Denmark	288 Ukraine
188 Finland	292 The United Kingdom
192 France	302 Yugoslavia
202 Germany	307 Europe's Smallest States
211 Greece	Andorra
218 Holland	Liechtenstein
	Monaco
223 Hungary	San Marino
227 Iceland	The Vatican City
231 Ireland	309 The European Community
237 Italy	311 Index

Foreword

The peoples of Europe are a fascinating mixture. Complicated by a long history of invasions, migrations, cultural contact and the formation of states, Europeans of every nation have today much in common, but their physical and cultural differences are still clearly evident to the traveller crossing modern frontiers. What are the origins of these differences? How ancient are they and what do they mean? Who, after all, were the early peoples of Europe and how are they related to the Europeans of today? How do they come to be where they are and how have their countries evolved? These are the questions which this book addresses, relying on a mass of information drawn from history and archaeology.

The answers are not always clear-cut. Europe has been extremely fertile in tribes and peoples who left their mark on the continent and then disappeared, merging with others or being dispersed and leaving little evidence of their passing. Some peoples originated as tribes, grew in importance and emerged as nations commanding a distinct territory. This was true, for example, of the Visigoths. But most present-day European peoples have their origins in the mediaeval period, or even later. There are survivals from a remote past, such as the Basques, but they are rare.

We are on safer ground with the formation of states, for which there is much historical evidence. Many European states are of relatively recent creation, the years after 1815 and 1918 being very important here. Others are of much greater antiquity and have long been associated with individual peoples. But there can be a feeling of nationality before a nation is born, as was the case with Italy before the mid nineteenth century. Many states, however, owe their creation to political forces, not to national sentiment. After 1918, the map of central and eastern Europe was substantially redrawn and several new countries emerged, some, including Yugoslavia, with the seeds of dissolution sown at their birth. Europe again stands at the beginning of a time of great change, which will witness the demise of some states, the birth of others and the association of powers old and new in a political structure which has never before existed in the continent. This book is offered in the hope that it will explain how Europe has arrived at where it is today.

The continent of Europe

Europe stretches from Iceland in the west to the Ural mountains in the east and from the Arctic to the Mediterranean. In the north, it joins Asia in a continuous landmass. In the south, the traditional division between the continents is the Bosporus, the narrow stretch of water leading from the Aegean to the Black Sea.

People have lived in Europe for more than forty thousand years; the division of peoples into nations is much more recent. Over the last two thousand years, European empires have flourished and declined, redrawing many national boundaries by force or persuasion. Rarely a peaceful continent, in this century Europe was torn apart by two major wars which changed the lives of millions of Europeans for ever. Today, a new movement is gaining strength as peoples and countries reclaim their identities and forge new links between east and west. This map shows the nation states of Europe in the last decade of the twentieth century: a future Europe may look very different.

11

Key to figures on map
1 Bosnia-Hercegovina
2 Croatia
3 Macedonia
4 Montenegro
5 Serbia
6 Slovenia
7 Moldova

The Beginnings of Europe

How the once uninhabited lands of Europe became today's nation-states is a story of human tenacity, ingenuity, co-operation and skill, and also of less laudable qualities such as aggression and greed. The long process began in the Stone Age when early humans crossed into the continent from Africa. After many thousands of years as hunter-gatherers they learned agriculture and settled in permanent communities. When metal-working became widespread for the first time Europe entered the Bronze Age.

Human life expectancy was about thirty years for the whole prehistoric period, but rising birth rates and major migrations swelled the population. The first European towns were built by the Greeks, and it was during their civilization that iron replaced bronze as the key metal for tools and weapons. As the Iron Age continued, Greece declined, and Rome emerged to become probably the greatest-ever European power. Further migrations from the north and east coincided with the disintegration of the classical world. But out of that collapse a new mediaeval European society was to arise.

The Time Scale

A hundred million years ago Europe did not exist separately but was part of the huge Laurasian landmass that became North America and Eurasia. By 50 million years ago continental drift had resulted in something like the present geographical shape of Europe. Much more recently, about half a million years ago, humans first set foot in Europe. The last Ice Age ended in about 10,000 BC.

Human development in the prehistoric and early historic period was not uniform for the whole of Europe. The south and east were generally more advanced than the north and west, and all dates are very approximate. The main stages, and some of their important features, were:

Old Stone Age (Palaeolithic): In Europe from about 500,000 to 10,000 BC. First an early form of man called *Homo erectus*, then more modern forms, including Neanderthalers. Truly modern humans, people like us, seem to have arrived in Europe about 40,000 years ago. All these different people were hunters and gatherers and used stone tools. However, modern humans had more specialized forms of stone tools as well as others made of bone and antler. They produced the first art, including figurines and cave painting. Europe's population 50,000–120,000.

Middle Stone Age (Mesolithic): From 10,000 to 6000 BC (south-east), 4000 BC (north-east). The end of the last Ice Age, about 10,000 BC brought great changes to the hunter-gatherer way of life. Migrating reindeer herds moved northwards and forest gradually covered the land, replacing the tundra and making it harder to find food because the rich herds had gone. In coastal areas people relied heavily on fish and shellfish. From about 6000–4000 BC agricultural techniques filtered into Europe from the south-east, with crop husbandry and pottery. Europe's population 500,000.

New Stone Age (Neolithic): From 6000 to 3000 BC. Farming: cereal crops and livestock; villages; clear-felling of forests with stone axes; pottery, leather-work and weaving; trade. Europe's population 2 million at start of agricultural revolution, 10 million by end.

Bronze Age: From 2500 to 1000 BC. Bronze tools and weapons; migrations of warlike peoples; warrior chiefs and elaborate burials; the wheel, wagons and carts; the horse and chariot; trade expands; bronze, gold, silver and amber ornaments; first civilizations in Mediterranean. Europe's population 25 million.

Iron Age: From 1000 BC. Iron tools and weapons; horses now widespread; more migrations; trade increases; first coinage; towns; literacy spreads; Macedonian and Roman empires. Europe's population reaches 50 million.

The Migration period: AD 200 to 600. As the western empire of Rome came to an end, a period of change began and major migrations of peoples took place throughout Europe. By the start of the Middle Ages (usually dated from the 5th century) Europe's population had reached about 80 million.

> It is very easy to see prehistory as a story of progress from ignorance to enlightenment and to berate our ancestors for not 'developing' more quickly. A rather different perspective is to suggest that people were well adapted to their environments for thousands of years and change occurred when they had to overcome problems, whether in their environment or their relations with one another.

The Continent of Europe

The first people to identify Europe as a geographical entity were the ancient Greeks. We define the continent as the mainland and islands bounded by the Atlantic and Arctic Oceans, the Mediterranean Sea and the Ural mountains and Ural river. Iceland, Ireland, Britain, Corsica, Sardinia, Sicily and Crete are included; Cyprus, Turkey and Greenland usually are not. Covering about 4.1 million square miles (10.6 million square kilometres), Europe is the second smallest continent.

Europe has offered many advantages to its inhabitants. The climate over much of the continent is generally even. The landscape is separated into many small regions by human-scale natural barriers, which allowed groups of people to establish themselves securely. Natural resources are plentiful in many parts of the continent. And Europe was accessible from Africa, the Middle East and Asia, with few obstacles to impede migration, cultural contact or trade.

The Land. The large low-lying north European plain extends from western France across to northern Russia, meeting there the Russian plain that descends from Finland to the Caucasus. With fertile soils and crossed by navigable rivers, these northern and central lowlands have long been important for human settlement. Western Europe has the additional advantage of a lengthy coastline with good access to the sea and food-providing continental shelves and estuaries. The central European uplands are well watered by rivers and were once heavily forested.

Several large mountain ranges span the south of the continent: the Pyrenees, Alps, Apennines, Carpathians and Caucasus, of which the Alps are the highest and most rugged. Among Europe's minor mountains are the Cantabrians of northern Spain, the Dinaric and Pindus ranges of Yugoslavia and Greece and the Balkan and Rhodope mountains of Bulgaria. All are crossed by accessible passes. The continent's only other major range is the Kjolen mountains of north-west Scandinavia.

Southern Europe has only small pockets of low-lying valleys and coastal plains. Some of these areas, however—in northern Italy, southern Yugoslavia, northern Greece and the Hungarian and Wallachian plains—were prime locations of early settlement.

Of Europe's great river systems, the Danube, Dniester, Dnieper, Don and

Volga of the south-east flow into the Black and Caspian Seas. The course of the major northern rivers—the Vistula, Oder, Elbe, Rhine and Seine—runs northwards to the Baltic and North Seas and the English Channel. Only two major European rivers flow into the Mediterranean Sea: the Rhône and the Ebro. Rising in the southern Alps, the Po ends in the Adriatic Sea.

> **Finding out about the past.** The analysis of rocks, soils and sediments provides much of our knowledge about the Earth's history. For human prehistory, before writing developed, archaeologists gather and piece together the evidence: human and animal remains, tools and artefacts, food debris and other refuse. The chronology of finds is worked out using carbon dating and dendrochronology—a comparison of tree ring growth that enables us to date events in the distant past. Geographical and site locations of finds are analysed and compared. Not all the evidence is clear cut, however, and many unanswered questions remain.

The Changing Climate. Over the past two and a half million years there have been dramatic changes of climate. Extremely cold periods known as Ice Ages or glacials, when much of north-west Europe was covered by vast sheets of ice, have alternated with relatively warm periods or interglacials, when the climate was similar, sometimes warmer than it is today. It is thought that there may have been as many as fifty glacial phases but scientists do not know precisely when these occurred or for how long each one lasted. The last major glacial phase reached its maximum extent around 18,000 BC, and was followed by a relatively short phase, lasting for a thousand years, from 11,000 to 10,000 BC.

The sea level was much lower during the Ice Ages, possibly as much as 125 metres lower than it is today. Britain was linked to the mainland, Scandinavia to Denmark and the Balkans to Asia Minor.

After the Ice Age, sea levels rose to cut off Britain and Scandinavia from the continent, and the Balkans from Turkey. Much of Scandinavia and north-west Russia enjoyed a milder climate than today, and vegetation zones reached further north. After this date the climate and soils of Mediterranean Europe are thought to have become gradually more arid.

Today, the climate of Europe is mainly temperate: few areas are so cold or so hot and dry as to be inhospitable to human occupation. Yet, with the continent's northern- and southernmost points thousands of miles apart, there are regions of more extreme climate: northern Scandinavia and north Russia, central Spain and the arid Caucasian steppes.

The continent has four distinct climate zones. Warmed by the Gulf Stream, the western oceanic region has plentiful rainfall, mild winters and cool summers. In the southern Mediterranean zone, summers are hot and dry and winters mild and wet, drier and colder in the east. Northern Scandinavia and northern Russia have a sub-arctic climate of long cold winters and short cool summers; winters are increasingly bitter and summers drier in the east. Finally, the central and eastern continental zones have a more extreme climate. West of the Carpathians, rainfall and summer weather are similar to those in western Europe, but winters are colder, with more snow; east of these mountains, there is much less rainfall, and summers are hot and arid.

Soils and Vegetation. Europe's soils and vegetation are largely determined by climate. Soils are very poor in the far northern tundra, where little but mosses, lichens and bushes can grow. It is virtually impossible to cultivate crops here and this region long proved hostile to all but a few hardy nomads and settlers. To the south, soils improve slightly in the northern conifer belt. Further south still, the plains and lowlands of north-central Europe have rich soils. Their mixed broadleaf and conifer forests once extended from Britain to Russia, but only fragments remain. With its long warm growing season, this fertile land was especially attractive to early farming peoples.

In the south grow dry-tolerant deep-rooted trees and scattered scrub. This was the earliest zone of human colonization in Europe, untouched by the bitter cold of the Ice Ages. Mediterranean farming was traditionally based on vegetables, hardy native trees such as the olive and vine, wheat, sheep and goats. Lack of year-round pasture tended to rule out cattle. Deforestation and intensive farming of the steep hillsides at an early date eroded and impoverished the soils.

East of the Carpathians, the dry grasslands lead eastwards to semi-desert, where settlement was difficult and mobility paramount. Hence the importance of the steppe horse.

The Old Stone Age: 500,000 to 10,000 BC

The First Europeans. The first of our ancient ancestors to leave Africa was *Homo erectus*, who had evolved perhaps a million years BC and arrived in Europe between 800,000 and 500,000 years ago. As populations grew, *Homo erectus* groups gradually moved further from their homelands, colonizing Europe and Asia, from Germany in the north-west to Indonesia in the south-west.

Homo erectus probably colonized Europe during one of the warmer 'interglacials' that separated the bitter Ice Ages. During the coldest periods, these early people would have stayed in the milder Mediterranean zone, moving northward again when the glaciers melted and the forests and animals spread north. This large-jawed, thick-skulled species used fire, made stone tools and ate meat. They were not full-fledged hunters, but pursued their prey into swamps, corrals or pits of pointed stakes, or over cliffs, and then hacked the animals to death.

The Neanderthals. Between about 80,000 and 60,000 BC a more advanced species, *Homo neanderthalis*, emerged in Europe and throughout the Old World. Few in number, perhaps less than 50,000 in all Europe, the Neanderthals had fire and a range of stone tools—in Europe, mainly flint. Their meat came from reindeer, bison and other large mammals, whose skins they wore as cloaks and blankets. It used to be thought that Neanderthals were generally extremely brutish looking. It is now clear from more recent finds that they were a very varied physical type. Those living in western Europe in the cold of the Ice Ages seem to have adapted physically to their environment by developing the heavy skull and skeleton we now associate with them. Their brains were if anything larger than ours and they must have communicated with gestures and a wide range of vocal sounds.

> **Fire.** Early humans observed how lightning set dry grasslands and woodlands alight, and accidentally discovered how to make fire when they struck flints together to make tools. They learned to use fire to drive off predators, to keep warm, to harden wooden spears and to cook meat. In later times people used fire to clear ground and to release soil nutrients for farming.

Human life was becoming more complex. The Neanderthals were probably the first to bury their dead, and they practised hunting rites or worship, as well as ritual cannibalism. They may have been socially advanced enough to look after incapacitated group members and orphans. It is unlikely that they were our direct ancestors, however. By about 40,000 BC the species had disappeared—but a new kind of human had already made its appearance.

Hunter-gatherers of the Ice Age. *Homo sapiens* arrived in Europe about 40,000 years ago. Like the first hominids, this large-brained species evolved in Africa, migrating through the Middle East and the Caucasus. How *Homo sapiens* replaced *Homo neanderthalis* is unknown. Genocide was once thought likely but it is now considered more probable that the Neanderthals died out in the extreme cold, perhaps as the better-organized newcomers took control of food sources or the less hostile territory. *Homo sapiens* looked relatively similar to modern humans and is often called Cro-Magnon man after a site in south-west France where the species was first identified.

Homo sapiens lived in large bands, extended families or tribes of about fifty individuals. People used increasingly sophisticated tools—now of bone and antler as well as of stone—and began to hunt animals successfully with spears and bows and arrows. Some groups depended on just one species for meat and hides, especially the reindeer, and followed the migrating herds.

The hunt was undertaken mainly by males, but females also had important occupations: food gathering, preparing healing herbs, cooking,

---

Tribes. The earliest tribes were little more than self-reliant extended families, perhaps with a leader. A minimum number of about fifty people must have been needed to ensure genetic diversity and healthy offspring. As early Stone Age tribes grew in size they subdivided. Once farming began in the later Stone Age, tribes grew larger and claimed possession of land. Chiefs' authority increased. By Roman times many European tribes had grown to the size of small nations of 100,000 members or more, made up of many separate smaller clans.

child care, making tools, clothes and utensils and building shelters.
   Based on comparisons with more recent hunter-gatherers, it has been estimated that population densities may have been as low as three individuals per 100 square miles (260 square kilometres). This would suggest a total European population of perhaps 120,000. Human groups were therefore extremely isolated.
   With insufficient resources all year round within range of any one site, settlements were temporary. People owned only as many possessions as they could take with them. As populations grew, groups split off from the main tribe and went into new areas.
Cro-Magnon culture. Social organization and customs continued to develop. The Cro-Magnon people worshipped common ancestors and had taboos against incest. They often buried their dead with the limbs folded or tied, as if fearing the corpses would rise again. Grave goods were placed in tombs—food, tools and crude artistic ornaments. By about 30,000 BC they were using engraving implements to decorate antler and bone—apparently for artistic rather than purely practical reasons and many clay figurines depicting mammoths and female fertility figures have been found. People used flint, iron ochre, the volcanic glass obsidian and marble and collected seashells and animal teeth as ornaments. The great cave paintings of Lascaux in France and Altamira in Spain have been dated to the late Cro-Magnon period, 15,000–10,000 BC. These show large beasts of the hunt such as the bison, boar and wild horse. The paintings probably had ritual significance—to promote good hunting or animal fertility, or for the initiation of hunters. Later cave artists included human figures.

The origins of art. What made people first decorate their implements and cave walls and try to make pictures of the physical world? The artistic impulse may have been celebratory, religious or a combination of the two but the increasing complexity of their artistry shows that people had time to use beyond supplying the needs of mere survival and were also developing a peculiarly human spiritual awareness.

The Later Stone Age: 10,000 to 3000 BC

The End of the Ice Age. Between about 12,000 and 8000 BC the ice sheets that had covered northern Europe melted, and sea levels rose. Grasslands and forests returned. The mammoth, mastodon and woolly rhinoceros were extinct, but the reindeer and bison survived. The Mesolithic period or Middle Stone Age had begun.

Europe's inhabitants continued to live by hunting and gathering but now had an abundance of temperate woodland species: deer, elk, wild cattle, wild pigs, birds, berries, nuts and fruits. They lived in more settled, though not yet permanent, communities. People kept to the same seasonal hunting grounds and had regular stopping places, following migrating herds of reindeer or steppe ass. This was the beginning of the nomadic way of life of the pastoralist.

Fish and shellfish were plentiful in the estuaries, lakes and rivers and along the coasts. Large mounds of shells, the refuse from eating shellfish, are found extensively on the coast of western Europe during this period and probably indicate permanent or semi-permanent occupation.

The population grew. Using the northern Amerindians as a rough guide, there may have been twelve people per 100 square miles (260 square kilometres). This would mean a population of about 10,000 in Britain at this time and 500,000 throughout Europe.

Communities of the Middle Stone Age. People lived in rock caves, animal-hide tents and thatched brushwood huts. Post-holes at many sites indicate circular and horseshoe-shaped shelters. With larger tribal communities, perhaps now numbering several hundred people, the chief wielded more formal authority; but at the same time a simple form of democracy probably emerged based on collective decision-making among

> **Nomads.** Not all wandering peoples are nomads. The nomadic way of life is that followed by pastoralists: people who raise sheep, goats, cattle, horses or reindeer and move with the animals on regular migrations, often between summer and winter pasture. Nomadism began when people first followed the movements of wild herds and flocks, and it developed as animals were domesticated.

the elders. Contacts of kinship and marriage may have kept different communities in touch with each other, but by modern standards they were still small and isolated.

Stone-working developed. Small flints, ground and polished for sharpness, were used to make axes, arrows, spears, harpoons and knives. Stones and shells were worked for jewellery. Grinding stones (for sharpening stone blades), amber, flints and other commodities were bartered, sometimes over long distances. Commerce went by boat, on foot and by sledge and ski.

People exploited a wide range of food plants. The dog was domesticated as a hunting partner relatively early. In northern Europe people followed reindeer herds, hunting them for food, for their hides, bones and antlers. Areas of forest were often burnt to produce grazing for animals. Some hunter-gatherer groups adopted elements of the agricultural way of life in advance of the appearance of a full agricultural economy.

From foraging to farming. Full-scale farming, based on cultivating cereals and breeding animals, began in the Middle East (and also simultaneously in Asia), where the main crops grown were wheat, barley, rye and oats. The first livestock raised (for meat and skins) were goats and sheep. The omnivorous goat was also useful for clearing ground and wild pigs were tamed. Next came the breeding of cattle.

Cereal cultivation and domesticated animals came to Europe during the New Stone Age (between 6000 and 3000 BC). Soils farmed without crop rotation rapidly become exhausted and this, together with the growing population, meant that agricultural communities constantly cleared new ground to farm. As livestock numbers increased new grazing land had to

The first population explosion? With the arrival of agriculture in Europe, human numbers rose rapidly. Far more people could be fed in a single area than by hunting and gathering. But while much more food was available, its variety was restricted compared with the previously large range of animal and plant foods. So deficiency diseases appeared, and there were times of starvation when the population outstripped the food supply. As farming and livestock raising spread, Europe's population rose from perhaps 2 million to nearer 10 million inhabitants.

be found and people moved with their animals into new areas. Farming reached the Balkans in about 6000 BC and spread to northern Europe along the great river valleys, advancing at about half a mile a year. There were cultivators beside the Danube in about 5000 BC and along the Seine a thousand years later. Farming was also carried westwards across the Mediterranean, then north along the Atlantic coast, as well as slowly into Russia, beyond the Black Sea.

It is not clear who these migrating farmers were. They may have been the first wave of Indo-Europeans. No-one knows exactly who the Indo-Europeans were or when they first appeared in Europe but it is thought that they came from western Asia. A language in the same family as most European languages was spoken in Anatolia and Syria until about 1200 BC.

Although settled farming was probably adopted by some hunter-gatherers in their own lands when they saw the newcomers at work, there must have been tensions between the farmers and those who continued to

The wheel. Before the wheel, heavy loads were rolled laboriously over logs. After learning to thin the logs in the middle, producing something like a pair of wheels joined by an axle, people in Mesopotamia and later in Europe began to make separate wheels and axles. These were at first cross-sections of tree trunks, then wooden sections tied together, lastly spoked wheels. Wheeled vehicles made the shifting of materials and goods infinitely easier. Long-distance folk-migrations, involving whole tribes and their belongings, became possible, and the increase in mobility transformed Europe.

Boats and ships. Middle Stone Age people were the first to make dugout canoes from tree trunks, paddling across the narrow seas to colonize Europe's coastal islands and to trade with each other. Smaller hide-covered boats like coracles were used on rivers. Larger sea-going rowing ships made of wooden planks stitched together, some perhaps with sails, were used for trade and travel by Bronze Age Beaker people, Greeks, Danes and others. Navigation was unreliable, so shipping hugged the coasts. Rome fought Carthage at sea in the second century BC with large sail-ships rowed by perhaps fifty oarsmen. Viking seafarers later built keeled, large-sailed long-ships.

live as hunter-gatherers. The two communities interbred, however, and the more numerous farmers gradually absorbed most of the older population.

There were significant regional variations in farming. In southern Europe, people grew cereals during the mild winters and harvested them in spring. They raised sheep, goats and pigs on the poor dry soils. Further north, grains were grown during summer and harvested in autumn; cattle did well in the moister climate. Rye was hardy enough to withstand the harsher conditions in north-east Europe and became important there. In Scandinavia and the far north, agriculture was possible only during milder periods. Few crops were grown on the south-eastern steppes, but livestock were raised there. By about 3000 BC a light plough was in use in some areas, making it easier to till the soil.

Progress was in any case uneven and incomplete, especially in more difficult terrain. Vast tracts of forest and wilderness remained, where people resisted the new way of life. Many northern nomads still relied on the reindeer herds.

Village life in the New Stone Age. Europe's first permanent agricultural settlements appeared in the Balkans. People now knew that cereals could be stored from harvest to harvest, so communities could stay in one place from year to year.

These early villages consisted of scattered rectangular one-roomed houses with gabled roofs. Built of wattle and mud on a wooden framework, and containing simple wooden furniture, each housed a family. Fifty to sixty houses per village (indicating a population of two to three hundred) was an average number. Farming people further north built timber long-houses in which extended family groups lived alongside animals and food stores in winter.

Europe transformed. The introduction of agriculture from the Near East transformed Europe, leading to more settled communities, clearance of large areas of forest and scrub and the development of mixed farming. The new-ways of life it brought rank as a true revolution in human society and Man's control of the environment.

People made and owned more goods than before, especially pottery. Cattle raids and other attacks must have been made by less settled, more nomadic groups and, not surprisingly, villages were often surrounded by protective ditches and earth banks or stone walls. Aerial photographs taken in western Europe show the outline of many such enclosures.

Ritual was important to New Stone Age communities. Tribes had rites and ceremonies intended to ensure a successful harvest or healthy livestock. Forms of burial became more varied, including cremation. Western Europeans began to build passage graves and stone burial chambers and circles, often with enormous effort and labour. The oldest of these predate Egypt's pyramids and the use of the wheel.

The Bronze Age: 2500 to 1000 BC

After about 2500 BC, and with the coming of the wheel, Europe was a continent in transition. Clans and cultures were on the move; languages, technologies and customs were changing; human populations and long-distance contacts and trade were expanding.

The first great civilizations had arisen in the Middle Eastern lands of Sumeria and Egypt. These wealthy and powerful cultures built large walled cities and developed the smelting of metal ores and the casting or hammering of ingots to produce copper, gold, silver and lead artefacts. With the discovery that bronze—a copper-tin alloy—was harder and more durable than copper, the Bronze Age was born. Seafaring Middle Eastern traders, prospectors and craftspeople soon took the knowledge of this metal to Crete, Greece and the Balkans, Sicily and Iberia.

The man in the ice. The mummified body of a man who died high in the Alps around 3000 BC was found by climbers in 1991. His equipment showed how well adapted people were to difficult conditions. He had a copper axe, which would have been rare at this time, and arrows flighted with eagle feathers. It has recently been suggested that he may have been a shaman, a kind of ritual specialist. Such people often go to remote places to seek spiritual experiences.

Battle Axes and Beakers. Before the beginning of the Bronze Age, around 3000 BC, major changes occurred in many parts of Europe. On the Russian Steppes north of the Black Sea the horse was domesticated and the population of this area expanded considerably; on the edges of the steppes old ways of life were pushed out. This steppe expansion seems to have had an impact as far west as Hungary, where burial mounds with material very similar to that of the steppes can be found. In the northern half of Europe, too, the old pattern of large villages, often associated with collective tombs, disappeared and was replaced by small, more ephemeral, settlements and individual burials; men were often buried with pottery 'beakers' and stone battle axes. People may have become more mobile and dependent on animals, but the forested environments of central and northern Europe would have strongly discouraged long distance migration, unlike the steppes.

Southern Europe was largely unaffected by these changes but about 1500 BC it saw the spread of a new pottery type called the 'Bell Beaker' which probably originated in the Rhineland, from the beakers mentioned

Horses. A small wild species of horse or ass had long been seen in Europe. Bronze Age migrants introduced larger and stronger breeds from the steppes. These impressive animals must have deeply impressed—or terrified—the native peasant farmers of Europe. Horse-drawn chariots were an important feature of later Bronze Age warfare, but horseshoes came into use later, in the Iron Age. War-horses were a potent symbol of political, economic and military power well into the Middle Ages; and some of these associations remain today.

The Age of Metals. Metals were slowly introduced to Europe from 5000 BC, beginning with gold and copper and extending to bronze by 2000 BC. By 2000, highly structured societies had also emerged, providing the basis for the growth of stable political powes in the Mediterranean and later in central Europe. It is possible that this upsurge in activity was connected with the arrival of the Indo-European peoples from western Asia after 2000 BC though some date their appearance much earlier and link them with the spread of farming.

above, before spreading down the Atlantic coast into Spain and Portugal and eastwards to Czechoslovakia and Hungary.

Metallurgy developed extensively at this time using local sources of copper in Spain, France and Central and Eastern Europe. Axes, daggers and ornaments were made. Many of the styles, of the daggers for example, probably originated in the Caucasus and the Russian steppes.

Warrior society. Before the coming of the Bronze Age warriors, neolithic farming communities and semi-nomadic herders had lived in rough equality. But now as Battle Axe and Beaker folk settled among them, a major social change occurred: the creation of Europe's first ruling class. Possession of metal and horses enabled newcomers to dominate natives. Despite intermarriage over the generations, this social division between peasants and warrior aristocracy, ruler and ruled, remained.

The Bronze Age chiefs and their followers extended their power through slave ownership, metal mining, horse breeding and the control of farm surplus and trade. They liked to exhibit their wealth and loved gold, silver and all forms of ornament. Livestock and metal artefacts became symbols of power and prestige, provoking an increase in raiding and warfare over the following centuries. Hoards of bronze and jewellery were sometimes hidden, and settlements were fortified with timber and stone.

Agriculture and trade in the Bronze Age. With vast areas of forest, heath, marsh and mountain still uninhabited, more land was cleared for agriculture as the population grew. Crops became more varied, now including cider apples, honey, peas, beans and more vegetable varieties.

The plough. The first plough in use when farming began was an enlarged pointed digging stick pulled by two people or, later, by two oxen with a pole attached. Fields were cross-ploughed to break up the soil and bring stones to the surface. Oak was used for ploughs, but some Stone Age people attached flints to them or wedged pebbles into holes in the wood for extra hardness. Then bronze and iron ploughshares, which turned over the soil better, were made. The Romans used iron ploughs. In the first century AD people in Gaul invented bigger ploughs, pulled by up to eight oxen, and able to cope effectively with heavier soils. These became common among the Slavs in later centuries.

Outside the temperate zones, however, there was little settled farming; on the steppe, life remained nomadic, and people in the far north still lived as they had during the Stone Age.

With the use of metal, long-distance trade expanded. People in southern Europe needed copper and tin to make bronze, but most of the ore was north of the Alps. As a network of sea, river and land routes developed, Irish axes reached Denmark, British tin was traded as far as Switzerland and Germany and amber from the Baltic coast was worn by the elites of the Mycenaean civilization in Greece.

Early Mediterranean civilization. By 2000 BC a remarkable civilization had developed on the island of Crete. Minoan civilization (named after Minos, a mythical Cretan king) grew out of a prosperous farming, metal-working, craft and trading island community. The Cretans were the first Europeans to have a written script, similar to Egyptian and early Phoenician hieroglyphs. Their decorated palaces were large, complex buildings that served as administrative and cultural centres and storehouses. Between 1800 and 1500 BC Crete was hit by earthquakes and a huge seismic wave from the volcano at Thera (Santorini), and its civilization went into decline. It had, however, a major influence on a new people who now became dominant in mainland Greece, the Mycenaeans.

Ancestors of the Greeks had settled in the peninsula by at least 2000 BC, some arriving from Asia Minor, some from the north. The Mycenaeans were warriors, travelling widely in search of riches and fighting to increase their wealth and power. After about 1700 BC the Mycenaean warrior chiefs divided Greece up between them and ruled as local kings. These were the heroes of Homeric legend—Agamemnon, Achilles, Odysseus and Ajax—who conquered Troy. Their power spread across the Aegean Sea, and their trading links were wide; Mycenaean cups and jewellery reached Wessex and Scotland.

> **Literacy.** Scribes were keeping written records in Crete by 1400 BC, using a script known as Linear A. Later, a different script was used, known as Linear B. When this was deciphered, it proved to be the earliest known form of written Greek. The scripts were used to record the economic transactions of the palaces.

The Iron Age: from 1000 BC

Iron-workers and iron warriors. Like most advances of the prehistoric and early historic period, the Iron Age came to the Balkans from northern Mesopotamia, Asia Minor and the Caucasus. Indo-European migrants from east of the Adriatic Sea and the Hungarian plain brought iron to northern Italy in about 900 BC, settling in the Po valley and either side of the Apennines. Phoenician and Greek traders and travellers who knew iron sailed to Italy, southern France and south-east Spain.

One Italian iron-using people was the Etruscans, inhabitants of Tuscany. Growing rich on farming and trade, they developed a civilization with cities equipped with public buildings, roads, sewers and water systems.

> **Iron in peace and war.** The introduction of iron was a major technical advance. The ores were more widespread than the copper and tin needed for bronze, and iron production was simpler and quicker. But the metal's greatest advantage was its superior hardness, especially when heated with charcoal to produce steel. In felling trees, ploughing, wheel making, carpentry and countless other tasks, iron was stronger and more durable than bronze, needing less repair and replacement. And in warfare men using iron weapons and armour easily overcame opponents who relied on bronze.

The Greek city-states. In Greece, Mycenaean civilization came to an end some time around 1100 BC, probably as a result of warfare between the small-scale palace states. The so-called Greek Dark Ages were a time of great upheaval, of rapid increase in human numbers and of mixing of races and cultures. The fast-growing hybrid population came to combine the vigour of the northern people with the skills of the eastern Mediterranean. New settlements sprang up; villages grew into towns; and the military leadership gradually settled down to become a landowning aristocracy. This was the beginning of the city-state civilization of classical Greece.

At first the city-states were tribal settlements controlling relatively small territories. Their brilliance as traders, seafarers, military strategists and public planners enabled them to grow into communities of up to 250,000 people. When the population became too large for a poor land to support, the Greeks spread out through trade and emigration, founding colonies around the Mediterranean and the Balkans.

In art, architecture, poetry, philosophy and science, the city-states enjoyed a golden age in the fifth and fourth centuries BC. Magnificent and graceful temples and public buildings were erected. Artists produced beautiful statues and finely painted vases. After Homer's poems were written down, there was a great outpouring of lyric poetry sung to an accompaniment of stringed instruments. The brilliant Greek philosophers taught and wrote. There was outstanding historical writing and tragic and comic drama. Greek thinkers began to speculate on the nature of the universe and to develop theories in mathematics, physics, acoustics and astronomy. The city-states shared a written script and a common religion. They despised the non-Greek-speaking northerners they came into contact with, calling them *barbaroi* in mimicry of their speech.

Alexander's Macedonian empire. As Greek city-state power came to an end, yet another wave of warriors from the north were entering the country. These were the Macedonians, led first by their king Philip and then, after his murder, by his son Alexander (the Great). These horse breeders came from the broad plains of Thrace and had grown rich on timber and gold from their mines. They spoke a rough form of Greek, but the city-states still regarded them as barbarians.

Greek democracy. The political life of the Classical Greeks was regulated by written constitutions and laws. Yet, although known as the birthplace of democracy, the city-states were ruled by small minorities for much of their history. A quarter or less of the inhabitants might be male property-owners and therefore citizens. The rest—peasants, women, children, slaves and foreigners—had no say in public affairs.

The early historians. Writers from Classical Greece and Rome provide us with first hand accounts of events of their time and often with descriptions of the different peoples they encountered. Sometimes the descriptions give details of appearance and customs; at other times, only the names of tribes or warriors are mentioned, or the habits of the people are compared (usually unfavourably) with the writer's own more civilized ways.

Using siege machines, catapults, a new infantry formation (the phalanx), iron armour, long javelins and huge numbers of cavalry, the Macedonians became masters of Greece. The wars they fought proved financially expensive, however, and Alexander set out to recoup his losses by conquering new lands to the east. He led his 35,000 victorious troops, with their Asian allies and mercenaries, as far as the river Indus. Short-lived as the Macedonian empire was, it fused southern Europe with the Orient for the first time. And it ensured a huge flow of wealth from east to west—not for the last time.

Mediterranean civilizations. The rise of civilization in the eastern Mediterranean world was no sudden apparition but a long process in which there were interruptions, overlaps and times of stagnation. After the civilization of Minoan Crete and the Mycenaeans there was a hiatus until about 800 BC when many of the small city-states in and around the Aegean opened the most extraordinary phase of early European history, the civilization of Greece. The Greek achievement embraced political life, literature, art and architecture. Nor was it confined to Greece and the Aegean, but reached across the entire Mediterranean world.

The Iron Age north of the Alps. It took longer for iron-working to reach beyond the Alps, where the Bronze Age lasted to about 700 BC. Here the Hallstatt people (named after a cemetery site in Austria), who emerged from central Europe, were industrious bronzesmiths, salt-miners, cattle and dog breeders, craftspeople and traders. Some of them still lived more like nomads but in time, however, they too began to use the iron ore found in abundance in their lands.

The Hallstatt people prospered, and their larger tribal centres became the first towns outside southern Europe. These were usually on a site of strategic importance, such as a hillfort overlooking a wide plain, beside a trade route or river estuary or near a source of raw materials. Each fortified town was controlled by a chief and his (or, exceptionally, her) retinue. Neighbouring tribes were often quarrelsome, and cattle raiding was widespread. Many sites were ransacked or burned and then rebuilt. Some may have been attacked by Scythians, nomadic horsemen from the Steppes, who were raiding central Europe around 500 BC.

Celtic tribal kingdoms. Population pressures and social tensions increased north of the Alps. More forest land and upland areas were clear-felled for farming, and iron-working became widespread. By the mid-fifth century BC the Hallstatt culture was being replaced by a later, Iron Age culture, called La Tène from a site in Switzerland. The La Tène period in central and western Europe was characterized by the growth of large centres which can justifiably be called towns. At the same time a new art style developed showing influence from the Scythian, Greek and Etruscan sources with which the groups north of the Alps had extensive trade contacts.

These people were the first to be called Celts (*Keltoi* in Greek); the Romans knew them as Gauls. Like the Battle Axe and Beaker folk, some of them migrated across Europe, sometimes as entire tribes. Place names bear witness to these movements of people: for example, the Boii tribe migrated from Bohemia in central Europe to Bologna in north Italy.

The Celts came to dominate much of the continent. Their tribal towns grew in size and number. They had priests, the druids, and bards, who sang poetry and made speeches on feast days. Some were literate, using the Greek and Roman alphabets. Their taste for plunder and piracy remained strong, involving them in raids on Rome, Greece, Egypt and Cyprus.

Centralized Celtic states and hereditary kingdoms were emerging. Gaul was divided between about sixteen tribes, such as the Parisi, the Carnuti and the Treveri; their capitals became modern Paris, Chartres and Trier. By Roman times some of these towns were larger than mediaeval cities with tens of thousands of inhabitants.

> **Wagon and chariot burials.** Bronze and Iron Age chieftains in many parts of Europe were buried under large funeral mounds of heaped-up earth. These funerals were arranged in great splendour, the bodies lying in state surrounded by weapons, ornaments, draperies, food and wine, richly dressed in fine robes, often in wood-panelled chambers or coffins. The richest burials included four-wheeled wagons or two-wheeled chariots. Burial practices became increasingly ostentatious and barbaric: women, slaves and horses were killed and interred with the lords.

The Roman Empire: 500 BC to AD 476

Rome's Beginnings. By the end of the first century BC Roman power had spread out from Italy to encompass most Celtic lands and much of the Mediterranean region. A hundred years later the empire stretched from the Black Sea to the Atlantic, from Mesopotamia and North Africa to Scotland and the Rhine. Many parts of Europe now benefited from a longer period of tranquillity than at any time before or since. How did this come about?

The earliest traces of permanent settlement at Rome date from the eighth century BC, coinciding with the traditional date for the city's foundation by Romulus: 753 BC. A century and a half later Rome was a substantial timber-built fortress-town. With the expulsion of the last king in 509 BC the city became a republic ruled by a senate, a popular assembly and elected magistrates. Later the common people elected their own representatives.

Rome's citizen army began to conquer their Latin neighbours. By about 500 BC more than 300 square miles (800 square kilometres), and a population of perhaps 40,000, were under Roman rule. Although north Italian Celts sacked Rome in 390 BC, massive new walls were built, and the city rapidly recovered. The Romans founded colonies and used a combination of shrewd diplomacy and military skill to isolate and defeat their Italian rivals. Some of their victories involved massacres; others were magnanimous.

By the time of Christ's birth the empire included parts of Spain, France,

The Roman military machine. Rome's military success was based on sound organization, firm discipline, high morale, good equipment and the skilful handling of siege engines and battering rams. The army was organized in legions of three to six thousand infantry and supporting cavalry. Battle tactics were highly methodical, and camps were always made according to a fixed plan. Legionaries were armed with long and short iron javelins and double-bladed iron swords. Early chain-mail was later superseded by jointed iron plate-armour. Soldiers were trained to build forts and roads to secure the territory they conquered.

the Alps, the Mediterranean islands, Tunisia, the Dalmatian coast, Macedonia, Greece, Asia Minor, Syria, Lebanon, Palestine and around the Black Sea. The expansion was unplanned at first, but more systematic later as the fruits of conquest became evident. There were failures, however, such as defeats in North Africa and by Germanic tribes.

Political troubles. As the Roman empire grew, so did its problems. Revolts and piracy sprang up, and it proved difficult to control the huge provincial armies. Aristocrat Roman landowners bought out the small farmers, swelling the numbers of the discontented proletariat. The administration was often incompetent and corrupt, and ambitious generals battled for power.

One of those involved in the civil wars was Julius Caesar. A ruthless conqueror (his conquest of Gaul involved appalling massacres), he was victorious in the civil wars and was appointed Rome's dictator for life and *imperator* (supreme commander). After his murder, another power struggle took place; then Caesar's great-nephew Octavian succeeded him as emperor, accepting the title 'Augustus'.

The Roman Achievement. Augustus ruled until his death in AD 14, bringing stability to the Roman world that lasted for a century during which the empire reached its greatest extent. Sixty million people lived under Roman rule. Many were peacefully assimilated and prospered, benefiting from the empire's single currency, language and legal system. Trade boomed. Postal and relay stations, roads, canals, lighthouses, docks and harbours were built. Vast quantities of goods came and went all over the empire and the Orient.

> **Roman religion and Christianity.** At first the Romans worshipped the Greek gods under Latin names. Gradually, however, many forgot the old ways, and a variety of religions became popular, including emperor worship and eastern mystery cults. Meanwhile the journeys of St Paul brought Christianity to Europe. Although Christians were persecuted for many years, their influence grew. In the early fourth century Constantine granted them free worship, supported the church and became the first Christian emperor. By the end of the century Christianity was the Roman state religion.

The Romans erected magnificent public buildings, monuments, bridges and aqueducts—their engineering skill was unequalled in Europe until the Industrial Revolution. The capital had an abundance of parks, theatres, forums, baths, law courts, temples, palaces and fountains. Piped water and sewage systems underpinned high standards of public health. Provincial towns and cities such as Milan and Lyon also boasted many such features. Rural areas benefited, too, through improved irrigation, drainage and agricultural tools and techniques. Latin philosophy, poetry, drama, oratory, legal writing and history rose to great heights inspired by Greek models. Standards of education were high, and literacy was widespread.

Byzantium and the fall of Rome. The Romans wanted to hold on to what they had. Their armies built wall-and-ditch defences and forts along the frontiers, such as Hadrian's Wall in Britain. But the resources required to secure all the conquered lands were immense. The legions became an economic burden. High taxes, inflation and devaluation dogged the economy. Soldiers mutinied when their pay failed to arrive. Parts of the Italian countryside were terrorized by bandits, and provincial cities went into decline.

Emperor after emperor failed to solve the state's problems. In 284 Diocletian decentralized the empire and split it between east and west, ruling the eastern half from Byzantium (modern Constantinople) and appointing a western co-ruler in Rome.

Constantine the Great reunited the empire temporarily, defeating all his rivals for power and making Constantinople his capital. He was the last emperor to control the whole empire effectively—something he achieved

Rome's legacy. The Roman empire was essentially a Mediterranean state. But it was the first political power to bring parts of northern and central Europe into a close relationship with the Mediterranean world and to provide a unified culture for much of the continent. Its legacy was immense: the Latin language and the Romance languages that derive from it; Roman law; the Christian faith; a great and influential literature; high standards of civic architecture and administration. After Rome the idea of a Europe-wide empire remained an alluring goal for later rulers, from Charlemagne to Napoleon and Hitler.

only through a massive expansion of the army to almost a million men. Over the next sixty years his successors tried to hold the empire together, but in 395 it was partitioned for good.

The western empire continued to fall apart under weak emperors, undermined by internal power-feuds and harassed by barbarian invaders who ransacked its towns and cities. In 476 the last emperor in the west was deposed by the barbarians.

The eastern or Byzantine empire continued. Its European territory included only Greece and the Balkans, but it also ruled vast areas of Asia Minor, the Middle East and North Africa. One Byzantine emperor reconquered some of the west, but only temporarily. During the seventh and eighth centuries the Byzantine capital of Constantinople itself came under attack. Although it survived the onslaughts of Germanic and Eurasian tribes, in the end the Arabs captured the city in 1453. The Roman empire was finished.

The Great Migrations: AD 200 to 600

The movements of large numbers of Germanic, Slavic and Eurasian peoples across Europe and into the remains of the Roman world were a long and complex process, beginning in the third century AD and continuing into the late sixth. Movements into the old Roman provinces affected chiefly Italy, France, the Low Countries, southern Germany, Spain and Britain. Some of the migrations resulted in the emergence of stable kingdoms like those of the Ostrogoths in Italy and the Visigoths in Spain.

> **Why the barbarians came.** Older views stressed the destructive aspects of the barbarian migrations as massive invading armies bent on plundering and destroying Roman civilization. We now see these great invasions more as folk-movements stimulated by the search for land and a better life, although armed conflict often occurred. Population pressure and a lack of natural resources probably triggered the German migrations, for example. Some barbarian peoples settled in the declining Roman world because it offered economic and political advantages; others came rather like today's economic refugees.

Others resulted in a mixed population of barbarians being settled in a land where a state or kingdom developed later—as in Frankish Gaul or Anglo-Saxon England.

The Northern barbarians. The Germanic tribes inhabited southern Scandinavia and the plains east of the river Elbe. The Roman historian Tacitus described them as large, moody, yellow-haired people, a tribal society inhabiting the northern forests and marshes. They hated cities, had little iron and were illiterate and poor farmers, he said. Ruled by hereditary kings and warrior chiefs, they were drinkers and gamblers, idle when not fighting, eager for honour and booty, but democratic in spirit.

In about AD 200 the first major movement of Germans took place. About 200,000 Goths—men, women and children—came south and split into two groups. The Ostrogoths established a kingdom north of the Black Sea, while the Visigoths continued south to the Danube. Both settled peacefully outside the empire; but when the Huns arrived from Asia late in the fourth century, the Visigoths came into conflict with Rome. Battles were fought and treaties made. Then the Visigoths invaded Greece and Italy, besieging and looting Rome, before moving north-west into Gaul to found a kingdom there.

A massive invasion of Germanic tribes across the Rhine followed. Among them were the Vandals, who drove south-west through Gaul into Spain, crossed to North Africa and attacked Rome by sea. In Britain, Picts and Scots raided across Hadrian's Wall, and sea-borne Angles, Saxons and Jutes arrived from northern Europe. By 442 eastern Britain had fallen to the invaders.

The Huns. The Huns were nomadic horsemen who for generations had grazed sheep and cattle on the arid central Asian plains. In the first century BC they had been attacked and beaten by the Chinese. Short of pasture for their flocks and herds, they had swept south-west across the steppes, arriving on the eastern fringes of Europe in 370. The sudden appearance of this great horde several hundred thousand strong was alarming. Devastatingly fast on horseback and deadly with bow, lance and sabre, Hun warriors were much feared.

The Huns never devastated the Roman empire as much as was expected, however. After overrunning the Ostrogoths, they moved from the Black Sea region to the Hungarian plain. They threatened Greece and the land route between Rome and Constantinople, and then fought the Romans along the Danube, burning and looting as they went. By the time the Huns crossed into Gaul, their power was waning, and a combined army of Romans and Germanic allies defeated them. The battered Hun army withdrew to the Danube; then the remnants of the tribes returned to the steppes, disappearing from European history.

Migrants from the East. As the German tribes migrated south and west, new peoples moved to take over their abandoned lands. The Slavs were a mixed group of peoples, related to the Germans but speaking a different language and originally from further east. Their homeland was probably the upper basin of the Vistula in Poland and the plains of western Russia and Ukraine. From there in the fifth and sixth centuries they moved west into northern and central Europe and south to Greece and the Balkans.

Less is known about the Slavs than about the Germans. Theirs was a more fragmented, less centralized tribal society, and their early history is poorly documented. Their lands and culture were often overrun and devastated by war in later centuries, and much less archaeological evidence survives or has been studied.

The Barbarian Kingdoms. By the late fifth century most of Roman Gaul was under Frankish, Visigoth and Burgundian rule. In Spain the Visigoths were dominant. Italy fell first to Saxon adventurers and mercenaries, then to the Ostrogoths, and for a third time to the Germanic Lombards or Langobards ('long beards'); the Italian region of Lombardy still bears their name. Western Europe was thus gradually transformed into a patchwork of barbarian kingdoms that maintained aspects of Roman civilization even though they had destroyed others.

Yet there was a lack of stability, and further great movements of people were to follow. By 562 the Avars, a race of horse-riding nomads from

Feudalism. The feudal social system came about during the Dark Ages because people were insecure enough to sacrifice some of their liberty in return for help and protection from someone more powerful. This produced a social pyramid that reached upwards from the landless peasant to the king. Feudal service usually involved an obligation to fight for your lord in wartime.

central Asia, together with Huns and Bulgars from south Russia, had settled beside the Slavs along the Danube. The races had merged by the tenth century and extended their territory north along the Elbe and south into the Balkans. Also in the tenth century, Magyars from the steppes were raiding in Europe, founding the forerunner of the kingdom of Hungary. In the following centuries Arabs conquered most of the Iberian peninsula and seafaring Viking raiders and merchants settled all over western Europe, into the Mediterranean and deep into Russia via its northern rivers. These great shifts of population and the cultural changes that went with them meant that large and stable nation-states did not emerge until long after the end of the Roman world.

A Time of Change

Classical Roman civilization had long been in decline, and Europe now entered its Dark Ages. This period was once thought to have been totally unenlightened, but the modern view is that it had redeeming features. Politically, it is true, Europe was much weakened from the time of Alexander's conquests or Rome's great expansion. The Germanic kingdoms were often fragmented and insecure, and a feudal society developed. Culturally, too, despite the efforts of a few enlightened rulers and the church, decline set in. Illiteracy and ignorance spread.

Yet the new Europe was not totally barbarian in the modern sense. The Germans and Slavs converted to Christianity, and Germanic societies produced religious literature, art, epic poetry and written legal codes. Most of all, their small, independent states helped preserve the continent from chaos and laid the foundations of mediaeval Europe—especially the kingdom of the Franks. While European civilization did not return to its greatest heights until the Renaissance began centuries later, the Middle Ages were still a period when many, and perhaps most, of the continent's inhabitants could live their lives in peace.

> **The foundations of modern Europe.** By 600 the major migrations of peoples in Europe were coming to an end. From a patchwork of small kingdoms came the first movements towards the nation states of later centuries.

Languages and Races of Europe

Genetic and linguistic research shows that human races and languages have diverged together as a result of tribal social patterns. In tribal societies, interbreeding groups of people develop more or less in isolation from others, creating their own genetic 'library', speech dialect and, ultimately, language. Since early European societies were tribal, genetic relationships were probably similar to linguistic ones. However, languages interact in a number of ways and after thousands of years of human change, the language someone speaks is no longer a reliable guide to their genetic inheritance.

In some cases conquest or invasion has wiped out the language of the conquered people completely although genetically the conquerors have a much lesser influence. The language of the Romans, for example, replaced Celtic languages in most of France, Spain and Portugal although Romans themselves must have been outnumbered by the indigenous population.

In other cases, the native language may live alongside and eventually replace the conquerors' own language. When Vikings, for example, settled in England in the ninth century, their language, Old Norse, survived there for a relatively short time, leaving only an estimated 900 everyday words 'loaned' into English like *gift, egg, skirt,* and some 1400 place names, for

A common vocabulary. Words for domesticated animals such as the sheep and horse, for some crops and for items like the wheel and yoke are similar in virtually all Indo-European languages, both east and west. Other common words, such as 'father' and 'mother', are similar in most European members of this huge language family.

Linguistic and genetic boundaries. In most European countries language is an unreliable guide to genetic descent. The Basques who inhabit the mountains of south-west France and northern Spain, however, show unique characteristics both genetically and linguistically, having been largely isolated from the main European migrations. Similarly in Wales, speakers of Welsh and English tend to have a number of different genes, while the Orkney islanders—speakers of a Scandinavian dialect—differ genetically from other Scots.

example Derby, Ormskirk, Skegness. The conquest of England by the Normans introduced French as the language of administration, the law, the ruling class, alongside English, the language of the lower classes, a situation which survived until the mid fourteenth century. It is estimated that some 10,000 words were 'borrowed' from French during this period, of which 75 per cent are still in the English word stock. But the language which developed into modern English remained basically the one brought centuries earlier by Saxons and other Germanic invaders.

The second course of interaction is cultural: where a language acquires prestige in some field it can 'lend' words to other languages. Greek and Latin, as the languages of Christianity and education until the late Middle Ages, have been major sources of new words into many European languages. Nowadays English, through the impact of American technology and media and also through British colonial expansion in previous centuries, and its status as a 'world language', is a major source of innovation.

Europe's language families. Linguists map relationships between languages by studying vocabulary, inflexions and grammar. From the many resemblances between different European languages they conclude that most have evolved from an ancient family of languages, spoken by Indo-European migrants who had arrived in Europe by 4000 BC and by people living in parts of south-west and southern Asia. Outside Europe the language family includes Romany, Persian, Kurdish and a number of Indian languages including Gujurati, Bengali and Urdu.

Europe's oldest language is Basque. Although Basque shares certain structural similarities with other languages, it is commonly believed that it is a true isolate, pre-dating the Celtic and Roman occupation of the Iberian peninsula. Dominated by its neighbours (indeed, proscribed for a period in this century) and under pressure from successive invaders, the Basque language is none the less spoken by over half a million people today.

The only other non-Indo-European group in Europe is known as Finno-Ugrian. Hungarian, with some 14 million speakers today, Finnish, with about 5 million, and Estonian, with 1.5 million speakers, are the best known of this group. Hungarian and Finnish are only remotely related, Finnish and Estonian much more closely. Lappish is spoken in Norway, Sweden, Finland and north-western Russia.

Celtic languages were once spoken over much of Europe. At the height of their expansion Celts occupied territory stretching from the Adriatic to Scotland, and from central Europe to south-western Spain; but by AD 400 the Continental Celtic language survived only in place names and today only the Insular branch survives. Irish, Welsh and Breton have some degree of political status, but Scottish Gaelic none, and although these languages are in school and university curricula, their numbers of native speakers have declined throughout this century.

The Romanic or Romance languages gradually replaced Celtic and other languages in most of the western Roman empire. The form of Latin that is still studied today was the formal written language of the Roman empire.

Romance languages. The Latin spoken in the provinces of the Roman empire developed into the Romance languages of western Europe.

In Iberia	In Gaul	In Italy	In Rhaetia	In Dacia
Spanish	French	Italian	Romansch	Romanian
Portuguese	Provencal	Sardinian		Vlach
Galician				
Catalan				

Alongside it, however, there was a kind of Latin spoken by the illiterate majority of the population, Vulgar Latin. Vulgar Latin was used in all the European Roman provinces. By the ninth century AD written and spoken Latin were separate languages and the spoken language was developing differently in the different countries. Latin continued to be used by the Church and for centuries was a common language among the educated.

Two minor branches of the Latin language family, Oscan and Umbrian, are, like Latin, now dead. Oscan was spoken widely in southern Italy in the last four centuries BC; Umbrian was spoken in northern Italy.

Germanic languages also belong to the Indo-European family but since they were spoken beyond the boundaries of the Roman empire, they were less influenced by Latin. Today the geographical distribution of Germanic languages is more extensive than that of any other group of languages, with some 440 million speakers worldwide. Among these, English is the most widespread, accounting for about 300 million (first- and second-language) speakers, while Frisian, its closest relation, and Faeroese have the fewest speakers.

Current Germanic languages belong to two branches of the family, North and West Germanic, but there was also a third branch, East Germanic which is now extinct. In this group were the languages of the Goths, the Burgundians and the Vandals and other tribes that migrated south, east and west in the early centuries AD. The earliest records in a Germanic language are the runic inscriptions dating to the third century AD, written in the special runic alphabet, the Futharc. The only extensive written records are a fourth century Gothic translation of the Bible, but relics of these languages can be found in names like Spanish *Rodrigo, Fernando*, and 'loan' words like Italian/Spanish *guerra* 'war'. A form of Gothic was spoken in the Crimea as late as the eighteenth century.

Germanic languages. Only one of the eastern Germanic languages, Gothic, was written down.

West	North	East
English	Swedish	Gothic
German	Danish	
Dutch	Norwegian	
Frisian	Icelandic	
Yiddish	Faroese	

One Germanic language has evolved outside Europe: Afrikaans, which developed from the sixteenth century Dutch in Cape Colony, has been one of the official languages in South Africa since 1925.

Slavic languages are more similar to one another than many groups, suggesting a fairly late break-up of their 'parent' language, Common Slavic, possibly as late as AD 600. In addition to the Slavic languages currently spoken, there are two extinct languages: Polabian (spoken in northern Germany until about 1700) and Old Church Slavonic (or Old Bulgarian) used in a large number of texts beginning in the ninth century.

The remaining European descendants of the Indo-European language

> **Slavic languages.** Some Slavic languages are written in Cyrillic script
> (e.g. Russian). Others, such as Polish, use the western alphabet.
>
> | West | South | East |
> |---|---|---|
> | Polish | Serbo-Croat | Russian |
> | Czech | Bulgarian | Byelorussian |
> | Slovak | Slovene | Ukrainian |
> | Sorbian | Macedonian | |
> | Polabian | Old Church Slavonic | |

family have not developed into groups of languages. Modern Greek, very different from Ancient Greek, evolved via the Byzantine Greek spoken in the eastern Roman empire from the sixth to the fifteenth century. Latvian, Lithuanian and Old Prussian are related to each other and are presumed to have a common ancestor in an unknown language, Baltic. Albanian descends directly from Illyrian, the language spoken by the Illyrian tribe in Roman times.

European Races. A few broad racial characteristics distinguish Europeans, who are often referred to as the Caucasian race, the so-called whites. Blond hair and fair skin are more predominant in the north of the continent; darker people are more numerous in the south—their pigmentation both an adaptation to and a result of greater exposure to strong sunlight. The chunkier build and greater amount of body fat common among northern Europeans are an adaptation to conserve body heat in a colder climate. There is much variation within populations, however.

There has long been disagreement between 'lumpers' and 'splitters'. The former emphasize the common racial characteristics shared by different peoples, resulting in a few broad racial groups, while the latter stress the differences between many more narrowly defined races. Numerous attempts have been made to classify Europe's distribution of races according to physical type, including studies of the geographical dispersal and predominance of head shapes, skin pigmentation, hair and eye colour, and so on. But today it is generally believed that no such racial and geographical classification of Europeans is possible, because the dispersal and intermixing of physical types has been so complete.

Since the discovery of the structure of the genetic code, scientific research into the origins of the human race has had a more scientific basis. Much still remains to be investigated but genetic research into DNA — the chemical molecules that transmit hereditary characteristics from parents to offspring — already provides fascinating information about human populations. Common DNA characteristics indicate common ancestry, and have been used to produce a genetic 'map' of Europe. Such studies confirm our picture of a sparsely populated continent gradually colonized by a large and expanding population of farming peoples who emerged from the south-east and spread north-westwards. It also tends to prove that throughout thousands of years of changing populations, mixing has been so thorough that no 'pure-blooded' races remain in any part of Europe.

The People of Europe

The Alamanni

A new grouping of western Germanic tribes, the Alamanni or Alemanni, is first mentioned by Roman historians in the early third century AD as living in the region between the upper Elbe and upper Main rivers. The name, a Latinized version of a Germanic word, signified 'all people', 'everyone', a clear indication that they were a confederacy of smaller groups, possibly formed after individual tribes had been unsuccessful against Roman armies in the warfare of the late second century AD.

The Suevi and a tribe named Hermunduri may have provided a large proportion of the new grouping but it is not known which other peoples may have joined them or how the separate warrior tribes came to co-operate. It seems to have been a successful coalition, however, for the Alamanni were soon attacking the Roman frontier between the Rhine and the Danube and in AD 233 they broke through it. By 260 they had forced the Romans to evacuate this exposed frontier line, and by the end of the same century they had begun to settle in the land which had once been part of the Roman province of Upper Germany (now south-west Germany). In the following century they raided eastern Gaul and the Rhine valley on numerous occasions and in 357 the Emperor Julian had to drive them out of the upper Rhine region. Not all their relations with the Romans were hostile, for during the same period, Alamannic soldiers fought in Roman armies and some of their leaders became high-ranking officers in the Roman forces.

Although some of the Alamanni were able to settle in Gaul when Roman authority collapsed there in the fifth century, the main body of the people remained in the territories that are now south-western Germany and northern Switzerland. To the north and west they were shut in by the powerful Franks, who won several victories against them late in the fifth century, and over the next century they were absorbed into the eastern part of the Frankish empire.

Throughout the fourth and fifth centuries the Alamanni remained a far from united political force, which helps to explain why these previously successful people were unable to keep their powerful neighbours at bay. No unified monarchy seems to have developed among them. A number of kings and princes often ruled at the same time, few of them with any lasting authority. The hilly and wooded character of the land where they had settled was to a large extent responsible for these divisions, for it isolated communities from one another, encouraging local organization. The power of local leaders can be seen in a number of hill-top strongholds of the fourth and fifth centuries, in southern Germany. One of these, the Runder Berg near Urach, has been excavated and reveals a small but powerfully defended chieftain's residence surrounded by the dwellings and workshops of his retainers and dependent craftsmen. Most of their smaller settlements lay in valleys or on lowland, many now beneath villages which have been continuously occupied ever since.

Much more fully recorded are the Alamannic cemeteries of the fifth to seventh centuries. Here the richer warriors and their families were buried, often with fine grave-goods and ornaments. These reveal trade and cultural contacts with the Franks and Bavarians, but also with the Ostrogoths in northern Italy, where some leading Alamanni went to serve as soldiers. One of the best preserved cemeteries is that at Oberflacht, where waterlogged conditions have preserved wooden objects, including furniture, vessels and even a lyre.

Although the Alamanni founded no lasting state, their name survives in the French name for all Germans, Allemands. Modern south-western Germans could regard them as remote forebears.
See: Germany, Switzerland

The Alans

The Alans were among the many nomadic peoples who ranged over the western Russian steppes from prehistoric times. Roman writers in the middle of the first century AD knew of several groups, some in and around the Crimea, others around the Sea of Azov and the Don valley, still others north of the lower Danube. These were mentioned because they assisted Roman emperors by raiding the Parthian kingdoms that lay beyond the eastern frontier of the empire.

In so doing they built up a formidable reputation as mounted spearmen, adept at breaking up massed ranks of infantry by their charge, and as horseback bowmen. Late in the first century they began to move westward and during the next hundred years they attacked the Roman provinces on the Danube, often in company with other similar nomadic groups.

The Alans were not a single, well-defined tribe or nation but they had an identity that was sufficiently unified and powerful to overwhelm that of other, smaller groups. It is not known what language they spoke, or even whether they did all speak the same language, but it is probable that the different groups could understand each others' dialects. Their material culture was very simple, consisting largely of artefacts such as weapons and ornaments which are difficult for the archaeologist to distinguish from those of other nomadic people. Roman accounts describe a highly mobile society, family groups moving in their wagons and driving flocks of animals over great distances. Their social organization seems to have been primitive and major divisions within society may not have existed. Little is heard of their leaders, whose power over their own people was limited.

Late in the fourth century, the Alans in south Russia were swept up in the westward drive of the Huns and joined in Hun attacks on the Roman Balkans. Several groups continued westward to the Rhine about AD 400 and at the end of 406 moved with the Vandals and Suevi into Gaul and from there on into Spain. There, they settled in the west and were absorbed into the mixed population of the region.
See: France, Germany, Russia, Spain

The Angles

The Anglii (Angles) were a small tribe who once lived in the north German coastlands, on the eastern side of what is now Schleswig-Holstein. Their name was later given to this region, which became known as Angeln. The tribe remained there, farming their land and engaging in a modest trade with neighbouring groups until shortly after AD 400, when they joined with Saxon tribes in a series of migrations to Britain. According to the historian Bede, writing early in the eighth century, Angeln was left virtually deserted.

In Britain, the Angles, along with other Germanic migrants, settled mainly in the east, in Northumberland, Yorkshire, Lincolnshire and East Anglia. The kingdom of the East Angles was named after them, but they were also largely responsible for founding the kingdoms of Northumbria and Lindsey. Otherwise, their activities and settlement in Britain are impossible to disentangle from those of the Saxons. But it was their name, only slightly modified to 'the English', which was later used for all the Germanic tribes who had come to live in Britain. So the land of England was named after a minor tribe which had once lived on the western shore of the Baltic.
See: United Kingdom

The Arabs

The homeland of the Arabs was the largely desert country of what is still Arabia. As a people they were always mixed in culture and lifestyle. Where agriculture was possible, for example in Iraq and the Yemen, they lived in settled villages and cities. In the barren interior and the uplands, Bedouin (the nomadic Arabs) lived mainly off their flocks of sheep, goats and camels. Arab civilization dates back thousands of years, but it was not until after their conversion to the new Islamic faith in 610 that they began to expand westwards. Egypt was conquered in 641–2 and over the next sixty years Arabs gradually conquered the whole of North Africa. By AD 700, they were at the southern gate of Europe: the Straits of Gibraltar.

In 710 a force of Arabs and Berbers landed in southern Spain and seized Gibraltar and Algeciras. In the following year a larger army under the Arab governor of Morocco invaded and captured the cities of Cordoba and Toledo from the Visigoths, later taking Merida and Seville as well. The Visigoths' resistance collapsed and the Arab advance through Spain was spectacularly rapid. By 718 they had occupied most of the peninsula and entered southern France. Charles Martel finally halted them at Poitiers in 732. After this phase of conquest new immigrants arrived from North Africa and the Near East to settle the conquered lands. For the next seven centuries there was a Muslim state on Spanish soil.

The Muslim regime in Spain was a relatively tolerant one. The old Visigothic landowning nobility was removed and their lands redistributed among Arabs, creating a new and more widely based landed class that contributed a great deal to the country's prosperity. Berbers from North Africa were prominent in the Muslim state, especially in the country districts where they followed their traditionally pastoral way of life. Non-Muslim groups such as Jews and Christians were numerous, well organized and generally tolerantly treated, so that internal strife was not common or intense.

Arab rule in Spain produced a rich and varied cultural life and their presence made the country a conduit by which Arab learning and literature reached Europe from the East. They improved the agriculture by irrigation and enriched it by introducing new crops, including oranges, cotton and rice. Many industries were developed: textiles, silk, paper, pottery, leather and armaments and in Cordoba alone there were said to be 13,000 weavers. Trade with North Africa, Egypt and Byzantium blossomed and merchants in south-eastern ports amassed great wealth.

In the ninth and tenth centuries Muslim Spain was the richest and most advanced state in Europe. Its political security came under serious threat, however, in the eleventh century, when a number of minor Arab rulers and princes divided up the peninsula into separate small kingdoms. This encouraged Christians in the north to advance southwards and begin the long reconquest of Spain. (It is to this phase of Spanish history that the exploits of El Cid belong.) In 1085 Toledo was recaptured by Christian forces and slowly the Arab frontier was pushed southward. Cordoba was taken in 1236, Seville in 1248. By the end of the thirteenth century, Muslim rule was confined to the province of Granada, where it was to continue for another two hundred years until its final extinction in 1492. To that final phase of Muslim Spain belongs its finest monument, the great palace of the Sultan, the Alhambra at Granada, one of the most magnificent buildings in Europe. Many Arabs chose to leave Spain for North Africa in and after 1492, others were ejected. Those who remained behind were required to become Christians, if they had not already been converted. These Christian Arabs, the Moriscos, were identifiable in Spain until the seventeenth century, but since then they have merged with the rest of the population. See: Portugal, Spain

The Avars

The Avars were one of a number of nomadic peoples who at different times moved westward into Europe from the central Asian steppes. First mentioned by eastern Roman writers in the fifth century AD, they were possibly related to or connected with the Turks, but otherwise their origins are obscure. About the middle of the sixth century they advanced across the Carpathian mountains into territories that are now western Romania and Hungary and there maintained a strong presence until the ninth century. Though from then on they operated from a permanent base, they remained at least semi-nomadic.

By 562 they were occupying land on the Danube and were strong enough to strike treaties with the Franks and Lombards, the leading powers of central Europe at that time. By 568, they were in control of most of the Carpathians, the middle Danube lands and territory as far west as the Elbe. They were also sufficiently strong to attack the eastern Roman empire of Byzantium and were able to extract from its emperors large sums of gold in exchange for peace. Under their ruler Bajan at the end of the sixth century, they reached the summit of their power. But in 626 an ill-judged campaign against the eastern Roman empire ended in failure. Avar power went into decline and was further undermined by internal strife.

From around 650 to 700, there may have been further migrations of Avars from the Asian steppes, but these did not greatly increase their overall strength in Europe. The Frankish king Charlemagne campaigned against them about 800, while their neighbours the Slavs and Magyars slowly came to dominate them more and more. Avar rulers were baptized as Christians not long after 800, but many of the common people remained faithful to their old gods for long afterwards. Both in eastern Europe and the Asian steppes, the Avars had disappeared as a distinct people by AD 900, presumably absorbed by the new rising powers.
See: Czechoslovakia, Germany, Hungary, Romania

The Balts

The name 'Balts' is a modern name for the peoples of the eastern coast of the Baltic Sea, who speak a distinct group of languages (Lithuanian, Lett, Old Prussian and Estonian) and are culturally and ethnically separate from the Russian peoples. The early Balts were recognized by Roman writers, who called them Aestii. Their modern descendants inhabit Latvia, Lithuania and Estonia. Although the three Baltic states are now small countries, the influence of the Baltic peoples at its peak extended far inland, to Moscow, Kursk and Kiev.

The early Balts arrived from the Eurasian steppes with other Indo-European migrants, possibly as early as 3000 BC. They settled in the lowlands between Lake Ladoga and the Vistula and in the period up to 1500 BC, their cultural influence reached from the Vistula basin in the west to the upper Volga and south to the Dnieper. As well as the resources of good agricultural land, Balts had access to amber on the Baltic shores, a material much in demand for ornaments in Russia, central Europe and Mycenaean Greece.

The great age of the early Balts was the period from about 200 BC to AD 500. Agricultural prosperity was at its height and the demand for amber from the Roman world, especially in the first and second centuries AD, greatly expanded. Other trade connections developed, with the Germanic tribes, the peoples of western Russia and the mixed cultures north of the Black Sea. The great migrations of peoples from east to west, which took place from the fourth century onward, had little effect on the Balts. Not until the Slavs moved northwards in the sixth century, and, later, when the Vikings expanded into the eastern Baltic, was there any significant external impact on their lands. The Slav conquests reduced the territory held by the Balts to an area not much greater than that of the three modern states, though without destroying their cultural identity, an identity which has survived 1500 years of change and is still alive today.
See: Estonia, Latvia, Lithuania

The Basques

The Basques of northern Spain and south-western France are descended from an ancient European people who are known to have been living in the same general area for around 4000 years, since at least the Bronze Age, about 2000 BC. Their language, which has several dialects, has no known relations with other European languages and is certainly a non-Indo-European survival from a remote prehistoric period. The Basques must thus be regarded as the oldest distinct people still surviving in Europe. The name Basque is derived from the Latin Vascones. In Spain, the Basques are known as Cascongadas and the name of the French region of Gascony derives from the same root.

The homeland of the Basques is the western Pyrenees and the foothills to north and south, a region in which there is little agricultural land but good pasture for grazing animals. Throughout prehistory, they seem to have followed the same pastoral life-style. Incomers seem to have made little or no impact before the Roman period. The Romans considered the Basques to have come from the mountains north of the river Ebro. The towns of Pamplona, Calahorra and Oeasso were their main centres, but the population was largely scattered across the valleys in many small settlements. The Basque way of life was only slightly influenced by Roman rule, for the region was not rich and its Roman towns remained small. Like other subject peoples, they provided troops for the Roman army, but they made little other contribution to the empire. Christianity was introduced to them during the fourth century AD, but it did not spread throughout the community until much later. When the Suevi and Visigoths conquered Spain in the fifth and sixth centuries, the Basques were confined to their more mountainous lands but they were never deprived of their identity.

They soon found themselves in a frontier zone between the Visigoths in Spain and the Franks, a situation which held some advantages as it gave them opportunities for raiding and infiltration to both north and south. Basque soldiers are heard of in the armies of the Frankish dukes of Aquitaine in the eighth century and in 778 Basque troops attacked and destroyed the rearguard of Charlemagne's army as it retreated through the pass at Roncesvalles. By 800, the Basques had spread from the mountains south into the Ebro valley and north to the plain of Aquitaine, greatly enlarging their area of settlement. This larger region took its name, Gascony, from the descendants of the Vascones.

More than half a million Basque speakers now live in Spain and more than 100,000 in France. Traditionally they have been expert herdsmen but they have also produced great sailors and fishermen, playing an important part in the development of whale and cod fisheries in the Atlantic. Many have migrated to the United States and South America but in their traditional homelands they have preserved their identity, their strong sense of separateness and still retain many aspects of their ancestral life. In their pursuit of national identity, some Basques are campaigning for DNA tests to prove they are, indeed, a separate people. In the past, however, tests made on other groups have proved only that over the centuries populations have usually become so mixed that no 'pure-blooded' individuals remain.

See: France, Spain

The Bavarians

The emergence of the Bavarians is among the most obscure events of early mediaeval Europe. Although reliable early historians mention other tribes and peoples in southern Germany after the collapse of Roman rule, there is no record of the Bavarians, or Baiuvarii as they were called, until about 550, by which date they were settled south of the old Roman frontier on the river Danube. Experts do not agree on where they originally came from or how they had come into being in the first place. Some suggest they migrated from Bohemia (western Czechoslovakia) to the region south of the Danube, others that they were in fact several different tribes who were already living in the Danube valley and who now banded together into a new population grouping. In any event their origins are likely to have been mixed, made up of migrant groups from the north and east, with survivors of the former Roman provincial population.

The historical Bavarians occupied a frontier position between the

Germanic Alamanni and the Slavs of eastern Europe. They had close connections with the Lombards in the sixth century and many of them took part in the Lombard invasion of Italy in 568. The Bavarians who stayed behind in southern Germany were threatened by Avars raiding from the east and in the late sixth century, accepted the protection of the Franks. They held out in their rather precarious position between the Germanic and Slav worlds until they finally submitted to the Frankish king Charlemagne in the late eighth century. After that, their importance as a major people declined, but their identity was preserved until modern times and the land they inhabited is still called Bavaria (Bayern).
See: Czechoslovakia, Germany, Italy

The Belgae

A group of Celtic tribes inhabiting what is now northern France and Belgium, to the north of the Seine and Marne, were called by Julius Caesar the Belgae, a name later transferred to the Roman province of Gallia Belgica and later still to Belgium. Caesar regarded the Belgae as the most warlike tribe of Gaul and although he conquered them in 57 BC, they continued to be troublesome to Rome for the next thirty years. Like the other northern peoples of Gaul, the Belgae occupied both large hill-top strongholds and extensive lowland settlements. They controlled deposits of iron in the north-east of Gaul, which enabled them to manufacture high quality swords and spears and there were frequent wars against their own Celtic neighbours, as well as against the advancing Romans. Like the other Celtic peoples, however, the majority of the population were farmers.

The Belgae themselves believed that their ancestors had crossed the Rhine into Gaul from the east and this tradition may reflect a prehistoric migration, perhaps in the second century BC. Some Belgae certainly crossed the English Channel and settled in what is now southern Britain about or shortly before 100 BC. This is unlikely to have been a mass movement and may have been confined to a warrior-elite seeking new lands to conquer. The immigrants brought the first coinage into Britain, gold coins that were copies of much earlier Greek ones. The practice of striking coinage spread to other tribes in southern Britain before the Roman conquest.

The Belgae in Britain are later mentioned by a Roman writer as being settled in what are now Hampshire and West Sussex, with their centre at Winchester, and other groups may have occupied the lower Thames valley. In Gaul, the main body of the Belgae had several tribal centres, including Reims, Metz, Trier, Chalons, Soissons and Arras, all of which later developed into Roman cities. After their conquest by Rome in the first century BC, the Belgae settled down and became Romanized subjects, making a substantial contribution to the development of Roman Gaul. See: Belgium, United Kingdom, France

The Bretons

The Bretons are descended from Celtic peoples who mingled with the earlier, non-Celtic inhabitants of the north-western peninsula of France before 500 BC. Like other Celtic societies theirs was class-based with a chief and priests at the head of the hierarchy and a nobility that was devoted to the arts of war. Large numbers of fortified sites can still be seen on their territory, both inland and on the rocky coastal cliffs. Their economy was largely based on farming and they produced a sufficient surplus of food to enable them to trade with the Roman world in the first century BC; they imported Mediterranean wine and pottery. One of the Breton tribes, the Veneti, were accomplished sailors and traded with the Britons across the Channel.

The Bretons were conquered, after a struggle, by Julius Caesar in 56 BC, but revolted against Roman rule in 52 BC. Although eventually organized as part of Roman Gaul, their area was remote from the main Roman centres and the Breton way of life was relatively little affected by Rome. They also retained their Celtic language.

In the fifth and sixth centuries AD, after Roman authority in Gaul came to an end, new Celtic immigrants arrived from southern Britain and Ireland. Christian missionaries followed the immigrants and the names of some of the leading Celtic saints are remembered in Breton place-names such as St Malo, St Brieuc, St Pol-de-Leon. The Bretons were at this time organized as a number of small lordships and were not able to resist the more united Franks who had taken over much of Roman Gaul. In spite of submitting to new overlords they still retained their own language, culture and social organization. In the ninth century, led by their hero Nemenoe, the Bretons rose in revolt against the king of France and extended their territory to include Rennes and Nantes. Later, they held off Viking invaders and strenuously maintained their independence, though they were formally vassals of the French king. They continued to be effectively autonomous until the French Revolution, and still consider themselves a distinctly Celtic people.

The Breton language is closely related to the now defunct Cornish and to Welsh and is still widely spoken in western and northern Brittany. It has been influenced over the years by French but in the nineteenth century there was a major literary revival in Breton, partly in reaction to official attempts to make French the only language of Brittany.

See: France

The Britons

The Celtic peoples of southern Britain were called the Britanni or Brittones by Roman authors of the first century BC and later. Although all now referred to as Britons, they were in no sense a unified people or group of peoples. Rather, they were a number of tribes at varying stages of cultural development. Those of the south-east, in Kent, Sussex, Hampshire and Essex had the most advanced societies, some including immigrants from the nearer parts of Gaul who came to raid but later settled permanently. These tribes lived a settled existence based on mixed agriculture and commerce. By the first century they had a market economy and used gold, silver and bronze coins, based on those used by the Gauls. Politically, they were still led by kings, though a warrior-elite was probably a dominant force within the tribal society. The Britons of the north and west, in the Pennines and Wales, were more remote and thus less open to external influence. In upland areas they may have depended on animal husbandry.

Most of Britain was productive land and supported a sizeable population by the first century BC. There were also rich deposits of minerals, especially iron, silver and lead, along with some tin and gold. The tribal leaders could therefore amass wealth and display their rank in fine ornaments and weaponry. An influential role within society was played by the Druids, a priestly class which was responsible for the preservation of learning as well as the conduct of religious affairs. The Britons spoke a variety of Celtic dialects, from one of which Welsh is descended.

Late in the first century BC, the Britons of the south-east were drawn increasingly into commercial and political contact with the Roman empire, which by then extended to the English Channel. British tribal leaders began to enjoy the products of the Mediterranean world brought to them by traders: wine, silver vessels, fine pottery and glass. In exchange they offered grain, metals and slaves. Some of the leading British rulers were recognized as kings by Rome and struck political alliances with the Roman emperor Augustus. Julius Caesar invaded Britain twice, in 55 and 54 BC. On these occasions the Roman army did not stay for long, but their invasion marked the beginning of the end for the tribal society of the Britons. In AD 43, the emperor Claudius sent a major expedition against them and over the next forty years much of Britain was subdued by Roman armies. Some of the tribal rulers threw in their lot with Rome and were allowed to retain a vestige of their authority. The Druids were seen as a dangerous and subversive force by Rome and were abolished. The main resistance came from the Britons of the north and west and it was these that preserved some sense of British identity through four centuries of Roman rule.
See: United Kingdom

The Bulgars

Originally the Bulgars came from an area in the Volga region of south Russia and were related to the Turkish nomads of central Asia. Led by chieftains called khans and nobles called Boyars, they were a ferocious warrior people, superlative horsemen who lived for raiding, plunder and war. During the seventh century AD, they took over territory in the northern Balkans and conquered the Slav peoples settled there, organizing them into a separate political unit. In the Turkish language, their name meant 'those of mixed race' and the first Bulgars to invade the Balkan region were probably descendants of the many different tribes with whom they had mixed during their migrations and conflicts in Russia and central Asia. In the Balkans, the Bulgars were a minority and were steadily merged with the more numerous Slavs, losing their language and their separate identity in the process. But their name survived and their kingdom maintained an independent existence among the other states of the Balkans until the fourteenth century. Under their rulers Asparukh (680–701) and Tervel (701–18), the Bulgars conducted major wars against the Byzantine empire based on Constantinople, thus beginning a struggle which dominated mediaeval Bulgar history and prevented them from building a strong Balkan state. The main aim of these long wars was to seize the city of Constantinople and take possession of its wealth. In the reign of the Khan Krum (808–14) the Bulgars won major victories against the Byzantines, killing one of the emperors, and greatly extended their frontiers both to the east and the west. But these contacts with the Byzantine world were to have profound effects on the Bulgar state. Their ruler Boris I (852–89) accepted the Christian faith, thus joining his people to eastern Christian orthodoxy. Influence on other aspects of Bulgarian culture followed, including the translation of the Bible into Slavonic and the introduction of the Greek (Cyrillic) alphabet.

The peak of mediaeval Bulgarian power was reached under Simeon (893–927). He was able to extend the borders of the kingdom to the Adriatic Sea and proclaimed himself 'emperor of all the Bulgars and the Greeks'. But at the same time Simeon engaged in further warfare against Constantinople and seriously weakened his country by his expenditure on armies. After Simeon, the Bulgars were subjected to a Byzantine counter-attack and to an offensive from their northern neighbours, and their power quickly waned. In the eleventh century, much of Bulgar territory was under Byzantine control, though from the late twelfth century their power was reasserted and their hold on the northern Balkans re-established. Under Ivan Asen II (1218–41) Bulgaria was one of the most powerful of the eastern Christian states. But after 1300 its political power declined sharply as the Ottoman Turks greatly extended their territory to the west.

See: Bulgaria

The Burgundians

The Burgundians were a Germanic people long settled in what is now southern Poland and eastern Germany. They are first mentioned in the second century AD, but they were probably a distinct people a century or more before that.

Early in the fifth century AD they migrated westwards to the middle Rhine, aiming to cross into the former Roman provinces of Gaul. They were beaten back by the Roman general Aetius and settled instead in the Rhine valley in the area of Worms. In 436 the Burgundians were set on and heavily defeated by an army of invading Huns from further east, who, as Roman power declined, were raiding and terrorizing what remained of the Roman empire in Europe. Those Burgundians who survived this defeat moved southward into eastern Gaul and the western Alpine foothills, and later into the valley of the Rhône where they gained the status of allies of Rome in return for military service. The great disaster at the hands of the Huns in 436 echoed down the centuries in Germanic legend and was remembered in the twelfth-century epic poem, the *Niebelungenlied*.

In 451, the Huns were again invading western Europe and Burgundian armies joined with Romans and Visigoths to defeat them, at the battle of Chalons. For the next century the Burgundians maintained a separate kingdom in eastern Gaul. As Franks replaced Romans as rulers of much of Gaul, the Burgundians allied themselves to the rising power and in 534 their kingdom was finally annexed, becoming part of Francia (later France).

Burgundian culture, although short-lived, was relatively advanced when compared with that of the other peoples of Gaul. Their most distinguished king, Gundobad (473–517) produced a law code for his own people, the *Lex Burgundionum*, and another for his Roman subjects. Christianity spread among the Burgundians while they were settled on the Rhine early in the fifth century. One of their princesses, Chlotilde, married the great Frankish king Clovis and it was perhaps through her influence that he was converted to Christianity. But after 534, Burgundian power was over and only their name survived in the land their descendants occupied.
See: France, Germany, Poland, Switzerland

The Celts
Belgae, Bretons, Britons, Gauls, Irish, Welsh

Various tribes and peoples who were referred to as Keltoi by Greek writers and Celti by the Romans lived over a large part of Europe during the Iron Age. They were by no means unified in any political sense and culturally there were great differences between the various Celtic groups. Aside from language and certain aspects of their social organization, there was little that linked together this great mass of peoples who once extended from western Britain and Ireland to south Russia and Turkey, and from the centre of Europe to Spain and Italy.

The Celts are first briefly recorded in Greek sources of the sixth and fifth centuries BC. Hekataeus and Herodotus were aware of them as people who inhabited that part of Europe where the river Danube rose (that is, south-western Germany), southern Gaul and northern Spain. Apart from their location and their name, virtually nothing else was then known about them, though archaeologists have discovered that their culture was already highly developed by that date.

No-one knows whether the Celts were migrants from further east who moved into central Europe and established themselves among the people already living there or whether these original inhabitants themselves developed a way of life which is noticeably different from their earlier more simple one. The first great flowering of Celtic culture occurred in the sixth and fifth centuries BC and is partly connected with more intensive exploitation of mineral resources. Although usually named after the famous and richly furnished cemetery site of Hallstatt in Austria, signs of the same kind of culture are found all over central and western Europe, most strikingly in Austria, Bavaria and Bohemia. The Hallstatt chieftains and their followers were the first people in central Europe to make widespread use of iron, using it in long swords, daggers, large cauldrons and other everyday utensils. The warrior society of Hallstatt was at its peak between 550 and 450 BC. By the fifth century, cultural changes had taken place to west and east of the original area of the Hallstatt, giving rise to a substantial number of local cultures grouped under the general heading of La Tène, a site on Lake Neuchâtel in Switzerland.

By the fifth century BC, Celtic peoples had spread over much of central and western Europe in a series of long-range migrations which are only sketchily recorded by ancient historians. Celtic peoples had reached the British Isles long before the first historical references to the islands. It is likely, though unproven, that this occurred early in the first millennium BC. Between 750 and 500 BC Celtic language and culture had spread into Scotland, and Wales and before 500 BC had reached Ireland. But in both northern and western Britain, pre-Celtic elements survived for many centuries, until long after the Romans had arrived.

Precisely when they arrived and how they spread over the two main islands are matters of dispute, but it seems less and less likely that a single major migration of Celtic people to Britain took place at any date. More probably, a warrior aristocracy imposed itself on the resident population, seeking to enlarge their wealth and prestige. Retainers and families would then have followed to establish more permanent settlements.

Celtic expansion into some areas, however, was certainly achieved by military forces of considerable scale. Early in the fourth century BC Celts swept into northern Italy in strength, taking Rome in 390 and severely curtailing Etruscan power. Further east, Celts were settled in the middle Danube valley in what are now Hungary and Yugoslavia before 350 BC. Fifty years later they began to threaten Greece, reaching Delphi in 278 and settling in parts of the northern Balkans. One group of tribes passed further east into Asia Minor and there founded the kingdom of Galatia (named from the Galli, Gauls). Some of these eastern Celts took service as mercenary soldiers with Hellenistic kings, serving as far away as Upper Egypt. Others found their way to the Black Sea coastlands and the Crimea in south Russia.

When first encountered by the literate cultures of the Mediterranean world, Celtic society was hierarchical and dominated by warrior-elites whose power depended upon their prestige and success in war. The Celtic tribes who had already settled in northern Italy were joined by others from beyond the Alps to fight in a major battle against the Romans in 225 BC. One Roman historian, Polybius, described them. The Alpine Celts, he wrote, fought in the front line of the battle wearing nothing but golden torques around their necks and golden armlets. The 'Italian' Celts were more practically dressed in breeches and short cloaks. Later Romans described the Celts as tall and muscular, with fair skin, fair curly hair and blue eyes. Some wore short beards, others had long moustaches but were otherwise clean-shaven. There are also descriptions of swept-back hair, held in place with a paste made of lime. Masks and stylized portraits found in some of the burial grounds confirm this style, perhaps a warrior's fashion. These descriptions are all, of course, of fighting men and may not have been typical of the ordinary Celtic people. They show, at least, that the Romans considered they looked significantly different from themselves.

From an early date and throughout their history, Celtic societies were geared to warfare, both against other Celts and against external enemies. For many warriors this was their way of life and not merely a means to achieve glory, though success in battle was of great moment for a man's prestige. There were major repercussions for the character of Celtic kingship. Kings had to maintain a successful record in battle if they wished to hold on to power. In general, a king had in any case little coercive power, the will of the leading warriors often carried much greater weight. Large political units of more than a single tribe thus rarely survived for long. The more usual unit was a warrior chiefdom controlling major resources such as land, metals and salt.

The more powerful of these chiefdoms were in contact with Greek and Etruscan traders, especially those who could provide fine bronzeware, pottery and other prestigious goods. These imports from the Mediterranean world frequently furnished the graves of Celtic leaders and their entourages, as is seen at Vix in central France and at Hochdorf in southern Germany. Imported luxury goods also stimulated Celtic metalsmiths to enlarge the range of their technical expertise and provided fresh designs which were adapted into new forms. The skill of these Celtic craftsmen was very great and they held high positions in society. Superb gold-work was produced in the last two centuries BC and excellent bronze vessels, weapons and ornaments throughout the heydey of the Celts.

The settlements of the earlier Celts include a wide variety of sites. The most impressive are the great hill-forts of central and western Europe, with defences that are still imposing and eloquent of a warlike age. Some of these strongholds were clearly the residences of chieftains and their followers. But there were many lesser fortified sites and still more enclosed settlements which were the homesteads and villages of peasants who worked the land. The single family unit played a central role in Celtic society and this is clearly reflected in the large number of small enclosed settlements, the holdings of nuclear families owing allegiance to a warrior-lord. Myths and legends are unreliable as historical sources but the epic stories of early Ireland describe a society akin to that discovered by archaeologists.

In the second century BC, very large, partly urban settlements emerged in Celtic central Europe (the *oppida* described by Roman writers) and quickly spread to the west. These were not only centres of political power, but also of commerce and industry, the forerunners of the cities that grew up under Roman rule. Outstanding examples of these oppida are Manching in Bavaria and Mont-Beuvray and Alesia in France.

A coinage in gold and silver, and later in bronze, was struck by Celtic chieftains, imitating Macedonian Greek coins from the late fourth century onward. These were originally high value coins, designed to reward warriors in precious metal, but by the first century BC a market economy had developed over much of the Celtic world and coins were used for commercial transactions.

Celtic agriculture was highly efficient, producing a surplus of grain which could be stored in timber granaries and underground storage-pits. Several hill-forts and farmsteads reveal large numbers of such structures, indicating an organized system of collection and storage. Animal husbandry was well developed; sheep, goats, cattle, pigs and horses were all raised and at Celtic feasts quantities of meat were consumed, especially pork, which was regarded as the champion's portion.

The supernatural world of the Celts was very rich in the observance of rituals and the power of magic. Like many other Indo-European peoples, their religious concerns lay with fertility and the afterlife, with war and the world of nature. Elements of Celtic religion survived the period of Roman rule and beyond. Although no pantheon of deities like that of the Graeco-Roman world existed a number of Celtic gods were worshipped over large areas of western Europe. Among these were Lug, whose name appears in several place-names (for example, Lugdunum, now Lyon), Cernunnos the horned god of the underworld, Epona, the queen goddess who appeared as mare, and Taranis, god of the sky and thunder. Triads of deities, or triple deities, were also widespread, notably the Matres or Matronae, mother-goddesses associated with particular places or regions, especially in the Rhineland and northern Gaul. Large numbers of Celtic deities were worshipped in Gaul, Britain and Germany during the life of the Roman empire, as many inscriptions, temples and votive objects reveal. Several old Celtic beliefs still survive as superstitions throughout Europe.

On the north-western fringes of the Roman world Celtic societies continued during the life of the empire and, after its fall, there was a resurgence of Celtic culture, though this was influenced by the earlier world of Rome and by the contemporary Germanic realms. Some of the finest achievements of the late Celtic world, such as the Book of Kells and the Ardagh chalice, were made under the influence of the Christian faith, of which Celtic missionaries and saints were formidable exponents.

Societies which are descended from those of the early Celts are still alive, along with Celtic languages, in Ireland, Wales, western Scotland and Brittany, though influenced by more recent cultures and experience.
See: Austria, Czechoslovakia, France, Germany, Greece, Hungary, Ireland, Italy, Russia, Spain, Switzerland, United Kingdom, Yugoslavia

The Croats

The Croats now settled on the eastern Adriatic coast, as neighbours of the Serbs, are one of the major western Slav peoples. Like the Serbs, the Croats speak Serbo-Croat, with minor variations, but use the Latin script while Serbs employ the Cyrillic alphabet.

Croats probably originated in western Russia and moved west into the northern Balkans in the mid- or late sixth century AD. In 614 they captured the Roman city of Salona on the Adriatic coast and consolidated their hold on the north-western Balkans and the Adriatic coastland. They had arrived as pagans and were gradually converted to Christianity from the seventh to the ninth centuries. From the beginning, they followed the Roman Christian tradition, in contrast to the neighbouring Serbs who adopted the eastern, Byzantine form. As a result, the Croats have always been more open to western European cultural influences than the Serbs.

In 925 the Croats founded their own kingdom under King Tomislav. They were surrounded by potentially hostile neighbours and strongly resisted attempts by the Byzantines, Bulgars and Venetians to encroach upon them: by the eleventh century, the Croatian kingdom was one of the leading powers of the northern Balkans. After 1100, however, it was annexed by the Magyars to the north and remained under Magyar rule for the next eight centuries. Conquest by the Ottoman Turks in 1526 and later rule by the Hapsburgs of Austria did not extinguish the Croats as a separate people and in the age of European nationalism after 1830 Croatian ambitions towards independence began to find a voice. Croatians took a growing interest in their own language, literature and culture, but the grip of Austria-Hungary was maintained until the end of the First World War.

Although the Croats were included in the new state of Yugoslavia after 1918, this was not welcomed by all of them. Tension with their eastern neighbours, the Serbs, was ever-present and under German occupation from 1941 Croatian nationalism found savage outlets for its intense dislike of Serbs. A Nazi-backed regime was responsible for atrocities against the Serb minority in Croatia and the bitterness which was then engendered survived through the following communist era until today.
See: Yugoslavia

The Czechs

The Czechs belong to the western Slavs and arrived in their present homeland in the late fifth or early sixth century AD, having migrated westward from beyond the Carpathians. They took over the area around the headwaters of the Vlata (a region earlier occupied by Germanic tribes), and during the seventh century became part of the earliest Slav state, founded by the Frankish merchant Samo. Two centuries later, Czechs were brought together with Slovaks in the Great Moravian Empire and from 863 were converted to Christianity by Byzantine missionaries. A Magyar invasion early in the tenth century separated the Czechs from the Slovaks again: the Czech kingdom was not conquered but the Slovaks fell under Magyar rule.

The power and influence of the Czechs grew significantly after AD 1000 with the kingdom of Bohemia coming to include Moravia, much of Silesia and Lusatia (now in Poland). The kingdom became a strong force in central Europe and attracted large numbers of German settlers, especially to the western and northern areas. These immigrants brought advanced skills in mining, agriculture, commerce and crafts, but were strongly resented by many native Czechs. In 1306, Bohemia came under the control of the house of Luxembourg and the rule of the Holy Roman Emperor Charles IV. This opened up a Golden Age for Bohemia; Prague became the political capital of the Holy Roman Empire and the Charles University, a major centre of culture and learning, was founded there. The city was adorned with many splendid buildings at this time in accord with its heightened status.

The Roman Catholic Church had become a wealthy and powerful force within Bohemia by the fourteenth century, though perpetrating the same abuses as elsewhere. Towards the end of the century, Jan Hus, rector of the Charles University, along with other Czech preachers, attacked these abuses, gaining much support from the population. When Hus was burned as a heretic in 1415, a massive revolt was sparked off in Bohemia, directed both at the Church and its mainly German hierarchy. This sequence of events is seen by Czechs as the first Protestant reformation and as one of the great episodes in their history. The followers of Hus later broke into factions which resorted to war to settle their differences. The more moderate Hussites clung to their faith throughout the following centuries, although with increasing difficulty after the Austrian Hapsburgs took control in 1526. Under the Hapsburg dynasty, the Czechs lost much of their nationhood, religion, leadership and, to an extent, language. Many became serfs on the estates of foreign landowners. Many more died in the chaos of the Thirty Years War (1618–48), these losses being counterbalanced by more German immigration. But the Czech nation did not disappear and from the late eighteenth century a small group of nobles and writers began a Czech national revival. The idea of a Czech state began to gain ground in the mid-nineteenth century, possibly in association with the Slovaks. Finally, in late 1918 the Czechs were incorporated in the new state of Czechoslovakia.

See: Czechoslovakia, Poland

The Dacians

The Dacians, or Daci, inhabited the Carpathians and the lowlands in what is now Romania. A tribal society, they were neither Celtic nor Germanic, but their metalwork, weapons and ways of fighting were influenced both by the Celts and by the nomads of western Russia. Like the eastern Celts, the Dacians evolved an advanced barbarian society in which a warrior-elite and powerfully defended hill-top settlements were major features. There were large reserves of gold on their territory and they carried on a busy trade with merchants from the Mediterranean world. Although they first came to real prominence in the first century BC, their ancestry can be traced back to the third or fourth centuries BC, when they may have arrived as migrants from the western steppes or the Black Sea region.

By the first century AD, they had become formidable military opponents of the Roman empire. Their warrior-king Decebalus organized his army along Roman lines and began to threaten the Roman frontier on the lower Danube. In AD 85 they attacked the Roman province of Moesia south of the Danube (now part of Bulgaria) and had to be forced back north of the river. In AD 91 peace was agreed, but Decebalus was left in position as king and even granted a financial subsidy by Rome. He thereafter continued to strengthen his power and expand his territory, so that in AD 101–2 the emperor Trajan was forced to mount a major invasion of Dacia. Decebalus was disarmed but was again left in control of his kingdom and another great expedition was required, in 105–7, to bring him down and force him to suicide. The wars of Trajan against the Dacians form the subject of the reliefs on Trajan's Column, set up in Rome to celebrate final victory.

After the defeat of Decebalus, his kingdom became the Roman province of Dacia with its capital at Sarmizegethusa. Its exposed position north of the Danube meant that it came under increasing pressure from invading barbarians in the third century and it was finally abandoned as a province of the Roman empire shortly after AD 270. The Romans who had settled there did not all move south of the Danube. Many remained and continued a Roman style of life for a generation or more. But from the fourth century

onward they were absorbed into the mixed population of the Carpathian region. However, modern Romanians tend to look back to Roman Dacia rather than the Dacians themselves as their ancestral culture.
See: Romania

The Danes

There is evidence that people were living in Denmark from at least 12,000 years BC. By 4000 BC there were settled farming communities and as early as 2000 BC there is evidence of craftsmen skilled in bronze work. After 500 BC they were working with iron and a more organized society developed with chiefs ruling over communities of farmers, craftsmen and warriors.

By the sixth century AD, when they were first mentioned as a separate people (by the Byzantine writer Jordanes), Danes were living in northern Denmark and southern Sweden. They had, however, been in contact with both southern Scandinavia and with the Roman empire for hundreds of years.

The Danish people were chiefly agriculturalists, though part of their wealth came from trade. Their society consisted mainly of prosperous farmers and a substratum of peasants or even slaves. There does not seem to have been a rich nobility in any organized sense, but the hoards of spectacular gold objects that have been uncovered prove that some people were able to accumulate great wealth. The Danes have a rich legendary history, some elements of which are founded on actual events and personalities. We hear of the kings Hrolf Kraki and Harald Wartooth, both of whom probably represent a period in Danish history when warlords ruled the land. Although warfare and conquest are the stuff of these accounts, it was agriculture and trade that made up the everyday lives of ordinary people and gave them what wealth they had. The social units which really mattered were not kingdoms, but the homestead, hamlet and village. From groups of these, men gathered for the *Thing*, the body which was responsible for law and government in a particular district. Within these communities there were craftsmen as well as farmers: metalsmiths, carpenters, boatbuilders, potters, weavers, ropemakers, and also learned men who conducted ceremonies for the dead and could recite the deeds of the people's ancestors. Certain individual places were of outstanding ritual and religious importance. At Lejre, near Roskilde, for instance, was an ancient burial place which much later came to serve as the site of a warlord's court and a heathen shrine where, every ninth year, ninety-nine men and the same number of horses, dogs and cocks were sacrificed to the gods.

During the eighth century AD Danes took part in Viking raids on north-western Europe and Russia as a result of which they settled in what is now northern Holland and eastern England during the ninth century. They conquered and held a large area of eastern and northern England and ruled that territory, called the Danelaw, from 876 to about 925. The major Danish towns of the Danelaw were the Five Boroughs of Lincoln, Leicester, Derby, Nottingham and Stamford. On the mainland, Danish power extended at this time as far south as the river Eider and northward into central Sweden, providing important bases and harbours for trade which were easily reached by sea from both east and west. A major trading centre existed during the early mediaeval centuries at Hedeby (Haithabu) near Schleswig where Ansgar, a Frankish monk, built the first Christian church in Denmark in 826. But Christianity did not extend throughout the Danish homeland until the tenth century and the reign of Harold Bluetooth (c. 940–85).

Harold extended Danish control into Norway and for a time the Danish Vikings controlled a North Sea empire which reached from Norway to western Britain. After the death of Cnut (Canute) in 1035, however, Danish power retreated to roughly its twentieth century boundaries plus the southern part of Sweden. In the tenth and eleventh centuries more people moved to live and work in towns and a striking series of military fortifications was built, at Trelleborg, Fyrkat, Odense and Aggersborg. The southern land border of Denmark was also partly marked by a frontier earthwork, the *Danevirke*.

Danish influence in eastern Britain was strong and distinctive laws and customs survived there into the twelfth century. Placenames containing the Danish elements -by (farm) and -thorpe (hamlet) are still common in Lincolnshire and Yorkshire.

See: Denmark, Holland, Norway, Sweden, United Kingdom

The Etruscans

In central Italy between the rivers Arno and Tiber (broadly Tuscany, Umbria and Latium), there originated one of the most striking of ancient Mediterranean cultures, that of the people called by the Greeks Tyrrhenoi, by the Romans Etrusci. Their homeland became known as Etruria.

Etruscan origins have been (and still are) debated with great passion, but there is a growing consensus that their culture was not imported by invaders from the eastern Mediterranean but developed within central Italy, under the stimulus of contact with a variety of external peoples, especially Greeks. By 700 BC their contacts with these more advanced societies had brought about a series of social and economic changes in Etruria and over the next two centuries the cities, communications and trade that developed there made it the most advanced civilization in the western Mediterranean before that of Rome, on whom the Etruscans were a major formative influence.

Etruscan culture was city-based from an early date, the older cities lying on or near the western coast: Veii, Vulci, Tarquinii and Caere. From this area Etruscan culture spread north and east across the Apennines into Umbria and towards the Alps. Invading Celts pushed them back southward in the fifth century. The Etruscans expanded south into Latium and Campania in the sixth century, but this was a short-lived venture, meeting resistance from the Samnites and later from Rome. For a time they built up naval power in the western Mediterranean but this was brought to an end by the Greeks of Campania and Syracuse in a battle in the Bay of Naples in 474 BC. On land, too, Etruscan power was challenged after 450 and during the third century Etruria was steadily swallowed up by Rome.

The cultural achievements of the Etruscans were for long known primarily from the princely tombs in cemeteries such as those at Tarquinii, Orvieto and Chiusi. The sophisticated paintings in these tombs give a vivid picture of aristocratic life, in which scenes of banqueting and dancing, wrestling, racing and hunting are counterbalanced by images of death and the underworld. The influence of Greek painting in southern Italy is evident, but the Etruscan artists created their own distinctive tradition.

Magnificent bronzes were also produced, the two most famous being the she-wolf from the Capitoline in Rome and the Chimaera from Arezzo. Sculpture in bronze and terracotta reveals the influence of Greek craftsmanship, as does their painted pottery, some of which may indeed have been made by immigrant Greeks. Bronze-working, both for large statues and small figurines, and for fine tableware, had a more distinctly Etruscan style. One of the most typical and attractive products of the bronzesmiths was a series of mirrors with their backs decorated with mythological and religious scenes. Etruscan vessels for the feast, winebuckets, cups and flagons as well as furniture, were widely exported to other parts of the Mediterranean and to the Celtic world of central and western Europe. The decoration of major buildings, especially temples, with painted terracotta was another Etruscan speciality which influenced the art of other Italian peoples, including the Romans.

We are no longer entirely dependent upon tombs and cemeteries for our knowledge of the Etruscans and their world. Much Etruscan monumental building was destroyed in later times, but the excavations of temples and other public buildings show work of high quality. Both in architecture and engineering, Etruscan achievements were in themselves considerable and had further impact on Roman practice. As more settlements are excavated, archaeologists are building a picture of their everyday life. Etruscan cities and their territories were taking shape in the sixth century BC along the familiar lines of the small city-states of the Greek Aegean. Planned layouts of streets are known, as for instance at Marzabotto, and the public buildings of a city, its temples, markets and public squares were clearly distinguished from the residential quarters. The richer houses were also carefully planned and some had sophisticated systems of drainage. Relations between city and country were close since the inhabitants of the cities depended on the rural community for food and much attention was given to the improvement and cultivation of farming land. At Spina in the delta of the river Po large areas of fertile land were reclaimed from the marshes by means of canals and sluices. When the Etruscans' sea-power ended early in the fifth century BC and trade with other countries became correspondingly more difficult, their exploitation of the resources of their own land increased, especially by the inland cities. Grain, olives and vines were produced and flocks of sheep and goats were kept. In many parts of Etruria agriculture was greatly assisted by irrigation through carefully constructed water-channels or *cuniculi*.

The cities came under increasing social stress from the fourth century, for reasons that are not yet clear, and the ruling urban-based landowners began to lose control of their own people. Tarquinii was badly affected and later the cities of Vulci and Caere both lost much of their territory to Rome. In 273 BC the Romans were able to found a colony at Cosa on Vulcian territory, without Etruscan intervention. Gradually, the Etruscan ruling class became Romanized. Some cities not only became impoverished but were abandoned or destroyed. This was the fate of the southern Etruscan city of Veii only twelve miles north of Rome. Others slowly declined as political and economic centres, but a number, including Arezzo, Perugia and Fiesole, continued to develop under Roman rule. There is still much to learn about Etruscan urban life and culture, especially in those cities which continued to be occupied after the Roman conquest, but it is certain that at their peak in the fifth century BC Etruscan centres were among the most imposing cities of their day.

The Etruscans were regarded by other peoples of the Mediterranean world as unusually devoted to religion and it is true that their beliefs and observances were marked by what is to us an uncommon attention to the will of the gods, to ritual practices, especially divination, to fear of supernatural forces and the immensity of time. But we cannot claim that they were any more or less religious than the other peoples of ancient Italy because we have insufficient evidence of the practices of others. One of the most clearly marked features of Etruscan religion was the dominance of the gods and the insignificance of mankind before them. Relations between the gods and human beings were therefore seen as matters of exceptional importance and were governed by complex rules. The wishes and purposes of the gods had to be discovered before any important undertaking, either public or private. The most important means of doing this was the interpretation of the entrails (especially the liver) of animals and the behaviour of lightning. Divination from an animal's liver (*haruspicina*) was adopted by the Romans from Etruscan priests. A bronze model of a sheep's liver, found at Piacenza, was apparently designed to guide the process of interpretation.

The underworld, the abode of the dead, also played a part in Etruscan religious thought. This is abundantly clear from the magnificent aristocratic tombs at sites like Caere and Tarquinii. Many of these were built and adorned like spacious houses, complete with domestic objects and walls decorated with scenes of human activity, generally pleasurable. The individuality of the dead person was to be preserved after death by maintaining the connection between earthly activities and possessions and the mortal remains. Family cults of dead ancestors also marked this link between the living and the dead. Although a pantheon of Etruscan deities was worshipped, most of them with clear Roman counterparts, Greek cults also had an impact on Etruscan Italy. The most important of these were the cults of Hercle (Herakles), Apulu (Apollo) and Aritimi (Artemis). Several of the purely Etruscan gods were ancient in origin and were connected with age-old human concerns, the fertility of the earth, the sky and death.

The language spoken by the Etruscans has presented problems ever since Etruscan culture was rediscovered in the Renaissance. It is known largely from about 10,000 inscriptions in an alphabet derived from that of the Greeks, most of them funerary inscriptions which simply give the names of the dead they commemorate. Etruscan was not an Indo-European language like Greek and Latin and its origins are still disputed, for it is not closely related to any other languages surviving from an early date. It is now usually thought to be an ancient Italian language, not one introduced from the eastern Mediterranean, but much still remains to be learned about its structure. No written works have survived and it is not known for certain whether any existed.
See: Italy

The Finns

The Finns are probably descended from the broad family of nomadic peoples of the wesern Asian steppes. The earliest known Finns arrived as migrants across the Gulf of Finland from Estonia and Russia in the early Christian centuries. The language they brought with them bears witness to their origin, for it is not Indo-European but instead belongs to the Finno-Ugrian group and is thus related to Estonian and Hungarian or Magyar. The newcomers entered a sparsely populated land, in which hunting and fishing were the prime means of sustaining life. They spread into the country along the river routes from the south in search of new hunting territories. Agriculture was established only in the south; for the next fifteen hundred years, hunting, fishing and trapping remained staple ways of life for the Finns. Furs became a major item of export to Sweden and Russia.

Three groups of early Finns can be distinguished before the eleventh century AD. In the south-west, the richest area of Finland, lay the Suomalaiset, who later gave the country its Finnish name, Suomi. Inland were the Tavastians and to the east the Karelians. The groups were hostile to each other and they were often at war. The Finns were therefore slow to form a single, strong political unit and so were vulnerable to their neighbours, the Swedes and Russians. In the mediaeval period, the Swedes in particular exercised a powerful commercial and cultural influence on them.

In origin the Finns are distinct from the Scandinavian peoples beside whom they live and this is evident in their physique, which tends to be shorter, with darker hair and eyes. Later genetic influence from the taller, fair Swedes, however, has also left its mark, especially in the south.
See: Estonia, Finland, Russia

The Franks

The people who were to give their name to France are first mentioned by name after AD 250. At this time they were a new grouping of small tribes, living between the Rhine and the Weser. The name Frank is derived from a German word (*frech*) meaning bold or courageous, a further indication that their origin was as a military confederacy. The later Franks had very hazy ideas of their own origins, resorting to myth to explain their appearance but all the other evidence is that, as a separate group, they began as war-bands bent on attacking the Roman provinces on the lower Rhine.

The Salian (or Salty) Franks lived north of the Rhine, along the River Ijssel, in what is now Holland. With the Alamanni and others, they raided

Gaul between AD 250 and 275 and caused widespread devastation far to the south. Some settled on the plains of what became northern Belgium and later as many as 100,000 may have followed the valleys of the Schelde and Lys to the more fertile agricultural lands of northern Gaul. The settlement of the Germanic-speaking Franks in Belgium is broadly the same as the spread of Flemish in eastern and northern Belgium today. They came to a halt around Tournai where the land was sufficiently thinly populated to allow them to remain. There they became allies of Rome, farming the land and providing troops for the Roman forces. Other Franks formed units in the Roman army and some of the major commanders in the fourth century imperial armies were Franks or men with Frankish blood. Late in the fourth century richly furnished burials of warriors in northern Gaul and the Rhineland bear witness to the close relations between the Franks and Roman provincial garrisons.

The contents of graves also show that the Franks were foot-soldiers rather than horsemen since the weapons that were buried with them were usually a short sword and a throwing axe. Roman writers described them as tall, rough people with fair or red hair worn long. Warriors shaved their beards but left a moustache.

As Roman power in northern Gaul waned, the Franks began to take control. Frankish settlement west of the Rhine steadily grew and several small kingdoms were established. After AD 450 Frankish enclaves around Tournai, Trier and Cologne assumed greater political significance, with Tournai forming the centre of the kingdom ruled by Childeric by about 460. Childeric's grave, dating from 482, reveals the wealth of this early kingdom and its widespread trade links with both the northern and the Mediterranean worlds.

Chlodovech, or Clovis as he is better known, raised the Frankish monarchy to a far more commanding height. He unified by conquest most of the petty chiefdoms of the Franks from the Channel coast to the Rhine and southward to the Seine, attacked the Germanic tribes east of the Rhine and swept away the last vestige of Gallo-Roman authority in the area about Soissons. Encircling the Burgundians from the north, Clovis compelled them to join in his most ambitious campaign, that against the Visigoths in the south-west. This ended in the great Frankish victory at Vouillé, near Poitiers, in 507, a battle which turned the Visigoths towards Spain and ensured that Frankish rule would be extended over most of what was to become France. At the death of Clovis in 511 the Franks had become the most powerful Germanic kingdom in the west.

That Frankish power did not progress in the sixth century was largely due to internal struggles within the ruling dynasty and to the competing ambitions of the nobles. The land which the Franks occupied was, however, rich and productive, and, without the pressures of campaigning, normal life began to return to the major cities and the trade network. Clovis had been baptized into the Christian Church, probably mainly for political reasons, and the faith made considerable progress among the ranks of noble families from 500 onward. Bishops were frequently leading figures in their regions and some were men of learning and literary attainment. Chief among these was Gregory of Tours who, in the late sixth century, wrote a notable history of the Franks, along with other Latin works.

Many elements in Frankish culture show a combination of Roman and Germanic elements, as the Germanic settlers mixed with the existing population. The social importance of the nobles is revealed in their wealthy burials, especially in the sixth and seventh centuries, at such places as Krefeld-Gellep, Cologne and Morken in the Rhineland, and at St-Denis near Paris. The contents of the graves show a warrior aristocracy fond of display and with the wealth to indulge in fine clothing, ornaments and weapons, often imported from other parts of the Germanic world. These nobles often lived in old Roman towns and cities, though their wealth came from estates in the country. The common people lived in relatively modest villages and homesteads, few of which have yet been excavated. In many cases the early Franks settled on or close to the sites of old Roman villa-estates, in some cases probably as peasants who worked the land. Many mediaeval villages came into being in this way and their successors are still there today. The communities of the time must have been very mixed, with Franks, Romans and Celts living side by side. The excavated Frankish villages, such as Neuwied and Brebières, are small, but no doubt larger communities existed, especially from the sixth century onward. Some of the major Roman cities retained their importance under the Franks, both as royal or ecclesiastical centres or as aristocratic residences.

The Franks learned from the Romans the value of an orderly, administered society and the Salic Law, drawn up originally in the sixth century, codified the rules for a rural, agricultural community, listing penalties for thefts and emphasizing the importance of the family over the individual. To protect family property from being transferred to other families through marriage, the law laid down that a woman could not inherit if any male heir survived.

The original Franks spoke a Germanic language and their linguistic descendants are not the modern French but the Dutch and the Flemings who still inhabit the Low Countries of the old Frankish homeland. In Gaul, the Latin language proved stronger than that of the Franks.

Frankish power was consolidated over France, the Low Countries and beyond the Rhine in the later sixth and seventh centuries. As they expanded eastwards into central and southern Germany they came into conflict with the Alamanni, whom they increasingly confined to the Alpine regions and south-western Germany, and also with the Thuringians, Bavarians and Lombards. Charles Martel ('the Hammer') strengthened the Frankish hold on Provence and began to exert greater influence in Bavaria and Italy. In 732 he also won an important victory at Poitiers against the Arabs, driving them back to Spain. Pepin continued this consolidation of Frankish power and was eventually succeeded by Charlemagne in 771, the beginning of a new era of conquest.

For the first ten years of his long rule, Charlemagne was at war in central Germany, northern Italy and Spain. He was not invariably successful. In 778 his forces in Spain had to fight their way out of a dangerous situation in the Pyrenees and the rearguard was severely harassed by the Basques in the Pass of Roncevalles. In the same year there were many revolts against Frankish rule in Saxony, in Italy and in Aquitaine, all of them firmly put down. Over the next twelve years Charlemagne extended his empire, conquering the Saxons and Frisians in the north, absorbing Bavaria and pacifying France as far as the Pyrenees. Within these years Charlemagne developed a strong sense of Christian mission and clergy were sent out to the newly conquered Saxons, and even to the Slavs and Avars. Scholarship, too, earned high respect at his court. Scholars and books were sought from Italy and England to advance the cause of learning. The king's admiration for the heritage of Rome found expression in the great palace which he built at Aachen (Aix-la-Chapelle), adorned with columns and marbles from Rome and Ravenna and enriched with treasures from many parts of the new Frankish realm.

On Christmas Day 800 the Carolingian empire was formerly created when Charlemagne was crowned emperor by the pope, an act designed to mark a renewal of Roman imperial power. His rule over western Europe could fairly be regarded as the most extensive of any since the late Roman empire. From a series of war-bands east of the Rhine, the Franks had emerged as the most powerful kingdom in early mediaeval Europe, ancestors not only of the French, whose country still bears their name, but also of many of the early inhabitants of Belgium and Germany.

See: Belgium, France, Germany, Holland, Italy

The Frisians

The prehistoric ancestors of the Frisians occupied the areas that are now northern Holland and the adjacent coastland of northern Germany for many centuries before their descendants were first mentioned by Roman writers in the first century AD. In origin they were a Germanic people who were famous as pastoralists, keeping cattle and sheep on the meadows and coastal marshes of their homeland. Because this coastal region was frequently flooded by the sea, it was periodically abandoned and the people who lived by the marshes developed a specialized lifestyle, often in settlements raised up on artificial mounds (*terpen*) for protection against floods.

They were subject to Rome in the reign of Augustus (late in the first century BC), but revolted when demands for tribute became increasingly heavy. Later, however, they seem to have co-existed peaceably with the Roman empire for three centuries, trading with Roman frontier provinces. When the Roman hold on the lands of the lower Rhine began to weaken, Frisians joined with Franks and Saxons in attacking Roman territory to the west, while some still moved eastward into the Weser valley. Still others accompanied the Saxons and Angles to eastern Britain.

Later, in the sixth century AD, the Frisians were conquered by the Franks and Charlemagne brought them within his empire in 785. They were, however, allowed a measure of independence within the empire, the so-called Frisian Liberty, which was later used to support various political claims. By this date the Frisians had become heavily involved in trade in the North Sea, the Channel and the Baltic and their reputation as merchants remained high into the Middle Ages.

The Frisians were very tenacious of their own ways. In spite of the efforts of Christian missionaries most Frisians were still pagan when in the mid-eighth century a group murdered St Boniface. Their social structure retained early features well into the mediaeval centuries, when other areas had turned to feudalism and the manorial system of land ownership.

Danes arrived as Viking raiders and settled in Frisia during the eighth century, but they did not dominate the region. Later, it was divided into a number of small independent states and managed to keep the rulers of the southern Netherlands at bay until the thirteenth century.

Even then, Frisia as a whole was not permanently conquered. After a period of anarchy and civil war much of the land passed into the control of the Holy Roman Empire. Frisian culture and language survived these vicissitudes and remains strong today. The language is a branch of north-western Germanic, related to Anglo-Saxon, and has been the vehicle for a rich literature, especially in the seventeenth century. Modern Frisians have retained a strong sense that they form a distinct people with a very long history, a feeling for which there is every justification.
See: Germany, Holland, United Kingdom

The Gauls

The Celtic peoples who inhabited the lands between the Alps and the Po valley (now France and northern Italy) were called Galli (Gauls) by the Romans. Their origins lie far back in the middle of the first millennium BC, when a number of Celtic chiefdoms were established in the centre and east of the territory that became theirs. They rapidly developed the rich agricultural resources of the land and traded their surplus with the Greek colonies on the southern coast, receiving in exchange luxury goods and Mediterranean wine. Over the following three centuries, the chiefdoms were replaced by a stable system of tribes, some of which covered large areas and developed quite sophisticated political systems in which magistrates replaced kings as the ruling authority. Before 400 BC, several Gaulish tribes had crossed the Alps and established themselves in northern Italy. From that base they were able to attack the Etruscans and in one massive southward thrust, in 390 BC, they seized the city of Rome and sacked it. But their hold on central Italy was brief and their forces returned to the north. The southern Gauls, close to the Mediterranean coast, came under increasing influence from Rome in the second century BC and their territory became a Roman province (Gallia Narbonensis or Gaul) from about 120 BC. Those in the centre and the north remained independent until their conquest by Julius Caesar between 58 and 52 BC.

The Gauls were a warrior people and fighting was a principal concern of the leaders and nobles, though not their only activity. The feasts and drinking bouts of their warrior elite were legendary even in their own time, occasions for extravagant boasting about their exploits. Although formidable at first sight, however, their armies were usually less effective against well disciplined Roman adversaries, but their courage was famed throughout the ancient world and many were recruited into the Roman army. The Romans, for their part, were impressed by the great size of the Gauls and their long, unkempt hair and the trousers they wore (a non-Mediterranean garment) merely seemed to underline their barbarity. The warrior aristocracy was extremely fond of display, as the superb ornaments and weapons made for them by their metalsmiths shows. Indeed, the art of the Gauls, especially in bronze, was outstanding and the best pieces are among the masterpieces of later prehistoric Europe. Their religion was administered by the Druids, who also transmitted the peoples' learning from generation to generation and presided over ceremonies in which human sacrifice could play a part, though this was probably not a common practice. Their religion was concerned with many aspects of human condition that in one way or another are still common today–fertility, death, the afterlife, warfare–but it could equally take forms that are alien to us. One cult involved the worship of severed heads, mainly those of prisoners taken in warfare.

Julius Caesar's conquest of the Gauls in the mid-first century BC brought them within the Roman empire, where they were organized in three

provinces. They adapted well to Roman forms of urban life, developing major cities which were to flourish throughout the Roman period. The Celtic language continued to be spoken over most of Gaul, but Latin was widely used in educated circles and provided a substantial part of the basis for French in due course. In the fifth century AD, Gaul was a noted centre of late Roman cultural life and letters. By 511, Franks had replaced Romans as the ruling power and the Celtic Gauls were gradually absorbed into the mixed population. Of all the Celtic tribes in Gaul, only the Bretons retained their language and culture into the succeeding centuries.
See: France, Italy

The Gepids

The Gepids were a shadowy Germanic people who originated in eastern Europe. They did not succeed in holding on to a block of territory for long enough to create a permanent state and thus little is known of their history and traditions. All we know is what is said of them in the history of other peoples with whom they joined or, more often, by whom they were attacked.

They first appear in historical accounts shortly after the middle of the third century AD when, together with the Goths, they attacked the Roman province of Dacia. Later they were subdued by a branch of the Goths north of the river Danube in Hungary and later still, in the early fifth century AD, they became vassals of the Huns. After the collapse of the Huns' power in the middle of the fifth century, they found a homeland in the Carpathian basin in Romania, but a century later they were forced out once more. They were dispersed in several directions in the mid-sixth century when the semi-nomadic Avars attacked them and never appeared again as a separate people with a clearly defined territory. Their descendants are now scattered among the peoples of Hungary and nations to the east.

Gepid culture is chiefly known to us from the wealthy burials of warriors and their womenfolk. Their metal jewellery and other ornaments are similar to those of the Lombards, near whom they were settled in the earlier sixth century.
See: Hungary, Romania

The Germans

Alamanni, Angles, Burgundians, Danes, Franks, Frisians, Gepids, Goths, Jutes, Saxons, Suevi, Swedes

The peoples whom the Greeks called Germanoi and the Romans Germani are not mentioned in the historical record until the early first century BC, though their tribal societies had clearly existed for long before that date.

The origins of the German peoples can be traced back to at least 1000 BC, by which time Indo-European peoples were living in much of northern and central Europe. It now seems unlikely that large-scale immigration into the north was responsible for the appearance of the Germanic peoples. The bulk of the population probably descended from those who had been settled on the land since before 3000 BC.

The early German heartland was the north German plain from the Rhine to the Vistula and the southern region of Scandinavia. Later, German peoples spread to the Danube valley and south-east to the Black Sea. In central Europe they were in contact with the other major peoples of the time, with Celts, Dacians and the various nomadic tribes who from time to time moved westwards in search of better land or to trade their goods.

The first Germanic contact with the Mediterranean world came in the late second century BC, when a large force of Germans (Cimbri and Teutones) descended on the middle Danube lands in search of land and plunder, defeated a Roman army and then swung westward into Gaul. They remained there for some years before being defeated in two battles by the Roman general Marius. Forty years later German war-bands were crossing the upper Rhine into Gaul under their king Ariovistus, giving Julius Caesar an ideal pretext for military intervention in Gaul. Caesar drove out the adventurers and later briefly crossed the Rhine on campaign. But the major Roman offensive against the German tribes was conducted by the generals of Augustus between 16 BC and AD 9. The area between the Rhine and the Elbe was overrun for a time, but the wooded and marshy terrain and the implacable hostility of most of the tribes brought the enterprise to an end in a catastrophic defeat for Rome in the Weser forests in AD 9. Thus, most of the territory occupied by the Germans remained independent of Rome, though a number of tribes maintained diplomatic relations with the empire over long periods.

The Germanic tribes included several large groupings (for example, Langobardi, Cherusci, Chatti and Marcomanni) and many small units (for example, Tencteri, Marsi, Naristi and Anglii). Warfare between, and often within, tribes was common and Germanic society was to a large extent organized for war. Although kings stood at the head of most tribes, their power was limited by the assembly of warriors and depended to a large degree upon the success, or otherwise, of wars fought under them. Often kings were removed and replaced by elected war-leaders for particular campaigns.

All leaders surrounded themselves with a retinue of warriors, whose loyalty was secured by success in battle, by booty and by rich gifts and other rewards. This institution of the retinue appears early in Germanic history and it retained its significance into mediaeval Europe. The bonds of the family were also very strong among early Germans, as is well illustrated in the prosecution of feuds as a means of righting wrongs and regulating justice.

The warrior-dominated society allowed only limited roles for women. They were concerned almost wholly with the home and the family and were reputed to be chaste and incorruptible. The penalty for sexual misconduct was severe: death by drowning in a marsh. In one particular sphere, however, women made a contribution which was not linked to the home. The leading seeresses of the Germans were held in high regard, as women who could predict the future, including the outcome of battles.

The Germanic economy was firmly based on agriculture, including both arable farming and animal husbandry. Settled agricultural communities existed long before the Germans appeared in history and many of these remained stable for centuries, making efficient use of natural resources. In the north-western regions, the raising of cattle was of great significance, as is evident in the many long-houses in which animals were stalled in one length and the family in the other. Settlements in the northern coastlands are particularly well known to us, as the waterlogged anaerobic conditions have allowed them to survive, and they provide a vivid and detailed picture of an ordered agricultural economy. Trade connections with the empire were very lively in the first two centuries AD. Surplus hides and meat were traded to the Roman frontier provinces and many Roman imports were received, especially bronzeware, pottery, glass and silver coinage. Apart from agricultural products, the Germans exported amber, iron and slaves to the Roman world, and also provided an increasing supply of manpower to the Roman army.

The stability of the Germanic world, and its relations with the Roman empire, were shaken in the later second century AD. An increased population with its consequent pressure for fresh land led several of the peoples of central Europe to break into the Roman provinces on the middle Danube with the intention of establishing communities there. The so-called Marcomannic Wars which ensued, from AD 166 to 180, mark a turning-point in relations between the early Germans and the Roman world. A generation later there were signs that the military initiative was beginning to swing towards the northern peoples as larger and more aggressive confederacies, such as the Franks, Alamanni and Goths, began to be heard of. Many of the lesser tribes disappeared in the third century and the main assaults on the Roman frontiers were conducted by the new confederacies (Franks, Alamanni and Goths).

There were also significant cultural and technological developments in this same period, including advances in metalworking, the introduction of runic inscriptions and the use of new decorative designs. Germanic culture was beginning to create its own identity. Contacts with the Roman world were responsible for some of these innovations; others were the result of internal development.

In the fourth century, many of the Germanic peoples close to the Roman frontiers continued to supply troops for the Roman armies, as well as attacking the frontiers. The attacks intensified after 350, especially on the Rhine and lower Danube, and also in the English Channel and North Sea. It was not until the Goths moved into the Balkans in 376, however, that there was a major settlement of Germanic people within the Roman empire. It was this invasion that marked the beginnings of the great migrations which were to take the Germanic peoples to most parts of Europe during the fifth and sixth centuries.

See: Austria, Denmark, Belgium, France, Germany, Holland, Luxembourg, Sweden, United Kingdom

The Goths

According to tradition, the Goths originated in southern Scandinavia and later migrated to the lower Vistula valley in Poland, where they were settled before AD 100. The Goths themselves accepted this account of their origins but it is supported by no independent evidence from historical or archaeological sources. More probably the tribal ancestors of the Goths had lived since prehistoric times in the Vistula valley in Poland and moved from there in search of better land in the later second century AD, travelling southeastwards into the fertile plain of the Ukraine and the lands bordering the Black Sea.

Once they had become established there, they began to attack the eastern provinces of the Roman empire, the first major raid being recorded in AD 238. About the middle of the third century their attacks on the Balkans became more frequent. One group broke into Greece and sacked Athens, while another group crossed the Black Sea and the Aegean to attack the rich provinces of Asia Minor. When the Romans evacuated the province of Dacia (western Romania) after 270, one section of Goths, the Visigoths, moved in and remained there for a hundred years. The main body continued to occupy the regions north of the Black Sea, creating two kingdoms there, that of the Eastern or Ostrogoths in the Ukraine and of the Western or Visigoths further west towards the lower Danube in territory that is now Romania.

By this time, the name Goth covered a wide range of peoples who had been drawn into these two power blocs, not all of them Germanic. They were a sufficiently coherent force to sign a treaty with the Roman empire early in the fourth century and many Goths took service in the Roman armies from this time onward. This relatively stable situation was shattered about AD 370 when the Huns arrived on the edges of Europe.

The westward drive of the Huns from the Asian steppes overthrew the kingdom of the Ostrogoths with awesome speed. The Visigoths were also unrooted by the Hun invasion and many thousands fled across the Danube into the Roman Balkan provinces in 376. Two years later, under their king Fritigern, they inflicted a massive defeat on the eastern Roman army.

Although they were victorious they were still without land of their own and were allowed to settle in the Balkans in the province of Lower Moesia in AD 382, remaining there in wretched conditions until 395.

It was during this time that many Visigoths became Christians, converted from their pagan religion by a man named Ulfila, who became their bishop and translated the Bible into the Gothic language, inventing an alphabet for the purpose. The Christianity he preached, however, did not agree with the teaching of the more powerful Catholic church and was considered by many to be heretical. Arian Christians, as they were called, after their founder, Arius, believed that Christ was a separate being from God the Father and was thus subordinate to Him. Several Germanic peoples were converted to the Arian form of Christianity and only later became Catholics.

When a new leader, Alaric, came to power in the last decade of the fourth century, Visigoth ambitions began to rise once more. They raided widely in northern Greece before moving west in large numbers and establishing themselves in northern Italy. From there they threatened Rome itself. They mounted three major invasions of central Italy, in 403, 408 and 410, finally briefly taking possession of Rome in August 410, an event which seemed to many contemporaries to mark the end of the Roman empire. Alaric then led his people into southern Italy and was planning an invasion of Africa when he died. The Visigoths had still not attained their objective: a land of their own.

They returned northward once more and settled in 418 in south-western Gaul with their centre at Toulouse where, in 475, they established an entirely independent kingdom. However, by this time the Franks were replacing the Romans as the dominant power in Gaul and the Visigoths were forced to move on once more, this time southward into Spain. There they created a Germanic kingdom, building on the systems established by the Romans in Spain. Late in the sixth century they were converted to the Catholic faith.

Most of the Visigoths settled on the land as peasant cultivators: the majority of the words they bequeathed to the Spanish language (only about thirty in all) concern rural life and affairs. Their villages were evidently small and most were swept away by later settlers in Spain. They can now be recognized by their cemeteries, in which the dead are buried with

Germanic ornaments, but no weapons or vessels. The leading Visigothic families, who may only have numbered a few hundred, attached themselves to the kings, as warriors and courtiers.

The Visigothic kingdom in Spain survived until early in the eighth century when much of Spain was overrun by Arab and Berber invaders from North Africa. It was a remarkably stable power for much of that time, though rather isolated from the political and cultural developments in the rest of Europe.

The Ostrogoths continued to live under Hun rule until 455 when the Huns were defeated in Europe. Almost immediately they began an aggressive expansion. They occupied the northern Balkans until 488, threatening Constantinople on several occasions. The rise to power over them of Theoderic was a turning-point in their fortunes. He had spent much of his youth as a hostage at the court at Constantinople, from where the Romans now ruled their reduced empire. There he acquired a great respect for Roman statecraft and learning. When his rule over the Ostrogoths was secure, he led them westward into northern Italy and in 489 overthrew its barbarian ruler Odoacar. Theoderic created a strong kingdom in which much of the Roman administrative framework was preserved and religious toleration was practised. He maintained friendly relations with other Germanic powers, securing them with dynastic marriages. Although Theoderic continued to recognize the authority of the Byzantine emperors, he was the most powerful single ruler in the west in the late fifth and early sixth centuries. His main residence was at Ravenna, where several fine churches (including San Apollinare and San Vitale) and a mausoleum were built for him and survive to this day. He died in 526. By this time the power of the Ostrogoths was in decline. Only ten years later the Byzantine general Belisarius began the reconquest of Italy.

The ending of the two Gothic kingdoms in the Mediterranean world did not mark the end of Goths as a separate people. Not all of them had left southern Russia when the Huns invaded in the late fourth century. The so-called Krim-Goths survived as an enclave in and about the Crimea, and when seventeenth century travellers encountered them there, they could still be recognized by their Germanic speech. But elsewhere Gothic identity was lost. The Gothic populations of Italy and Spain had already intermingled with the other inhabitants of those lands during their days of

power. Later, they merged with the mass of population and left little trace of their earlier prominence. When the adjective 'Gothic' was applied to an architectural style or a script in the seventeenth century, it was an archaism which the true Goths would not have understood.
See: France, Italy, Poland, Portugal, Romania, Russia, Spain, Ukraine

The Greeks

The origins of the Greeks can be traced back at least to the early second millennium BC. At this time Greek-speaking people were living in the land which is now Greece, though it is not known whether the language was developed by the indigenous population or by a mixture of natives and incomers, probably from the north or north-east. The language belongs to the Indo-European family and is thus related to Sanskrit and Latin, and to the Celtic and Germanic languages.

Earlier scholars believed that three main waves of northern invaders moved into Greece from about 2600 BC onwards: the Ionians first from Asia Minor, followed by the Achaeans from the Greek mainland about 1500 BC and the Dorians from northern Greece after 1200 BC. Such population movements are not convincingly distinguished in the archaeology of early Greece, and the idea of a major migration through the Balkans is no longer strongly supported. It is, however, interesting that the Greeks themselves maintained a tradition of a Dorian invasion into the Peloponnese and there were certainly later invasions from northern peoples. That Greeks, or a people directly ancestral to Greeks, were settled in the peninsula by at least 2000 BC seems certain. The spread of Greek settlement was by no means confined to what is now the Greek mainland. The Aegean islands and the western coast of Turkey were also studded with Greek communities during the second millennium BC.

The development of Greek culture in the second millennium is closely bound up with Mycenaean civilization. This arose in the northern Peloponnese after 1700 BC, influenced by the cultures of Minoan Crete and the Near East as well as Greece itself. Mycenaean wealth and power were centred on strongholds of local kings and their retinues, a warrior aristocracy which used warfare as a means of enriching itself. Mycenaean adventurers travelled to Crete, Cyprus, Sicily and southern Italy, across the Aegean to Asia Minor and the Levant. This is the general background to the most famous story of early Greece, the Trojan War, a rich mixture of history, myth and legend, given poetic shape by Homer in the *Iliad* and *Odyssey* around the middle of the eighth century BC. Mycenaean traders also crossed the Aegean to Asia Minor and penetrated west to Sicily and Italy, creating a network which was to be reformed and enlarged by later Greeks. After about 1125 BC, Mycenaean power collapsed, an event still not adequately explained. It was followed by a long period of disturbance, migration and change, often called the Greek Dark Age. The many small Mycenaean kingdoms vanished and when the political outlines of Greece are again evident they take a very different form, one which provided the basis for the greatest period of Greek culture.

After 900 BC there were major political and cultural developments which affected Greeks on both sides of the Aegean. The emergence of the *polis*, the autonomous city state with a recognizable bloc of territory, lay at the centre of the new order. The early *poleis* appeared at Corinth, Sparta, Megara and in Crete: Athens emerged later as a progressive force. Cultural stimulus came from Asia Minor, where cities were rapidly developing into commercial centres after 800 BC. Greece was a poor land agriculturally and as populations grew, Greek colonies were founded in the northern Aegean, the Black Sea coasts, Italy, Sicily, Spain and North Africa. Some cities, including Miletus and Corinth, had a large number of colonies, several of which became major cities in their own right. It was in Ionia, the coastland of Asia Minor, that literature flourished from the eighth century, and later philosophy and science.

Coinage was adopted by the eastern Greeks before 600 BC. Growing wealth and increasing population led to change in the political organization of the city-states. Kingship disappeared in most states, to be replaced by oligarchies of the wealthier citizens or by 'tyrants', strong rulers who held competing factions under control. Other states had different arrangements. At Sparta, kingship was retained, along with a Council and Assembly, while the free men of the state were required to live within the confines of a military organization to the age of sixty, thus providing an army of exceptional quality. Relations between states were assisted by major religious centres and festivals, the most important being the athletic contests at Olympia, the oracle of Apollo at Delphi and the sacred island of Delos in the Aegean. But war between states was frequent and common aims were rarely pursued, except in religious matters. By the later sixth century the main lines of classical Greek civilization were drawn and all seemed set for further brilliant development.

This progress was threatened, but not as it turned out interrupted, by the rise of the Persian empire and its westward advance through Asia Minor in the later sixth century. The Greek cities of the coastal areas were brought under Persian control, not all of them unwillingly. A further advance against the Greek mainland was thwarted by the Greeks in the great campaigns of 490 and 480 BC, in which the land power of Sparta and the naval might of Athens proved decisive in the battles of Marathon, Thermopylae and Salamis.

The late sixth and fifth centuries witnessed an astounding series of developments in art, literature and philosophy. Superb sculpture in the fine marble of Paros and Naxos included figures of *kouroi* (young boys) and *kourai* (young girls) produced by workshops in Attica. After the wars with Persia, several schools of sculptors explored the use of marble and limestone with increasing confidence and skill. Pride of place must go to Pheidias and his associates who were responsible for the Parthenon sculptures, the great cult-image of Athena which that temple housed and the greatest statue of the ancient world, the image of Zeus at Olympia, adorned with gold and ivory. But a host of other sculptures of outstanding quality stood in the cities and sanctuaries of Greece, to be admired and imitated for centuries to come. In literary achievement, no single century can approach fifth century Greece, in which the histories of Herodotus and Thucydides, and the plays of Aeschylus, Sophocles, Aristophanes and Euripides were written. Among other magnificent artistic achievements were the black and red figure painted pottery. These are not only superb and moving compositions in their own right, but also exceptional sources of information on Greek life, especially in Athens. They also offer a tantalizing glimpse of the large-scale mural paintings which once adorned great buildings in the cities and sacred places and which are now almost totally lost to us.

The glories and freedom of Greek culture were not open to all members of the Greek community however. Slavery was basic to the Greek economy and it seems to have existed from at least Mycenaean times. The work of slaves in the household, on the land and in workshops enabled the free citizens of the advanced cities of Athens, Corinth and Sparta to enjoy a great deal of leisure. Slaves were relatively cheap in Classical Greece. Most were acquired from slave-dealers in the eastern Mediterranean, though others arrived as war captives, sold after a defeat. It is thought that at least one slave existed for every free citizen in fifth century Athens. A wealthy general, Nicias, is said to have owned a thousand slaves at one time.

The life led by women in Classical Greece was also strictly limited, in the great cities as in the countryside. The woman's domain was the home and she was largely excluded from the public activities which made up so much of the life of a free man. But at least some women could and did play a part in life outside the family circle. Some high-born women had influence on the conduct of public affairs, though this was normally expressed through their menfolk. Many social occasions could not be attended by respectable women.

Greek houses tended to be simple in plan and were usually modest in their decoration and furnishings. Much of Greek life was conducted out of doors, so that far more attention and wealth were devoted to public buildings and amenities than to private dwellings. The wealthier citizens had houses which were often arranged around a central court, on to which the main rooms looked, turning away from the hot and busy streets. Many rooms were small by modern standards, the larger chambers being those in which guests were received and entertained.

The dominant power in fifth century Greece was Athens but her power was repeatedly challenged by Sparta and her allied city-states and in 405 BC the Athenian empire ended. It was succeeded by a new military power to the north, Macedonia.

Macedonia had long been regarded by the Greeks as virtually a barbarian kingdom but when Philip II became king in 359 BC, he commanded a professionally trained army and rich resources of precious metals. By 338 he had strengthened his kingdom in the northern Balkans and Thrace and defeated the old city-states who were exhausted by a century of war. Under Philip's son, Alexander the Great, the Macedonian forces spread Greek culture eastwards to the borders of India.

After Alexander's early death his vast domains were divided among his leading generals and the empire was broken up. Rome became the new dominant power in the Mediterranean: Macedonia became a Roman province and mainland Greece, the province of Achaea, became a backwater, although it retained its intellectual drawing power. Athens continued to serve as an academic centre to which the young men of wealthy families flocked for instruction in rhetoric, philosophy and science. Greeks were much sought after as tutors and doctors in the Roman world. Men of culture would still expect to learn Greek and be conversant with Greek literature and learning. Several areas of the Greek world, especially the coastal provinces of Asia Minor, attained a high level of prosperity under the rule of Rome. The prevailing culture of Rome's eastern provinces was Greek and this continued even after the Roman empire had declined and moved its court to Constantinople. Greek culture had more influence on the later history of Europe than any other, not only directly but via Rome and Byzantium. The rediscovery of Greek literature and learning in the Middle Ages had further cultural impact, still felt in the twentieth century.

Greek colonization carried Greeks into many parts of the Mediterranean world, especially to western Asia Minor, southern Italy, Sicily, southern Gaul, eastern Spain and the North African coastland. Italy and Sicily, in particular, retained their Greek culture and population into the Middle Ages.

See: Greece, Italy

The Gypsies

The Gypsies' origins are remote from Europe but groups of this people are found today in many European countries. They received their first mention in European records in the fourteenth century, having moved west from India via Turkey and Armenia. From Asia Minor they passed into Greece and thence to Romania, Hungary, Germany, France and Spain. The name they were given reflects a mediaeval belief (probably fostered by the Gypsies themselves) that they came as pilgrims from Egypt; their own name for themselves is

Rom. The Gypsy language still retains a link with their Indian origin for it is related to Sanskrit. The ethnic identity has been preserved to the present, partly by their own determination to follow their traditional style of life wherever they may be, and partly because of the long history of official repression with which they have met.

From the fifteenth century Gypsies have been viewed with suspicion, if not hatred, in most parts of Europe. They were freely persecuted in Spain, France and England and, in eighteenth century Prussia, were condemned to death. The Nazi regime in Germany treated Gypsies as sub-human and attempted to exterminate them, killing over half a million in German-occupied Europe. Despite this long period of repression, they still survive in considerable numbers in certain countries, notably Russia, Hungary, Romania, Bulgaria and Greece, and many still pursue a largely nomadic way of life. Other Gypsy groups have become sedentary and taken on many of the cultural characteristics of the lands they inhabit.

A well defined social organization exists among the nomadic Gypsies. Tribal groups or *witzass* are brought together into larger assemblies *kumpanias* for communal occasions. Above these in turn is a court of justice *kris* which meets when need dictates. Family life is very strong. Marriages are usually arranged by parents and, once married, a couple will stay close to the husband's family. Bride-prices are still often paid. Although formally Christians or Muslims, Gypsies adhere to worship of their own ancestors whose aid they seek in prayer. Funerary customs of great age are still honoured, at which coins are thrown into the grave and alcohol poured on to the earth over the dead. Ritual feasting for over a year following burial provides a release from mourning. If a Gypsy dies in his tent or wagon, his possessions are destroyed by fire.

True Gypsies are still a distinct ethnic group, well defined in physical terms: dark skinned, dark eyed and black haired. Their traditional occupations, such as horse-dealing, copper-working, violin-making and fortune-telling are still practised by the nomad groups and, needing no essential daily routine, this allows spontaneous and fairly frequent social contact whether for specific celebrations or in more general gatherings. The total number of Gypsies in Europe today is unknown. Probably most (perhaps half a million) are in Russia, followed by Hungary, Romania and Bulgaria.

The Huns

Although the Huns formed their nation on the steppes of central Asia, they had a major impact on Europe in the late fourth and fifth centuries. Their early history is obscure but they are often identified with the nomadic Hsiung-nu who are described by Chinese writers as living in the southern Gobi desert in western China during the first century AD. They later moved westward into southern Russia and in the later fourth century had reached the steppes east of the river Don. About AD 370 they attacked the Ostrogoths of the Ukraine and quickly overthrew their kingdom. The Visigoths immediately to the west were forced to seek refuge in the Roman Balkan provinces south of the Danube.

For a time the Huns advanced no further into Europe, being content instead to provide troops for Roman armies and to receive payments of gold in return for not invading the Roman empire. But in 433 two leaders came to power among them with far more ambitious aims: Bleda and his brother, the greatest of Hun rulers, Attila. Under their leadership, raids on the Balkans and Greece increased and the Roman emperors in Constantinople were required to pay ever larger sums of gold in tribute.

The Huns now began to push further into western Europe but, although their army roused widespread terror, they were not successful in the long term. In 451, under Attila, they invaded Gaul and penetrated as far as present-day Orleans before being disastrously defeated by an allied army which included Romans and Goths. Undeterred, the following year they entered Italy, only to be stopped at Lake Garda. In 453 Attila suddenly died (the cause is unknown) and without him, Hun power quickly disintegrated. After another major defeat, in a battle on the river Nedao in Hungary, the peoples the Huns had terrorized rose in revolt. Within a few years the scattered Hun empire had ceased to exist.

Historians of the late Roman empire, who feared and hated the Huns, described them as 'short, sturdy, swarthy, thinly-bearded, with round flat faces, and surpassingly ugly.' Their habits were said to be disgusting and their culture nil. They had no written language but their speech was known by the Romans to be different from the Germanic tongues of the more familiar barbarians. All that remains of the language now are some names and titles, over which experts are divided. The best guess is that most Huns spoke a dialect closely related to the Turkic languages.

Whatever their appearance and language, they were by all accounts superb horsemen, riding the short, tireless ponies of the steppes with saddles but probably without stirrups. They exploited their skills in warfare to devastating effect, especially against infantry. Their soldiers were hardy, tough, brave and cruel. They were particularly effective as mounted archers, shooting arrows as they rode, a tactic which their opponents at first found impossible to counter.

As nomads, they led a pastoral life, living in felt tents, tending herds, following grass and water. But large mass graves show they also had some kind of settlements. Believers in shamans and spirits, the Huns did not convert to Christianity, though they were tolerant in religion and easygoing with subject peoples, so long as they paid their tributes.

Their nomadic way of life was somewhat modified when they settled in eastern Europe but they continued to depend on animal husbandry for their main livelihood. Their material culture was generally poor, much being derived from the peoples they subdued. But several of their royal or noble graves contain magnificent gold and silver ornaments and vessels, not all of them the result of loot and extortion. The brutality of the Huns, for which they were notorious in the late Roman world, was real enough, but their reputation for utter savagery was grossly overstated by Greek and Roman writers.

See: Hungary, Italy, Romania, Russia, Ukraine

The Iberians

The Iberians were early inhabitants of what is now Spain and Portugal although they were not the first to live there. They possibly came from North Africa in the thirteenth century BC but they were not documented until the sixth century BC when Greek navigators made the first reference to the people who lived on the east coast of Spain along the river Iberus (Ebro) as Iberians.

Very little is known about these early Iberians, although they apparently were typically small in stature with long or oval skulls and tended to bury their dead in caves.

Throughout prehistoric time different peoples moved into Spain from the north, and early Mediterranean civilizations influenced the area from the first millennium BC. Celts crossed the Pyrenees and mingled with the native peoples before 400 BC and tribal groups in the north and north-west were referred to by ancient writers as Celtiberians, a mixed race of Celts and Iberians. The true Iberian areas lay in the east and south-east and by the fifth century BC those who had lived there had developed a lively and innovative culture, influenced by Phoenician trading posts in the south (from the sixth century BC) and Greek colonies along the east coast. Western Mediterranean cultures also influenced Iberian styles of metalworking, pottery and art.

Many of the Iberian settlements were fortified hill-top sites, showing there was a need for protection against neighbouring groups, but there were also lowland town sites, some with sizeable communities. Certain of the towns show obvious planning and contained private houses of some sophistication.

Before the Roman conquest was completed the Iberians were producing their own coinage based on Roman denominations. The inscriptions on these coins, though, show a unique alphabet which is similar to the Greek and Punic forms rather than the Roman. The inscriptions include the names of towns and the reverse side shows a charging horseman or one man leading two horses or brandishing a sword or bow. On the obverse is a male head, sometimes inscribed with what appears to be a native name. These coins have been found throughout Spain and also near Narbonne. A few other inscriptions using a similar alphabet have also been found.

Those who came in direct contact with them found the Iberians a warlike people. They were known to be ferocious in battle, where they rode on horseback or fought on foot with javelins, swords and slings. They were devoted to their leaders and carried the leaves of a poisonous plant so that they could commit suicide if defeated. According to the Roman Pompeius Trogus, 'Their bodies inured to abstinence and toil, their minds composed against death, all practise a stern and constant moderation. They prefer war to ease and, should they lack foes without, seek them within. Rather than betray a secret they will often die under torment, setting a silent reserve before life itself. Active of body, restless of spirit, they commonly set more store by their horses and fighting accoutrement than by the blood of their kin.'

Politically, the Iberians were organized in a large number of small states, often at war with each other and sometimes bound in temporary alliances. When Rome became involved in Spain in the third century BC, her influence quickly spread among the tribes of the east and south. The Celtiberians of the interior and the north were much more resistant to Roman rule and major campaigns had to be fought to bring them under control in the second and third centuries BC. Once conquered, though, the Iberians entered enthusiastically into Roman provincial life and made southern Spain into one of the most Romanized parts of western Europe. After the Roman conquest of Spain, little else is heard of the Iberians as a separate people.

See: Portugal, Spain

The Illyrians

A group of several Indo-European tribes occupied the western side of the Adriatic seaboard from the Balkan mountains to the eastern Alps and north to the Danube. Some may have arrived as early as 2000 BC from the western steppes, though by the time they were recorded, the group included others from the northern Balkans. The name by which these tribes were known to Greeks and Romans was Illyrioi or Illyrii, originally the name of one small tribe settled near the river Scodra. Greeks gave the name Illyria to the southern area of their settlement but the Romans gave the name Illyricum to the entire region from the eastern Alps to what is now Albania.

The Illyrian tribes were famous for their prowess in war on land and sea. They frequently raided Macedonia and northern Greece, and their pirate raids terrorized the Adriatic and the central Mediterranaean. Although there were Greek colonies on their coasts, with consequent development in trade, the Illyrians of the interior remained tribal and never developed a unitary state with common aims. Several individual tribes exerted considerable local power, however, notably the Liburni, who were famed as sailors; the Dardani, who controlled important mineral resources, including, iron; and the Ardiaei. When the power of the kingdom of Macedonia declined in the third century BC, the Illyrians expanded southward. But the Romans were also advancing into the Balkans and they blocked the Illyrians' further progress. In the course of time they were included in the Roman province of Illyricum, later Dalmatia.

Modern Albanians, who speak a language derived from Illyrian, are their direct descendants.
See: Albania, Yugoslavia

The Irish

Ireland was first colonized after the end of the last Ice Age, about 7000 BC, probably from south-western Scotland. Irish Stone and early Bronze Age cultures produced remarkable ritual and funerary monuments, such as Knowth and New Grange, and the working of metals, especially gold and bronze, reached high peaks of excellence between 2000 and 1000 BC. Gold was plentiful in Ireland and no doubt drew prospectors and traders to the country during the Bronze Age. The question of later immigration, particularly by Celtic peoples, is still debatable. Celtic speakers are likely to have arrived between 600 and 500 BC, but there is no secure evidence for a major wave of immigration. High-level contacts were maintained between Ireland and Britain from 500 BC and throughout the Roman period, though without profound alteration to the native cultural tradition. There was trade with Roman Britain, but not on any large scale.

Ancient Ireland, like contemporary Ireland, was a predominantly agricultural land and the Irish depended heavily upon their animals and the crops they could grow. Much of the land was fertile and easily supported the small population. That the standard of living was reasonably high is indicated by the high quality of goods which have been found from the Early Christian period, the fifth century onward.

The Irish entered on a most important and formative phase in their history in the fifth century AD, when they were converted to Christianity, largely by the work of one man, St Patrick. This brought Ireland firmly into the western European Christian community and by the sixth century Irish monks and missionaries were making a large contribution to the spread of the faith on the European mainland and in northern Britain. Irish settlement was scattered, with few large urban centres. The small farmers and local lords owed nominal allegiance to the high king who had his court at Tara, but had barely any coercive power. This fragmentation meant that the Irish were not able to resist a formidable military threat when it came, first from the Vikings, later from the Normans.

The Vikings settled in Ireland in the mid-ninth century, after decades of raiding. Under their influence, town life increased, most notably in the trading centre of Dublin. There was a good deal of intermarriage between Irish noble families and Vikings and thus a degree of cultural fusion took place. The Norman invasion of 1170 and their conquest of much of eastern Ireland led to no such cultural relations. Norman England now became the ruling power, though never one that was acceptable to the bulk of the population. Outside the main towns, of which there were few, Irish life continued in its traditional ways for centuries, in places until the twentieth century. The essentially Celtic character of Irish life can still be encountered in the remote countryside and in Irish literature.
See: Ireland

The Jews

The Jews originated as groups of nomads in the Near Eastern desert lands, following a pastoral life and only later settling in areas where agriculture was possible. During the twelfth century BC, according to Jewish lore, settlement concentrated on Palestine. This was a long, slow process involving many small tribal groups separately, not a single mass movement. The Jewish hold on this territory was precarious and they were long exposed to hostile neighbours. About the middle of the eleventh century BC, a unified monarchy was established under Saul and the state was given a firm basis by King David shortly after 1000 BC. Thereafter, the Jewish kingdom suffered division and was later dismembered by the Assyrians and

Babylonians. But despite the fact that Jews were scattered widely over the Near East, the idea of a homeland in Palestine, with Jerusalem as its capital, was never lost. Late in the first millennium BC, the Jews were influenced by Greek culture and then were conquered by Rome, becoming unwilling subjects of the Roman empire.

The movement of Jews into Europe began in earnest during the Roman empire, usually to the larger cities and ports around the Mediterranean. Certainly by the middle of the first century BC there was a small Jewish community in the city of Rome. Generally tolerated under Roman law, their Judaic faith was no bar to their progress in social and commercial life. When Christianity was adopted as the official religion of the empire early in the fourth century, the position of Jews underwent a change for the worse. Legislation restricted their activities and their faith, and this was followed by further limitation under the Germanic kingdoms from the fifth century onward. The most severe restrictions, amounting to proscription and expulsion, were applied in Spain under the Visigoths.

From the sixth century AD Jews were increasingly concerned with both local and long-distance trade. Their wide dispersal throughout Christian Europe and the Muslim world helped them to establish a commercial network and they had the further advantage of a single system of commercial law based on the Talmud. Moreover, as Jews were progressively excluded from the possession of land by the countries in which they settled, they were indirectly encouraged to create portable wealth. Within Europe, the position of the Jews was most secure in areas controlled by the Franks, whose rulers granted them protection, commercial privileges and the right to administer their affairs under their own law.

The main Jewish communities were in the larger towns, especially in the Mediterranean lands. After the Muslim conquest of Spain early in the eighth century, Jews found themselves welcome there and exploited the opportunity. By the tenth century, Jewish merchants were active in the Rhineland and they spread eastward in the thirteenth and fourteenth centuries into Poland and Russia. The emergence of a Christian merchant class then began to restrict Jewish enterprise in pure commerce and they turned more and more to the field of banking and, a practice that was forbidden to Christians, moneylending. They often acted in these capacities for kings and cities as well as the urban poor. By 1200, Jews were actively engaged in usury in Germany, France, Italy and England. About this time, too, the Church started to adopt a more hostile attitude towards the Jewish community and public feeling turned sharply against them. Further restrictions were imposed on their trade, they were often confined to special quarters within cities (ghettos), and frequently falsely accused of ritual murder, poisoning and mockery of Christian ceremonies. Mass expulsion of Jews began, from England in 1290, from France in 1394 and from Spain in 1492 after the fall of Muslim Granada, though they sometimes had to be recalled to restore order to local finances.

By 1500 Jews had been expelled from most of western and central Europe. Their main centres now were northern Italy, Poland, Russia, a few German cities and the Ottoman empire. In these areas their numbers grew, though not without provoking animosity and persecution. After the early seventeenth century Jews were allowed to return to France, England and the Low Countries, and social opportunities for them slowly enlarged. But anti-semitism was still strong in Poland, Russia and in Germany and there were numerous local pogroms against them. There was still active persecution of Jews in Poland and Russia early in the twentieth century, but the worst was still to come. The anti-Jewish policies of Nazi Germany culminated in the attempt to exterminate the European Jews. By 1945 some six million had been murdered and many others had fled to Israel and elsewhere. In 1948 the state of Israel was founded as a homeland for the Jewish people. Many, however, remain dispersed throughout the world.

The Jutes

The Church historian, Bede, writing in the early eighth century, included Jutes, with the Angles and Saxons, among the peoples who migrated from Germany to Britain in the fifth and sixth centuries AD. He reports that their descendants were settled in Kent, the Isle of Wight and Hampshire.

It is now reasonably well established by archaeological evidence that the Jutes who took their pottery, jewellery and other ornaments to Kent came

from Jutland in northern Denmark. They were probably descended from the Iron Age farming communities which steadily developed during the early centuries AD. In England, those who settled in Kent helped to establish the most advanced of the Germanic kingdoms in Britain. After the early phase of settlement, however, their identity as a separate people was lost as they merged with other immigrant Germans and with the native Britons.
See: Denmark, Germany, United Kingdom

The Lapps

The Lapps occupy the northern parts of Norway, Sweden, Finland and the Kola peninsula of Russia. The original population arrived here from central Asia shortly before the beginning of the Christian era, perhaps as a result of disturbances in the steppe lands. In the early Christian centuries, the Lapps came under Finnish influence and the Finnish language was adopted. Their original language is unknown. The name Lapp derives from a Finnish word meaning nomad. Their own name for themselves is Same.

For centuries the Lapps lived by hunting and tending herds of semi-domesticated reindeer. Since the nineteenth century, they have adopted increasingly settled lifestyles and have declined greatly in numbers. The traditional Lapp reindeer-herding, however, is still practised on the Finnmark plateau in Norway. The majority of Lapps now live in Norway, with fewer in Sweden and Finland.

Physically, Lapps have tended to remain distinct from their neighbours. They are short, often about five feet in height, black haired and have noticeably Mongolian features. Their legs are short in relation to the body and frequently somewhat bowed. They are noted for their stamina and endurance. The long Arctic winter which compels traditional Lapps to live for months in confined spaces, can induce the so-called Lapp Panic, a form of neurosis brought on by lack of sunlight. Modern Lapps are highly skilled artists and designers who have heavily influenced Swedish artists. They are also now receiving acclaim as innovative and accomplished musicians.
See: Finland, Norway, Russia, Sweden

The Ligurians

The Ligurians were first mentioned by Greeks who colonized southern Gaul in the sixth century BC. Their territory then extended from the Rhone valley along the coast into Italy as far as the river Arno. They were fierce warriors and effective seamen who often turned to piracy. They frequently allied themselves with the Celts to whom they were culturally related. When the Romans advanced into northern Italy in the third century BC, the Ligurian tribes became Roman subjects, but they remained hostile for a century and a half. Only in 123 BC, when the Celts and Ligurians were defeated near Aix-en-Provence, was their power neutralized. Even then minor tribes in the hills remained unconquered and resistant. Ligurian territory was organized as one of the regions of Roman Italy by the emperor Augustus. See: France, Italy

The Lombards

The Lombards or Langobardi were one of the Germanic tribes settled in the lower valley of the Elbe. First noted there by the Roman historian Tacitus in the late first century AD, they remained in the region until after the collapse of the western Roman provinces in the fifth century. They then moved south and about 485 took over land in what is now northern Austria, north of the river Danube. Twenty years later they moved on again, this time into the former Roman province of Pannonia (broadly speaking Hungary). There they established themselves as a major power with diplomatic links with the Byzantine empire and with the Franks in Gaul. Christianity spread among some of the Lombard leaders at this time and many of their warriors took service with neighbouring peoples.

To the east, the Avars were becoming powerful and threatened Lombard territory by the mid sixth century. In 568 under their king, Alboin, the majority of the Lombards (along with other peoples) invaded northern Italy and quickly carved out a new homeland in the north-east of the peninsula. This included the fertile valley of the river Po and many of the old Roman cities of the region. They were able to extend their influence into central and southern Italy in the next ten years, but the main focus of the Lombard kingdom remained the north. For a decade (574–84) the Lombards were without a king and power was in the hands of a number of military leaders (*duces*). Their warrior-bands found the land of Italy a rich source of plunder. Many of the old land-owning families were killed or removed from their estates and their land passed to the invaders.

The Lombards at first kept themselves separate from the surviving Roman population of Italy, preserving their own social structure and language for longer than most other Germanic invaders of the Roman world. Their main social unit was the group of families (*fara*), organized for war and led by a warrior-noble, based in a stronghold from which the surrounding countryside could be controlled. Plunder was their principal source of wealth, and even their daily livelihood in the early years of their occupation of Italy. Later, they integrated rather more with the other inhabitants of the peninsula, but without losing their warlike disposition. They retained their Germanic language and a number of place-names in northern Italy contain Lombard elements. Otherwise, the language is almost entirely lost.

For some time, no organized system of government existed in Italy and great damage was done to the cities, churches and countryside. The monarchy was re-established in 584 in response to growing pressure on the Lombards by the Franks and Byzantines. After this, a more ordered' state began to emerge, the main unit in which was the land ruled by a military leader and controlled by his army. A law code was drawn up for the Italian Lombards by their king, Rothari, in 643 and this reveals much about their views on justice and retribution, especially on the use of the vendetta, the exercise of personal vengeance, to redress a wrong or insult. A Germanic kingdom had replaced a Roman provincial order. For the next century, the Lombards were the most powerful tribal group in Italy.

The Lombards who invaded Italy in 568 were either Arian Christians or pagans. It was clearly desirable for the Pope to convert them to Catholic Christianity, not only for religious reasons but also to make it easier for them to be integrated politically with the other Christian peoples of Italy.

A Bavarian Catholic princess, Theudelinda, was influential in the spread of her faith, though Arian doctrine retained a hold among the Lombards until the eighth century.

By 600, the Lombards were masters of most of Italy. The walled cities of the north remained their major centres, along with further strongholds such as Castel Trosino and Nocera Umbra. Archaeological evidence comes mainly from cemeteries in the north, from Piedmont to Friuli. Among the earliest of these are graves outside the little town of Cividale, some of which are richly furnished burials of seventh century nobles. Of other wealthy burials, the most important is the grave of Theudelinda, found under the cathedral at Monza.

From the middle of the eighth century, Lombard power was increasingly threatened by the Franks and by the rising authority of the popes. A Frankish invasion of Italy in 755 signalled the end of the kingdom, though it held together until 773, when Charlemagne led another Frankish army into Italy and took control of the main Lombard centres. Within a relatively short time, all trace of Lombard rule had disappeared. The Lombards who remained in Italy became part of the general population, no longer a separate people with a Germanic social order. Their presence is recorded by that region of Italy which is still called Lombardy.

See: Austria, Germany, Hungary, Italy

The Magyars

The nomadic Finno-Ugrian people known as the Magyars are first known of in the upper basin of the river Volga. By the ninth century AD they had moved south to the steppe around the river Don, in seven tribal groups or *bordes*. The whole people was called On-Ogur (meaning ten arrows), the origin of the later name, Hungarian. Other nomads were pushing the Magyars westward when, in 892, the ruler of the Frankish empire invited them to fight with him against the Slavs of Moravia. This brought them further west and after defeating the Moravians in 906, they settled in the Hungarian plain. There they created a kingdom, the forerunner of modern Hungary.

In the tenth century the Magyars were notorious for their savage raids across Europe, as far west as the Rhine. But in 955 they suffered a massive defeat on the Lechfeld near Augsburg in southern Germany by the German emperor Otto I and after this they were more susceptible to political and diplomatic controls. On Christmas Day 1000, their leader, Stephen I, was crowned king by the pope, an event which led to the conversion of the Magyars to the Christian faith and the establishment of closer links with other western states. Over the next two centuries Hungary prospered, until, in 1241, a great Mongol invasion devastated the land and killed half of the population. Within half a century of this disaster they had recovered some prosperity but soon fell under the control of foreign rulers.

The language of modern Hungarians is descended from that of the Magyar settlers of the ninth and tenth centuries, a Finno-Ugrian language which is unrelated to other European tongues with the exception of Finnish and Estonian.
See: Hungary

The Minoans

The people of the brilliant Bronze Age civilization of Crete have been known as the Minoans since the name was applied by Sir Arthur Evans, the discoverer of this lost culture early in the twentieth century. The name was derived from Minos, a mythical king of Crete, whose story may be a faint memory of the prominence of Crete before 2000 BC.

The remarkably advanced civilization which emerged on the island in the third millennium BC, was centred on a number of palaces with associated townships. The greatest of these lay at Knossos, itself built over a very substantial prehistoric settlement. Other large palaces were at Phaistos, Mallia and Khania: smaller centres were at Zakro, Gournia and Monastiraki. Their main period of development began about 2000 BC. The larger structures at Knossos, Mallia and Phaistos were striking architectural achievements, planned around central courtyards and containing smaller courts and staircases. At their peak around 1500 BC, they were adorned with fine frescoes depicting scenes from myth and cult. Other arts, including painted pottery, gem-engraving and jewellery manufacture, flourished at the same time. The uppermost level in society used two systems of writing: a hieroglyphic form used on stone seals, and a linear script, known to us as Linear A, mainly used on clay tablets.

At its peak in the centuries after 2000 BC the Minoan civilization was one of the most inventive of the ancient Mediterranean. The population was clearly numerous and a developed social structure emerged and remained in being for several centuries. Aside from the palaces and their satellite towns, there were also smaller settlements and villas. Large temples, such as those in Egypt at the same date, are unknown and religious cults were probably based in the palaces and other houses. Ceremonies took place in cult-chambers in the palaces and also sacred caves and at hill-top sites. The dominant deity was a goddess, or group of goddesses, concerned mainly with fertility and the after-life. Dancing and acrobatic leaping over the backs of bulls played a part in one group of ceremonies.

Around 1800 BC, the palaces at Knossos and Phaistos were destroyed, though whether through warfare or an earthquake is unknown. Again, about 1500 BC a major destruction occurred at Knossos when a volcanic eruption and a great earthquake shattered the island of Thera. A disturbed period then followed in Crete, and there may have been invasions from outside. Only Knossos seems to have made a substantial recovery from this series of disasters and entered upon a final phase of prosperity which lasted from 1450 to 1400 BC or a little later. After this, Minoan culture faded away, to be superseded by that of Mycenaean Greece.

The Minoans had a major influence on the world of the Mycenaeans and thus made a great contribution to the later development of civilization in the Mediterranean world. They can justly be regarded as the first advanced European civilization and it is a sobering fact that after their demise they were almost completely forgotten until their rediscovery late in the nineteenth century.

See: Greece

The Mongols

Although they were (and are) a people of the central Asian steppes, the Mongols played a significant part in the history of mediaeval Europe. In the thirteenth century, a major Mongol invasion swept across western Asia and eastern Europe, affecting particularly Russia and the Ukraine. At its peak the Mongol empire under Ghengis Khan stretched from the Pacific Ocean to the Red Sea and into western Russia as far west as Moscow and Kiev. In 1241 a double invasion of Europe was launched, one Mongol army driving into Poland and eastern Germany, the other invading Hungary and thrusting forward to Vienna. Both armies won crushing victories and it seemed as if the Mongols might settle in Hungary for good. Late in 1241, however, the Great Khan died and his people withdrew to the Asian steppes, never to return to Europe.

The Mongols have always been essentially a nomadic people, from their first certain emergence in the early centuries AD. They appear to have been related to the Huns. They depended heavily on the herding of animals, especially sheep, goats, horses, cattle and camels, the last being used to convey them across the vast deserts of Asia. Their nomadic movements were seasonal, dictated by the availability of pasture for their flocks. Their homes were portable tents made of felt stretched over a wooden frame (*yurt*). Their animals supplied all the food they needed, supplemented by tea and a powerful drink consisting of fomented mares' milk. Many of the modern descendants of Mongols are still nomadic, though in the past half-century they have been subject to Chinese influence, which has led them to become more settled. Until recently, a large proportion of Mongols were illiterate, as theirs is a mainly oral culture. Their physical appearance is highly distinctive. Most are short (standing up to 5 feet 6 inches), stocky in build, with short legs. Their faces are noticeably flat, the eyes slanting and the hair coarse and thin.
See: Russia, Ukraine

The Normans

Early in the tenth century AD an army of several thousand Scandinavian warriors, Norsemen or Vikings, under their leader Rolf (Rollo in the later French form) entered northern France along the river Loire. In 911 Rolf's force was defeated at Chartres by the French king Charles III; Rolf himself accepted baptism into the Christian faith and a few years later he and his people were given land for settlement on the lower Seine in the region of Rouen. This settlement of Norsemen (Normanni) was the basis of the dukedom of Normandy, which was to play a vital part in shaping mediaeval western Europe. Northerners continued to enter Normandy during the tenth century and there is little doubt that considerable damage was done to this part of France by these pagan intruders, monasteries in particular suffering at their hands. Rolf himself reverted to paganism and for decades pagan worship was still practised. As late as 1013, Richard II, Duke of Normandy, could welcome as allies a pagan Scandinavian force which had just devastated neighbouring Brittany.

The Scandinavians who settled in Normandy were probably not numerous. Place-names do not reveal a massive change in the population and the ownership of many estates continued without break. But the newcomers formed a militarily powerful ruling class which rapidly became a dominant political force in northern France. In the eleventh century they extended their sphere of interest in western Europe and into the Mediterranean world. From about 1010 onward Norman warlords attacked southern Italy. The most successful was Robert Guiscard ('the wily'), who went to southern Italy in 1047, pillaged widely and established a power base in Capua and Apulia. Later, Norman power was extended to Sicily. By 1120 the whole region formed a single kingdom with Sicily, its capital at Palermo, as its centre of power.

Strong links were developed between the ruling families of Normandy and England from the beginning of the eleventh century. Normans of high rank settled in England when Ethelred II of England married the daughter of Richard I of Normandy, and more followed in the reign of Edward the

Confessor (1042–66). When Edward died in 1066, the Duke of Normandy, William II, claimed that Edward had named him as his heir. This was disputed by the Earl of Wessex, Harold, the most powerful figure in England. William mounted the great expedition of 1066 to assert his right to rule in England. The Norman victory at the battle of Hastings decided the issue and England quickly passed under Norman rule.

Although notorious during their rise to power for their ferocity and ruthlessness, the success of the Normans was not confined to the building of strong kingdoms. In the twelfth century a notable revival of learning took place in Europe to which the Normans made a considerable contribution. Scholarship, literature, philosophy and science were all affected and there was renewed interest in legal studies. All this led to the foundation of universities in the later twelfth century. Interest in Roman literature stimulated the writing of works in Latin, while the Greek heritage was explored afresh through contacts with the Byzantine world. The learning of the Arabs, especially in science and mathematics, was also made more accessible through Muslim Spain. Romanesque architecture produced great Norman churches like those of Jumieges, Winchester and Durham, as well as the many lesser churches of England and France. From an unpromising beginning as a warband, the Normans brought new life to the culture of mediaeval Europe. As a people they are no longer distinct from the populations of the lands they conquered: their descendants are present in France, England and southern Italy.
See: France, Italy, United Kingdom

The Phoenicians.

The greatest trading people of the Near East were the Phoenicians (the Poeni as they were known to the Romans). A semitic people, of mixed Middle Eastern origin, their ancestors may have been metal traders from Babylon. Culturally they were cosmopolitan, mixing Mesopotamian, Egyptian and local traditions. About 1200 BC they were well established, operating from the major trading ports in the eastern Mediterranean. By 1000 BC, and probably earlier, they had invented the alphabet.

The most important of the Phoenician ports were Tyre and Sidon in what is now the Lebanon. Before 900 BC their traders had explored the whole of the western Mediterranean and founded trading-posts in southern Spain (Cadiz, Utica) and North Africa (Algiers). Later, by the sixth century they were active in Sicily and Sardinia. They made little attempt to take over land in these areas: their aim was to trade from secure harbours, often sheltered behind an offshore island. By far and away their most important trading post was Carthage, near modern Tunis, which they founded in the ninth century. This developed into the greatest port of the western Mediterranean, its merchants travelling far and wide in search of outlets for all manner of commodities, metals, foodstuffs, pottery and slaves. In the fifth century BC Carthaginian traders had to compete with expanding Greek interests and after 300 BC came up against the rising power of Rome. After long and fiercely contested wars at sea, in Spain, in Italy and finally in North Africa, Carthage was defeated, and Roman commerce expanded.

The Phoenicians in the eastern Mediterranean, however, continued their trading activities, despite being attacked by the Assyrians and subjected for a time to the Babylonians. Merchants from Tyre traded eastern goods including purple dye, for western metals, acquiring foodstuffs from their own hinterland, and buying and selling slaves in all markets. The Persian empire absorbed the Phoenicians without altering their activities. Their fleets simply entered the service of the Persian king. Alexander the Great's conquests brought their separate history to an end. As traders and craftsmen their achievements over a thousand years had been astonishing. In art and literature their attainments were less impressive, but the alphabet they invented in 1000 BC was eventually adopted throughout the western world.
See: Italy, Spain

The Picts

The Picts are first mentioned by a Roman writer in AD 297. By then they were recognized as a separate people, a combination of two tribes, the Caledonians and the Maeatae who were settled north of the isthmus of central Scotland. Elements in their language seem to go back to a pre-Indo-European tongue, spoken in Scotland before the arrival of the Celts. In Latin, Picti means 'painted ones' and the name was presumably applied to them by Roman troops. It is not known what the Picts called themselves.

The heartland of the Picts lay in the lowlands of eastern Scotland, the most fertile part of the entire region and their power may have extended over much of Scotland north of the Forth-Clyde line. The centre of their kingdom was in Perthshire and Angus, though important ecclesiastical centres lay further north.

The Picts had a variety of types of settlement. Their leaders and their immediate entourage lived in large fortified strongholds, but most of the ordinary people lived in small farmsteads. Larger villages seem not to have existed, so that the population was scattered across the landscape. The organization of society was simple. Farming was the main occupation. Kings were supported by a commander of the army and a revenue official but there seems to have been no fully developed noble class. Almost nothing is known of their religion except that a group of pagan priests or magicians had influence before St Columba introduced the Christian faith late in the sixth century.

The Picts' kingdom had certainly taken shape by AD 500 and probably earlier. About AD 800, the Picts in the north were raided by Vikings, who then settled on their land. Only forty years later, in 843, the Scottish king Kenneth McAlpin absorbed the Pictish people into his own realm, bringing to an end their kingdom and their history as an independent people. Only the faint memory is left that they were the ancestors of the inhabitants of eastern Scotland.

The most striking of Pictish monuments are a series of about 250 stones bearing symbols and, from a later date, sculpted cross-slabs. The symbol-

stones depict a mixture of ordinary objects, animals and abstract designs which clearly had a definite meaning, probably connected with the ownership of land or marriages and succession within the leading families. Some may be memorial stones for important figures. The cross-slabs with their wide range of Christian and secular references are often vigorous and original works of sculpture in low relief. Pictish craftsmen also produced fine metalwork, especially in silver. Several major hoards of silverwork have been discovered, including those at Norrie's Law, which contained huge silver chains, and St Ninian's Isle, which was a collection of bowls, sword-fittings and personal ornaments of high quality, concealed about 800. Aside from small fortified sites and farmsteads, Pictish settlement is still poorly recorded.
See: United Kingdom

The Romans

Roman origins have been much debated since at least the fifth century BC. According to Greek myths, Rome was founded by the Trojan hero Aeneas, who fled from the destruction of Troy to Italy, there to fulfil his destiny by founding a world empire. It is very doubtful whether the myth rests on any historical foundation, but it was current among Greek historians before 400 BC. According to the native Roman tradition Rome was founded by Romulus, who was abandoned as a child near the Tiber with his twin brother Remus and suckled by a she-wolf before being saved and brought up by shepherds. Romulus killed Remus in a petty squabble and went on to found the city of Rome at a date which later Roman scholars placed in the mid-eighth century BC. The firm date of 753 BC was finally accepted by the late first century BC. Dates were thereafter reckoned *ab urbe condita*, 'from the foundation of the city' in this year. These two traditions were brought together by early Roman historians, the awkward gap between the fall of Troy (early twelfth century BC) and the mid-eighth century being filled by a fabricated dynasty of local kings.

Archaeological finds on the site of Rome agree with the native tradition that a settlement began there around 800 BC. At this date Rome was a series of small villages, or one scattered village, similar to other agricultural settlements in the region of Latium. The economic life of such villages was modest, their inhabitants subsisting on wheat, barley, beans and peas, with milk and meat from domesticated goats and pigs. After 750 BC, the settlement of Rome began a period of major growth, influenced by contacts with the Greek cities of Campania and the south. Elsewhere in Latium similar developments were taking place: extravagantly furnished burials show that a local aristocracy was emerging. By about 650 BC the settlement of Rome had grown and extended into the marshy valley of the Forum and on to the Esquiline and Quirinal hills. Shortly afterwards, it began to take on the appearance of a city, with stone buildings, sanctuaries and a public square where the Forum later lay.

At this time, the king was Tarquinius Priscus (Tarquin I), certainly a historical figure, unlike most of the earlier kings of Rome. Tarquinius Priscus was an Etruscan who was elected as king after he arrived in Rome and ruled there for at least 35 years. Etruscan cities had been established long before Rome became important and in the late seventh and sixth centuries, cultural and political relations between Rome and the Etruscans were close. But Rome may never have been subject to direct Etruscan rule, or at least not for any length of time. Some Etruscan families settled in Rome; Etruscan goods such as pottery vessels were imported and Rome took over Etruscan political and religious traditions such as the ceremonial triumph, the public games and the fasces, (the bundle of rods and axes which symbolized supreme political power). Later rulers continued to expand the city of Rome by ambitious building projects and to extend Rome's contacts beyond Latium.

The later sixth century saw several significant changes in the developing state. There were changes to the basis of Roman citizenship, so that more people were eligible. Equally important for the next phase of Roman expansion were reforms to the organization of the army and its fighting methods. The infantry forces were organized in sixty centuries (containing a hundred men each) and the cavalry in a further six centuries. This force was the forerunner of the later legion. More disciplined methods of fighting at close quarters were also introduced, probably adaptations of Etruscan tactics, themselves derived from the practice of Greek hoplites. These developments made a major contribution to the conquest of Italy.

The later kings of Rome were populist rulers. They followed policies which appealed to the widening citizen body, and controlled the powers of aristocratic families, as well as reducing their wealth. A clash between the nobles and the kings was inevitable and it came in 509 BC, when Tarquinius II was expelled by a group of nobles and the monarchy abolished. Thereafter, the very notion of kingship was abhorrent to Romans. In place of kings a joint magistracy was instituted, in which power was shared by two men, the consuls, who held office for one year and could not be re-elected. In times of extreme crisis, power could still be invested in one man, the dictator, who could act as supreme military commander for a six-month period. The republican organization which emerged about 500 BC was a surprisingly sophisticated system of government, but it did not guarantee stability. Within Roman society powerful groups clustered about influential individuals and competition between these factions often led to disorder. The forces which were ultimately to destroy the republic can be traced back to its very origins.

During the sixth century BC Roman authority extended over several of the cities of Latium and began to spread to the neighbouring peoples of central Italy: Sabines, Volsci and Aequi. Rome's great rival, the Etruscan city of Veii, only 10 miles to the north, was subdued shortly after 400 BC, thus doubling the size of Roman territory. Rome was now set to dominate much of Italy, but there was a major setback when, in 390 BC, a raiding force of Gauls from northern Italy swept south, defeated the Roman army and sacked Rome. The setback was temporary. By the middle of the next century, Rome was expanding once more. From 330 to 240 BC large expanses of central Italy were annexed and colonized by the Romans. Late in the fourth century, major contacts with Greek cities in the south were forged and Rome was able to exploit the declining power of those communities by offering the weaker ones protection.

The next phase of Roman advance involved half a century of struggle with the trading empire of Carthage in the central and western Mediterranean. Beginning with a minor incident in Sicily in 264 BC, the struggle for mastery of the sea and its surrounding lands was fought out in two major Punic Wars, the first conducted largely by sea between 264 and 241, the second ranging widely on land in Spain, Italy and finally North Africa between 219 and 202. The Carthaginians' brilliant general, Hannibal, led his army across the Alps into Italy and there joined with the Gallic tribes of the north to wage a skilful series of campaigns. He was finally defeated in 202. The power of Carthage was broken and in the following half-century Rome's position as the greatest power in the Mediterranean was assured. Next, the Gallic peoples of northern Italy and Liguria were conquered and Roman power in Spain was also greatly expanded. In the Balkans, diplomacy won over many of the Greek states, who preferred the protection of Rome to the threat of attack from Macedonia. Roman statecraft was joined with military might in the pursuit of imperialist aims. In the eastern Mediterranean the Romans generally avoided direct annexation of territory, preferring to rule through existing local regimes or kings. In the west, the barbarian or tribal societies seemed more suitable cases for conquest.

Internal crises and disputes put enormous strain upon the Roman republic during the second century BC, arising partly from the effects of the long wars on the agricultural economy of Italy, and partly from the rising ambitions of leading politicians. Urbanization and the growth of a market economy brought further difficulties. Julius Caesar's astonishing conquest of Gaul between 58 and 52 BC brought him enormous prestige and personal power and after a bitter civil war, Caesar was victorious and began a major programme of reforms and ambitious building schemes. Caesar's dictatorship naturally antagonized those who still clung to the remnants of republican traditions. His murder on March 15 (the Ides) 44 BC was carried out not as a *coup d'etat* but as the removal of a tyrant by a mixed group of his opponents. Further civil war followed, and, amid the ruin of the old republic, Octavian emerged as sole ruler of the Roman world. An age of prosperity began, not only in the Mediterranean provinces but also in areas closer to the frontiers.

The first and second centuries AD were for the Romans an age of building in the provinces, not only of great public structures such as temples, public squares, baths and amphitheatres, but also of major amenities such as aqueducts, bridges and roads. The achievements in architecture and engineering were not approached for many centuries, as the potential of stone, brick and concrete was fully exploited.

The Romans brought unprecedented stability to those areas of Europe which they conquered and administered. The 'Roman peace', enforced by the highly organized armies, ensured prosperity for a large proportion of the inhabitants of the empire, including many native peoples who never saw Rome or even Italy. Most of the peoples who were conquered by Rome were quickly absorbed within the Roman order. Only a generation or so after conquest, natives of conquered territories might adopt a life-style that was not far removed from that of Roman Italy and they could aspire to Roman citizenship.

Social mobility was a marked feature of the early Roman empire. Men of humble rank, even slaves, could rise to fortune and high office if they followed the right path. The boom of prosperity was reflected in the growth of cities in most parts of the empire. Merchants and craftsmen found enlarged markets for their wares. Farmers produced more from their land and fed the rising urban population. Freedom from external warfare provided the conditions for economic growth.

Not everyone shared in the benefits of Roman rule. The larger cities contained many disadvantaged and poor inhabitants. Slavery was an integral part of the economic system, supporting large agricultural estates, industrial workshops and the households of the better off. Household slaves were usually well treated, not least as they were valuable chattels, and often acted as nurses and tutors to the children. Many slaves in industry and on the land lived wretched lives, however, alleviated only by early death. The place of women in Roman society was largely concerned with the home and the upbringing of children. The lives of wealthier women were freer and some played an active role in urban and religious life, though magistracies and other offices were held exclusively by men.

The Romans worshipped a wide variety of gods, many of them related to the deities of Classical Greece, others deriving from native Italian gods. It is frequently argued that religious feeling among the Romans was shallow, but this is belied by the thousands of religious dedications found all over the empire and by the number and splendour of temples and shrines. Perhaps the most striking feature of Roman religion is its tolerance of the deities of other peoples, both inside the empire and without. Many Celtic gods continued to be honoured in western Europe under Rome and several deities from the east, including Mithras and Dolichenus, were introduced by their devotees. The Christian faith, too, was tolerated for the most part, though some of its ceremonies gave rise to suspicion from time to time and there were intermittent persecutions.

Large city populations required entertainment and this was provided in a number of ways. Most popular were the games in the amphitheatre, which included combats between gladiators, beast-fights, in which one animal was set upon another, mock naval battles and other spectacular displays. Criminals could also be condemned to fight each other to the death in the arena. Less costly of human life were the plays and farces which were performed in the theatres. These included revivals of Greek tragedies and comedies, but also pantomimes and Roman comedies. Among the educated classes, recitations by writers and historians were the usual means of bringing new work to the public. The production of books, on scrolls of papyrus, was a laborious and expensive business, and only a few people would be able to own them. Writers like Livy, Tacitus, Vergil, Ovid and Horace, who tell us so much about the Roman world and its people, were read and enjoyed by the more literate Romans only.

The early Roman empire was remarkably free from major revolts, except for that led by Boudicca in Britain (AD 60–1) and that of the Batavians on the lower Rhine in 69–70. The extension of Roman citizenship via urban foundations, military service and individual rewards did much to cement loyalty to Rome among the native peoples, as did the material benefits of the Roman peace. Some regions easily adapted to the forms of Roman life after conquest or annexation and rapidly became Romanized. This was true of much of Gaul, southern Spain and North Africa. In provinces such as Britain and Lower Germany, the process was much slower and the results less spectacular. In most provinces, a strongly urban culture developed in which the cities enjoyed a considerable degree of local independence.

After about AD 160 serious problems began to manifest themselves. Economic difficulties and external enemies in central Europe and the Near East led to a major collapse after 230, and for some decades the integrity of the empire was severely tried. A new political order was required and this was eventually provided by Diocletian after 284 and Constantine from 312. The political centre of gravity had shifted from Italy to the eastern provinces by the early fourth century, a fact underlined by Constantine's foundation of a new imperial capital at Byzantium, which became known as Constantinople (now Istanbul). Christianity had spread throughout the

Mediterranean world in the second and third centuries and was strong in the eastern provinces when Constantine was himself converted in 312. Later, the faith became the official religion of the state.

The western provinces were increasingly attacked by barbarians from the later fourth century, especially on the Rhine and Danube frontiers. Increasing numbers of barbarians (from the Latin *barbarus* meaning foreigner) tried to settle within the empire and many were enrolled in the Roman armies or settled in the provinces. Early in the fifth century the frontiers began to buckle under the pressure and barbarian settlement spread ever more widely throughout the west. Power was now in the hands of military commanders, often themselves of barbarian origin, but even they could do little to fend off the heavier assaults. By the 470s the western provinces were largely in barbarian control and even nominal rule by emperors ended in 476. The eastern Roman, or Byzantine, empire continued as a major power through this troubled period and revived in the sixth century, when the emperor Justinian attempted to restore Roman rule to Italy and North Africa, with some success. But from the later sixth century Byzantine power was mainly confined to the eastern Mediterranean and Asia Minor. Here it was to survive through many vicissitudes until the capture of Constantinople by the Turks in 1453. See: Albania, Austria, Belgium, Bulgaria, France, Germany, Greece, Holland, Hungary, Italy, Portugal, Romania, Spain, United Kingdom, Yugoslavia

The Sabines

The Sabines were an Italian Iron Age people from the central Apennines north-east of Rome. They were famous for their bravery and their devout religious practices. Wars between the Sabines and the Romans are recorded for the fifth century BC and these may be the background for the legend of the Rape of the Sabine Women, in which brides were forcibly seized by Roman intruders. In 290 the Sabines were soundly defeated by a Roman general and lost much of their territory. From then on, they were steadily absorbed into the population and culture of Rome, becoming full Roman citizens in 268 BC. See: Italy

The Samnites

The Samnites inhabited the southern Apennines in Italy during the Iron Age. They were a warlike people, composed of four main tribes in a confederation which was governed by a central assembly. In time of war an army of the entire people was led by a single warlord. Their settlements were mainly large agricultural villages and strongholds. Like certain other peoples of this part of Italy, the Samnites spoke the Oscan language, an ancient Italian language related to Latin. The Samnites came into contact with the expanding state of Rome in the fourth century BC and in a treaty of 354 the river Liris was fixed as the boundary between their territory and that of Latium. But Roman power continued to spread southward and in 342–1 BC the Romans seized part of Samnite territory in Campania. Despite a major Samnite victory at the battle of the Caudine Forks in 321, Rome continued to take over Samnite land. The Samnites supported Hannibal against Rome when he invaded Italy late in the third century BC and lost further territory and power when he left the peninsula. By the first century BC the Samnites had all but vanished as a separate people.
See: Italy

The Sarmatians

The Sarmatae or Sarmatians were a short, powerfully-built people known as superb horsemen. They were related to the Scythians and may represent a later branch or tribe of that people. They are first reported living in the basin of the river Don, and had possibly moved there from the Asian steppes. From the third century BC they began to move steadily westward towards the middle and lower Danube. Two main branches of the Sarmatians are distinguished by Roman writers. One, the Roxolani, advanced to the area around the Danube estuary; the other, the Iazyges, crossed the Carpathians and took possession of the plain between the rivers Tisza and Danube. After a trial of strength with Roman armies on the Danube frontier, both groups settled into more or less friendly relations with the Roman empire, punctuated by occasional raiding. From the later second century BC onwards, however, they figure more prominently as opponents of Rome, allying themselves with Germanic tribes to attack the Danube provinces. In an attempt to neutralize their threat many Sarmatians were settled in the Roman provinces, most notably by the emperor Constantine. During the fourth century they were absorbed by neighbouring Germanic peoples and ceased to figure in history as a separate population.

Although the Sarmatians were a nomadic or semi-nomadic people when they arrived on the Danube, they settled in fertile areas for a long time and adopted an agricultural economy and a stable way of life. Their social organization remained simple and they failed to develop the kind of strong, centralized power structure which might have provided the basis for a Sarmatian state.

See: Bulgaria, Romania, Russia, Ukraine

The Saxons

Although they are first mentioned by Ptolemy, in the mid second century AD, the Saxons played no part in European history until the later part of the third century. From their homeland in Schleswig-Holstein in northern Germany they then began to harass the coasts of western Europe and Britain, along with the Franks and other neighbouring peoples. Their attacks on Britain and Gaul intensified in the fourth century and by the end of that century or early in the next they were seeking to settle within the Roman provinces. When the Roman frontiers could no longer function, bands of Saxons began to move into eastern Britain, attracted as others had been by the easily accessible, rich land.

The Saxons who migrated to eastern Britain helped to create several small Germanic kingdoms which were only much later brought into a unified kingdom of England. Together with the other Germanic settlers of the time, the Angles and Jutes, they came to be known as Anglo-Saxons, to distinguish them from the Saxons on the European mainland.

The early Saxon settlers came in small groups and established themselves, or were established, in East Anglia, Essex, Oxfordshire, Lincolnshire and South Yorkshire, often at or close to Roman towns, as at Caister-by-Norwich and Dorchester-on-Thames. The tradition reported by Bede that Saxons were brought to Britain by the British leader Vortigern to serve as soldiers and only later turned against their employers, may be regarded as resting on fact, though the full story was almost certainly more complicated than the one that has been handed on to us. By the middle of the fifth century, Saxon immigration markedly increased. In eastern Britain there were Saxon settlements from Yorkshire to Kent, inland to the middle Thames valley with more and more of southern Britain falling under their control. They did not, however, have matters all their own way. About 490, a Saxon force was defeated by the Britons at Mount Badon and for a time the Saxon advance was checked. But after 520 more expansionist Saxon regimes began to emerge in Sussex, Essex and Wessex, laying the foundations of later minor kingdoms. Contacts with the continental Saxon lands were not lost and new settlers probably came to Britain during the sixth century. There was also intermarriage with surviving ruling families, as the king-lists of Wessex and Lindsey reveal. Christianity spread slowly through the Anglo-Saxon kingdoms after Augustine was sent to Kent by Pope Gregory in 597. The following century was the age of conversion.

After AD 600 minor kingdoms began to emerge among the Saxons settled in Britain. Kent was the earliest and most advanced. Wessex developed steadily through the seventh century to become the dominant power in the south and the nucleus for the kingdom of England. In the Midlands, Mercia expanded by taking over territory which had been in British hands. The Kingdom in the North, Northumbria, subjugated wide areas west of the Pennines and even north of the Tweed. Fighting between these petty states was commonplace, not least as kings had to reward the warriors in their retinues with treasure won by conquest.

The early English kingdoms were far from isolated political units. They not only had links with each other but also with Frankish Gaul, northern Germany, Scandinavia and the British in the north and west. The royal burial at Sutton Hoo (Suffolk) of about 625 tells us much about these contacts, especially those with Scandinavia. By this date, however, it is impossible to talk in any meaningful way about a peculiarly Saxon identity in the English kingdoms as there had been so much interaction with other Germanic settlers in the island and with the native British. The Saxon name continued to be used, however, not least by the Welsh (*Seisneg*) and the Scots (*Sassenach*). (In the German homeland of the Saxons, too, the name was transferred to major territorial divisions, Lower and Upper Saxony–*Niedersachsen* and *Obersachsen*.)

England offered considerable tracts of productive land to the Saxon colonists and that is what had attracted the migrants to the island in the first place. Much of the land had been cleared of its woodland in the preceding centuries so that large areas were accessible without immense labour. The great majority of the Saxons, and the other Germanic immigrants, were peasant farmers, living in small villages and hamlets. Their houses included long rectangular halls as well as small huts with floors dug into the earth. Larger villages and small towns appeared in the seventh century, especially after 800 as trade within England and with the European mainland increased. Towns also gained in importance when King Alfred founded fortified places or *burhs* to provide strongholds against the Danes in the ninth century.

Cultural life in certain circles was far from primitive. The epic poem *Beowulf*, composed in the eighth century, describes many features of aristocratic Saxon life. Among the descriptions of fighting and feasting there are also reflections on the human condition, the most moving being the image of human life as the flight of a swallow through a lighted hall, from darkness to darkness.

Saxon settlement in Gaul is less well known, but is recorded for the area between the Pas-de-Calais and the Somme, and for parts of Normandy and the lower Loire. These Saxon enclaves were later absorbed into the Frankish kingdom. A large proportion of Saxons had not left their homelands on the lower Elbe and the adjacent coasts and though they, too, were always vulnerable to the Franks, the power and influence of these continental Saxons grew during the sixth century.

The name Saxon was generally applied by this time to a loose grouping of tribes which lay in northern Germany between Frisia and Mecklenburg. There was no unified political power among these peoples. Influential nobles were in control of such policy as was pursued, in which warfare was the dominant factor. Kings were unknown. Leaders in war were chosen by lot, behind which divine guidance was believed to lie. The Saxons remained pagan until the eighth century and their conversion to Christianity thereafter was a slow process in which Anglo-Saxon and Frankish missionaries played a leading part.

The threat which the Saxons posed to the eastern border of the expanding Frankish empire was not to be tolerated for long by Charlemagne. In 772 his troops seized the great Saxon sanctuary of Eresburg and destroyed their great idol, the Irminsul, and from then until 785, Frankish armies invaded the Saxon territories using the river routes of Lippe and Main. With great difficulty the Saxons were beaten down and their land studded with fortified strongpoints and royal palaces as centres of administration. In 785 the Saxon leader Widukind accepted Christian baptism, but this did not mark the end of the struggle. The Saxons revolted in 792 and for the next decade there was fighting every year. Many were deported, their crops and villages destroyed, until finally Saxon resistance was worn down and their lands brought into the Frankish empire.

See: France, Germany, United Kingdom

The Scotti

The inhabitants of Ireland during the later Roman period were referred to as Scotti by Roman writers. The word may be derived from an Irish word meaning raider or plunderer. In the fourth century AD the Scotti are recorded as raiders of Roman Britain, along with the Picts of Scotland and the Saxons from northern Europe. They themselves were probably of Celtic origin. They are otherwise poorly known both in literature and archaeology and no physical description of them survives. Their metalwork and settlements alone identify their culture. At an uncertain date, possibly in the fourth and fifth centuries AD, the Scotti, or some of them, migrated across the Irish Sea to western Scotland, giving that land its name. There, too, their settlement and culture are very difficult to identify, except perhaps in a number of strongholds, such as Dunadd in Argyll.

By the seventh century, if not earlier, the Scotti had established a stable kingdom, Dalriada, with its centre in Argyll. This may have been made up of several lesser groups under their own leaders. There were attempts to enlarge the kingdom at the expense of the Picts of the east and the Britons further south, none of which seem to have been particularly successful. In 843 Kenneth MacAlpin, a king of Dalriada, merged his kingdom with that of the Picts, thus establishing the kingdom of Scotland which was to survive until the Union with England in 1707.
See: Ireland, United Kingdom

The Scythians

The Scythians or Scyths were nomads, reportedly a squat and square-bodied people. They were first recognized by Greek writers as inhabitants of the steppes between the Carpathian mountains and the river Don. Their origins, though, may have been in central Asia north of the Caucasus, from where they moved progressively west into the steppelands from 1000 BC onward. By 500 BC they occupied a broad swathe of steppe north of the Black Sea, with some groups advancing as far west as the modern territories of Hungary and Poland. The Scythians controlled important resources in the Black Sea hinterland, trading wheat, fish and furs with the Greeks. They were famed for their horsemanship, their mounted archers being especially effective.

The art of the Scythians reached a brilliant peak in gold-working; magnificent ornaments, weapons and vessels have been found in the graves of their chieftains. These graves were often large timber structures sited beneath earth mounds in which the ruler's horses as well as his treasure were buried. Their art also found expression as physical adornment in tattooing.

Scythian power was on the wane by the third century BC and by the first century AD they had merged with the other peoples of the steppes. The Sarmatians had taken over as the leading force. But their reputation for savagery in war was not forgotten and their name evoked terror for long after they had disappeared.
See: Russia, Ukraine

The Serbs

One of the Slav peoples who entered eastern Europe in the later sixth century AD were the Serbs, who settled in the western Balkans in what is now Yugoslavia. For long organized along tribal lines, the Serbs expanded their territory after AD 900 creating a kingdom which spread across Bosnia, Hercegovina and Kosovo, and survived until the Turks advanced into the Balkans in the fourteenth century. Serbia's most able ruler was Stefan Nemanya (1168–96) whose rule established Serbia as the strongest state in the Balkans during the period of Byzantine decline. By 1350, the Serbian empire reached from the Danube to central Greece and from the Adriatic to the Aegean. Most Serbs followed the eastern form of Christianity and the Orthodox Church gave them powerful support, its monasteries forming focal points of learning, art and culture.

In 1371 and 1389 the Turks defeated the Serbians and for the next four centuries they were vassals of the Ottoman Turks. After 1800, a movement for independence gathered momentum under the leadership of George Petrovic and in 1830 the Serbs won a substantial measure of self-government. In 1856 an independent Serbia was guaranteed by all the great powers. In 1878 Serbia won its complete independence and began a major phase of economic and military growth. Serbs helped to liberate large areas of the Balkans from the Turks, but the murder of the Austrian Archduke Ferdinand by a Serbian revolutionary in July 1914 not only brought Austria-Hungary to declare war on Serbia, but also precipitated the general European conflict of 1914–18. In 1918, Serbs joined Slovenes and Croats in the Kingdom of Serbia, Slovenia and Croatia, later Yugoslavia.

Their relations with the Croats were never easy and deteriorated still further under German occupation in 1941–44. Increasing friction between Serbs and Croats after the death of the communist president, Tito, in 1980 flared into civil war in 1991, as both Serbs and Croats sought independence for their respective republics.
See: Yugoslavia

The Sicels

The indigenous peoples of eastern Sicily were called Sicels by the Greeks who founded colonies in the island from the eighth century BC onwards. Greek tradition records that the Sicels had arrived in Sicily from Italy, but there is no independent support for this. Instead, for at least some of the early settlers on Sicily, the archaeological links seem to be with the eastern Mediterranean. The Greeks called the other native peoples of the island Sicans (those in the centre-west) and Elymians (west). By the fourth century BC Greeks and Sicels had thoroughly mixed and the Sicels thereafter disappear from history. The main tangible memorial to them is the name of Sicily, the land of the Sicels. Sicilians today are descended mainly from Greeks and Italians rather than from Sicels.
See: Italy

The Slavs

Bulgars, Croats, Czechs, Russians, Serbs, Slovaks, Slovenes, Ukrainians

Slavs are first specifically mentioned in the sixth century AD by Byzantine writers; by this time they had begun to occupy large parts of eastern Europe. It is possible, however, that the ancestors of the Slavs were the people whom earlier Roman writers called the Venedi and who occupied part of the Vistula basin in Poland.

It seems certain that the middle and upper basin of the river Vistula in Poland and western Russia formed the general area of Slav origins, with other groups from further east, in the Dniester and Dnieper valleys of the Ukraine. In the late fifth and sixth centuries AD there were also links with Germanic peoples immediately to the west. They seem to have been a loosely linked group of peoples, not a distinct tribe or confederacy.

The language of the early Slavs was Indo-European, though a much later development than Latin, Celtic and Germanic. It was a language spoken by all Slavs from the Baltic to the Balkans and from the Elbe to the Ukraine, down to the ninth century. Later, as various Slav states were established, different languages developed in three main groups: western (Polish, Slovak and Czech), eastern (Russian and Ukrainian), and southern (Bulgarian, Slovene and Serbo-Croat). The survival of early Slav river names in the region between the Oder and the Dnieper may be a strong indication that this was the first area of permanent Slav settlement.

The colonization of the land was essentially achieved by peasant cultivators, moving into the better land provided by the great river valleys. Agriculture was the main basis of life and the settlements of the early Slavs were mainly villages and hamlets. During the sixth century, small fortified sites appeared, perhaps the strongholds of local leaders, and after AD 600 some of these began to develop into towns. Trade grew in importance from the seventh century and was organized from a number of commercial bases on the Baltic coast (for example, Wollin) and in the valleys of the Oder and Vistula.

The Slavs migrated from their homelands in three main directions: south to the Balkans and the Adriatic; west into Central Europe and north-eastwards from the Ukraine into Russia. The movement into the Balkans began early in the sixth century. In 517 they crossed the Danube and raided Macedonia and northern Greece. These raids continued into the middle of the century and the emperor Justinian was compelled to settle some Slav groups on Byzantine territory to lessen their attacks. By 536 they had reached the Adriatic, opening up areas for new settlement in Croatia and Serbia. When Avars arrived in Hungary, more Slavs moved southwards. By about 580 Slavs were settled in all the former Roman provinces on the lower Danube and others were beginning to settle in central Greece. Shortly after 600, yet another wave of Slav settlers swept into the Balkans and continued westward to the Alps and eastward to Asia Minor. This was a major migration of population and was only contained with great difficulty by the Byzantine rulers.

The Slav states in the northern Balkans today are the result of these migrations: Croats moved into the coastal areas of the Adriatic, Serbs into the central Balkans.

There is no record of how and when the Slavs moved into central

Europe, but the archaeological evidence indicates that they were pushing into eastern Germany and Czechoslovakia from the Ukraine in the first half of the fifth century. They were thus taking part in the general migration then affecting most of eastern Europe. As Germanic groups moved westwards, there was land available for the Slavs and they advanced steadily into the Oder and lower Elbe valleys, reaching the Baltic during the sixth century. This settlement in northern Germany was consolidated in the seventh and eighth centuries but was finally checked by the advance of Charlemagne's Franks. Cultural contacts were maintained with the neighbouring Germanic peoples and the clear divide between Slavs and Germans, carefully fostered by later rulers and modern politicians, certainly never existed. The nomadic peoples of eastern Europe also left their impress on Slav cultural development, especially in metalworking and art.

The earliest of the Slav states was founded in unusual circumstances, about which we are well informed. In 624 a Frankish merchant, Samo, went with other traders to a Slav area close to the border with the Avars. These Slavs were at the time engaged in an uprising against their formidable neighbours and Samo joined their cause, taking a leading role in the conflict. For this, he was elected ruler of the Slavs, a position he held for the next 35 years. The precise location of Samo's state has been much discussed. As it was close to Avar territory it was probably an area just north of the Danube, perhaps in Slovakia and Moravia.

Other Slav states were slow to emerge. Moravia was an organized entity in the eighth century but was overthrown by the Magyars in 906. The minor Slav states along the Elbe remained weak and disunited, but to the east of them a stable kingdom was created in Poland by Miesko (960–92) and his son Boleslav Chrobry (992–1025). The latter had dreams of a greater Slav state which would reach from the Baltic to the Danube, an ambition which foundered in civil war. Bohemia, too, became a state in the early tenth century, though retaining strong German connections.

The third Slav movement, into Russia, began in the eighth century. By about 880, with strong support from Viking merchants, they had established a realm with centres at Novgorod in the north, Smolensk in the centre and Kiev in the south. Kiev quickly became the capital of this emergent state, the first in Russia. It had close commercial relations with

Byzantium and from there it received the Christian faith about AD 1000.
The major threat to Kiev Russia came at first from the steppe nomads, Khazars and Pechenegs. Weakened by long warfare, the state began to break up into warring chiefdoms in the late eleventh century. But its greatest trial was still to come. After 1220 the Mongols began to attack from the south-east. In 1237–40 much of eastern Russia was overrun and in 1240 Kiev itself was taken and sacked. The Mongols later withdrew, but the effects of their invasion were lasting and Kiev Russia never recovered.

The different Slav groups were converted to Christianity at different times. The Croats were among the earliest to become Christians through contacts with Rome. The Slavs further east were influenced by Byzantine Christianity and later by the Orthodox Church, leading to a divide between the eastern and western Slavs. Today, the Slav peoples owe allegiance to a wide variety of faiths: Orthodox (Russians, Bulgarians, Serbs), Catholic (Poles, Czechs, Slovaks, Slovenes and Croats) and Muslim (Bulgarians).
See: Bulgaria, Czechoslovakia, Poland, Russia, Ukraine, Yugoslavia

The Slovaks

One of the western Slav peoples, the Slovaks inhabited the mountainous area east of the Czech settlement in Bohemia. From the beginning of the sixth century AD they were overshadowed by more advanced and powerful neighbours, especially the Magyars. By the 1400s, the Slovaks had begun to establish links with their Czech neighbours and like them came under the rule of the Hapsburgs in the 1520s. The Slovaks retained their language and culture throughout this period, but their sense of national identity was not strongly expressed until after 1800. A Slovak rising against Magyar domination in 1848 was put down and there was no further opportunity to break free until the collapse of Austria-Hungary in 1918. The Slovak people were then brought into the new state of Czechoslovakia, where they remain as a distinct ethnic group.
See: Czechoslovakia, Hungary

The Slovenes

The Slovenes are one of the southern Slav peoples; they speak their own distinctive language and have a clearly defined national consciousness. They settled in the northern Balkans in the area that is now Slovenia in the sixth and seventh centuries AD. Unlike the other southern Slavs, they fell under strong German influence from the ninth century, their aristocracy and much of their landed class becoming markedly Germanized. Most of the Slovenes were living within the Austrian state in the Middle Ages and it was not until after 1848 that a Slovenian nationalist movement gathered strength. Together with the Serbs, Croats and the other neighbouring Slavs, they were brought into the new federal state of Yugoslavia in 1918 and since then have been recognized as forming the most advanced and industrialized of the constituent republics, as well as that with the strongest orientation towards the west. In 1991, they broke away from the Yugoslav federation to form the independent republic of Slovenia.
See: Yugoslavia

The Suevi

A large grouping of Germanic tribes who lived east of the upper Rhine in the early Roman period bore the name Suevi or Suebi. Julius Caesar confronted them when they tried to settle in eastern Gaul in the mid first century BC under their war-leader Ariovistus and pushed them back across the Rhine. Little is heard of them again until early in the fifth century when they joined the Vandals and Alans in crossing the frozen Rhine on the last night of 406. For the next three years they moved around in Gaul, raiding freely and then, in the summer of 409, they crossed into Spain where they settled in the north-western hill country of Galicia. There the Suevi founded a kingdom which lasted from 411 to the late sixth century.

What is known of this kingdom suggests it was a warlike, even barbaric, state. From their mountainous base, the Suevi raided widely, even taking Merida in 439 and Seville in 441. Their activities were curtailed in 456 when they were defeated by the Visigoths near Astorge, but they continued to be a thorn in the side of the other peoples of Spain until they were finally absorbed into the Visigothic kingdom in 585. Catholic Christianity spread through their upper ranks from the mid fifth century, though how this process began is unknown.

The Suevi developed no distinct culture of their own and soon after the merger of their kingdom with that of the Visigoths they vanished as a separate people, to the regret of no-one.
See: France, Germany, Spain

The Swedes

The earliest historical references to the peoples settled in Sweden date from the late first century AD. By this time, the Svear, the ancestors of the Swedes, were living around Lake Mälaren in central Sweden, while further south were the Gotar, once thought (incorrectly) to be the early Goths. The origins of the Svear and the Gotar lie much further back in prehistory, quite probably in the middle of the first millennium BC, and may have had connections with Denmark and the southern Baltic coastlands.

In the first centuries AD, the land was occupied by small farming groups, who were ruled by local lords. More organized political units may have emerged by the fourth century. Although relatively remote from the rest of Europe, the Iron Age inhabitants of Sweden received Roman trade goods, especially bronze and glass vessels, coinage and pottery. In the fifth and sixth centuries AD, large quantities of gold coins were imported into Sweden, Öland and Gotland from the Byzantine world. From this time onwards there are signs of considerable disturbance in the region, probably due to a rise in population and the consequent pressure on land. In the seventh century the Swedes began to look outward to the eastern Baltic for land and trading opportunities and after 700 very many Swedes took part in the Viking raids and colonization.

A major centre of political and religious power in this period lay at Old

Uppsala near the modern city. Royal burials were placed there in vast mounds, which still survive. In the seventh century another focus of power existed around Vendel and Valsgärde in eastern Sweden, again revealed to us by richly furnished graves which show links with England and specifically with the Sutton Hoo burial. The importance of Swedish trading ventures is illustrated by the major trading post situated at Birka on Lake Mälaren which was in contact with wide areas of Europe and the Near East.

Throughout the long period from their first appearance in recorded history to the time when they were thoroughly established in the comings and goings of the world, the Swedes retained their old religion and although the first Christian mission to them was sent in 829, Christianity was not adopted by many Swedes until the twelfth century.

The burial practices of Swedish leaders and their followers are a rich source of information on their religious beliefs. Entire ships, along with furnishings, clothing, food and drink, horses and dogs were placed in the burial mounds at Vendel and Valsgärde. Some graves here and elsewhere were surrounded by stone settings in the form of boats, underlining the importance of the sea and perhaps also symbolizing the journey of the soul into the next world. The myths and stories which abound in Scandinavia during the early mediaeval period appear in graphic form on a fascinating series of engraved memorial stones on the island of Gotland. Some of the scenes may record actual events from the lives of leading figures of the fifth to twelfth centuries.

The modern population of Sweden can claim direct descent from these early Swedes, though there have been important contacts between the southern Swedes, Danes and northern Germans in particular.
See: Denmark, Finland, Sweden

The Thracians

The tribes who inhabited the Haemus and Rhodope mountains and the plains below them in the northern Balkans were known to the Greeks as *Thrakoi*, Thracians. They were a warlike group of tribes, living in open villages, not cities. They were certainly of Indo-European stock, but their language and many aspects of their culture are still poorly known. The Greeks themselves knew little about them, although the coast of Thrace was settled by Greek colonists at Abdera, Perinthus, Aenus and Byzantium. Their early recorded history is very sketchy. They fell under the domination of Persia late in the sixth century BC, but were later able to reassert their independence and establish a strong and militarily formidable kingdom in the fifth century. In the mid fourth century Thrace was invaded by Philip II of Macedon and became a protectorate of Macedonia. The kingdom re-emerged when the Macedonian monarchy declined and was recognized as a political entity by the Romans in the second century BC. Thracian kings continued to rule the territory until AD 46 when Thrace became a Roman province.

The cultural life of the Thracians has been revealed by major new discoveries of the past forty years. Greek legend derived Orpheus and possibly Ares, the god of war, from Thrace. Thracian religion contained a number of deities who could be identified with Greek gods, e.g. Bendis (Artemis) and a Thracian counterpart of Dionysus. Rider-gods were later important and at all dates gods of the Underworld were powerful.

In craftsmanship, especially the work of metalsmiths, the Thracians were outstandingly skilled. The burial monuments of their kings and warrior nobles have yielded an enormous wealth of gold and silver vessels, jewellery and other ornaments, fine weapons, glass and decorated pottery. Silver coinage circulated freely in Thrace, particularly the coins issued by the Greek cities on the coast. The precious metal vessels are often of superb quality, displaying high skill in technique and exuberance in design. There is clear evidence of the influence of Greek artists, but Persian and Scythian craftsmen also left their mark on Thracian art.
See: Bulgaria, Greece, Yugoslavia

The Thuringians

The Thuringians (Thuringi, Thoringi or Toringi) are first mentioned about AD 400, but had probably developed a separate identity during the previous century. Not until after the middle of the fifth century is it possible to speak of a recognizable archaeological culture in their heartland, which was the region about the confluence of the Saale and the Elbe, along with the valley of the Unstrut to the west. Although they are rarely mentioned in the historical sources for the fifth and sixth centuries, the Thuringians were a force to be reckoned with for over a century. They did not attempt to move south towards the Danube with other Germanic tribes in the late fifth century, probably because they had sufficient territory to support themselves. However, they were vulnerable to Frankish expansion east of the Rhine from the early sixth century onward. About 530, most of the Thuringians were made subject to the Franks and thereafter they rapidly declined in influence. Some of them accompanied the Lombards to Italy in 568, others were absorbed by the Bavarians. Like the Burgundians in Gaul, little more than their name survived on the map of central Europe to record their existence.

See: Germany, Italy

The Turks

The name 'Turks' was applied by Arabs to all the Turkic peoples in the Middle Ages, the word itself being originally Turkic and probably meaning simply 'people'. It is therefore a non-specific term for a large range of peoples who extended from Siberia and northern Iran to eastern Europe and not merely to the Turks who settled in Asia Minor and gave their name to Turkey.

The first Turks to be mentioned in historical sources were the Kirghiz, who are noted in Chinese writings of the early first century AD, though they may have originated centuries earlier. The Kirghiz came from central

Asia, from the wooded regions about the Altai mountains. Unlike most of their neighbours they were fair-haired and blue-eyed. Like the Scythians and Huns, they were pastoral nomads and like them, they moved westward across the vast plains of Asia towards the Caspian and Black Seas. After AD 500, they controlled an immense area from the eastern Black Sea to western China. Their language was related to that of the Mongols, though it developed its own distinct character. By the eighth century, they had become at least partly literate.

Another major group of the Turkic peoples were the Oghuz, who appeared in Mongolia during the eighth century. They, too, moved westward, through Iran towards Asia Minor, conquering on the way the Caliphate of Baghdad and Syria. By the twelfth century they had reached the eastern borders of the Byzantine empire, which they constantly harassed. One of their chiefs, Osman, founded an energetic and ambitious dynasty, the Ottomans, who eventually overthrew the last remnant of the Byzantine empire by capturing Constantinople in 1453. They swept on to the Balkans, conquering Greece, Bulgaria and much of the land of the southern Slavs. The Ottoman Turkish empire, ruled from Istanbul (the former Constantinople), was a dominant force in eastern Europe from the fifteenth to the late seventeenth century, but then entered upon a slow decline until it finally collapsed in the late nineteenth century.

The Turks are an overwhelmingly Muslim people, but their ethnic mixture is very varied. Physically they may be fair with blue eyes, dark with dark eyes or Mongoloid with high cheeks and narrow eyes. Their cultural heritage is also very mixed, including Byzantine Greek, Arab, Iranian, Kurdish and more recently Mediterranean elements. The traditional Turkish society is now breaking up, as many leave the countryside for the cities. Many others have sought employment in Europe as migrant workers. In the traditional communities, men and women live in separate worlds. Popular culture is very strong away from the cities, especially in music and minstrelsy, narrative stories and shadow plays performed by dolls. The Turkish language is spoken by over 90% of the population.

See: Albania, Bulgaria, Greece, Romania, Yugoslavia

The Ukrainians

Ukrainians are a distinct Slavic people, who speak their own Slav language and have a well defined folk culture and identity. They have settled the broad, fertile plain of south-west Russia north of the Black Sea, a region where many different peoples and cultures have lived since the first millennium BC.

Apart from Slavs, various nomad peoples moved into and through the Ukraine, or 'borderland' (of Russia) and both Goths and Huns were nourished by its rich land. The Ukrainians probably emerged as a nation in the making after AD 1200, though the name is not recorded until the sixteenth century. For most of their history, Ukrainians have been ruled by outsiders. The Mongols conquered them in 1240 and the Lithuanians in 1392. In the sixteenth century they passed under Polish rule and suffered greatly when their property was forcibly taken over. Many of their farmers fled to the lowlands around the Dnieper river, where they established the military society of the Cossacks, famed and fearsome horsemen. The Cossacks led a great revolt against the Poles in 1648 and for a time created an independent state. But this was too weak to stand against Poland and they asked for military help from Russia. Gradually, the Ukrainians were submerged in the Russian empire, where they remained until 1917. After the Russian revolution an independent Ukraine was recognized by Soviet Russia but it was not until 1991 that independence became a reality.

Ukrainians possess one of the liveliest folk cultures in all Europe. Their dress is a mixture of western and traditional steppe garments. Their singing, both choral and solo, is famous and the range of their folk songs is among the widest in the world. Their festivals are also accompanied by dancing, in which many traditions are represented. Literature and drama are also very lively in the Ukraine, as are films and pictorial art. The Ukrainian language has now largely given way to Russian, but is far from extinct. The richness of the black earth of the Ukraine means that the great majority of the people are farmers and have long been so. But industry has also developed and Kiev is one of the major cities of eastern Europe.

See: Poland, Russia, Ukraine

The Vandals

Vandilii are recorded in what is now Poland in the second century AD and were fairly certainly the ancestors of the Vandals. They were probably a group of tribes, not a single political unit under unified control. In the late second century there were two main divisions, the Asdings and the Lacringes. At the end of 406, they crossed the Rhine with Suevi and Alans and pushed into Gaul and later into Spain. Some settled in the north, but the main body of Vandals moved south into Andalusia and found there a wealthy land which was ripe for plundering.

Unlike most of the other Germanic invaders of the empire, they learned seamanship, took over vessels found in the harbours of southern Spain and raided the coasts of Africa across the Straits of Gibraltar. Once there, the Vandals swept eastward with astonishing speed, taking city after city. Within two years, only three major centres held out against them: Carthage, Cirta and Hippo Regius. This was a peaceful land and the savagery and destruction of the Vandal invasion must have seemed all the more horrifying. In 439 Carthage fell and the conquest of the wealthy coastlands of Africa was complete. Even this did not satisfy the Vandals. In 440 they landed in Sicily and threatened to attack Italy from the south. In 455 they invaded both Italy and Spain, and sacked Rome itself. Vandal rule in Africa continued until 533, when a Byzantine army under Belisarius invaded and quickly overthrew their kingdom. The Vandals had not made any attempt to integrate with the late Roman population and in material terms little was left to mark the kingdom's hundred years of existence.
See: France, Poland, Spain

The Vikings

Danes, Norwegians, Swedes

The Vikings were not a distinct people, tribe or nation. The name was applied to raiders and merchants whose homelands lay in the Baltic and Scandinavia, in the lands that are now Norway, Sweden, Denmark and the islands, and who broke out in the eighth century AD to range widely across northern and western Europe, Russia, Byzantium and the Mediterranean world. The name seems to mean 'adventurer by sea' or 'sea-raider', and reflects the understandable reaction to their sudden arrival and their rapid and often devastating raids. But Vikings were also notable explorers, especially in the North Sea and the Atlantic, accomplished merchants who established trading-posts over an astonishingly wide geographical spread, and settlers in regions which until then had been under-exploited.

The origin of the Vikings is not easily explained. There had long been contacts, both in trade and diplomacy, between Scandinavia, the eastern Mediterranean and western Europe, and these had been relatively stable and controlled from the Roman period to the eighth century. During all this time, the often warring tribes of central Europe formed a major buffer between the northern peoples and the wider European world. After 780, however, the Frankish king Charlemagne brought most of western Europe under his rule and this more stable situation may have encouraged the northerners to widen their horizons.

The first Viking raids fell heavily upon eastern England and the western coastlands of Europe. After 786 they attacked the south of England and in 793 they sacked the monastery of Saint Cuthbert on Lindisfarne off the Northumberland coast, an event which reverberated through the courts of western Europe. After 835, Viking attacks on England intensified and by 851 they were able to winter in the island and later (in 865) extorted tribute (Danegeld) from the English king. More permanent settlement of Vikings followed in Northumbria and later in the eastern Midlands, the area of the Five Boroughs of Lincoln, Nottingham, Stamford, Derby and Leicester. Their further expansion over southern and western England was checked by King Alfred in the later ninth century. By this time, Viking attention was already turning elsewhere, towards Ireland, Scotland and the Western Isles, the Low Countries and northern France. In the 840s the French coasts were ravaged and shortly after 900, Norwegian Vikings (Norsemen) began to settle in what was to become Normandy. Even Spain was subjected to Viking raids between 900 and 1050.

The greatest of Viking explorations by sea took place in the Atlantic. Iceland was certainly known to Vikings in the ninth century and settlers from Norway, Denmark and from the Viking areas of Britain were living there by 870. Greenland was settled in the later tenth century, traditionally by Erik the Red and his followers. Although it was a forbidding land, its coasts were rich in seals, whales and walrus, providing skins and ivory for export. Newfoundland and the mainland of North America were certainly known to the Vikings and a Viking settlement is known in Newfoundland, at L'Anse aux Meadows. America was probably first seen by Vikings in 985 by a group aiming for Greenland but sailing by mistake well to the west. Leif, the son of Erik the Red, later landed on the continent and gave various names to it: Vinland, Helluland and Markland. There is, however, no proof that Vikings settled permanently in mainland North America.

Viking sailors and merchants also penetrated far to the east of their Baltic homes, into Russia. After 860 the local inhabitants of the centre of European Russia invited men from the north to restore order to the country. They seem to have called them Rus and it is highly likely that Viking adventurers had already reached this part of Russia, travelling along the major rivers, Vistula, Dvina and Bug, and were becoming a power in the land. Trade took them deeper into Russia along the rivers Dnieper, Don and Volga, where the trading towns of Novgorod, Kiev and Smolensk provided major markets visited not only by local traders and Vikings but also by Arab and Asian merchants. Archaeologists are increasingly discovering Viking material along these major trade routes. Some of the Scandinavian merchants were men of considerable wealth and were important enough to be allied with the ruling houses of the Slavs among whom they had settled. Viking soldiers also found military service far to the east, with the Byzantine emperors, the Varangian Guard being recognized as a *corps d'elite*. (*Varangias* was the late Latin word for a Scandinavian settler in Russia, derived from the Old Norse *Vaeringi*.)

In their explorations both to east and west, the Vikings were in search of wealth, in one form or another. Their most effective trading activities were those which centred upon a central market, such as Birka, Novgorod or Dublin. Birka in southern Sweden was probably the greatest of these. It lay on an island in Lake Mälaren, which linked the royal centre of Uppsala with the wider world. Its heyday was the ninth and tenth centuries, and to it came merchants from western Europe, Byzantium, Russia and the Near East. Local craftsmen were at work here, aiming to catch the attention of the foreign traders. Hedeby, near Schleswig, was another trading-post which was visited by merchants from many parts of Europe. The Vikings founded other forms of town which had considerable impact on urban development in western Europe. Dublin, for example, began as a fortified palace and administrative headquarters. Later it became a major port and industrial centre. The impact of the settlers on existing towns could also be considerable. York, Lincoln and Nottingham all became prosperous through Viking trading enterprise.

Viking expansion by sea was only possible with the aid of fine ships and skilled seamen. Sailing ships of outstanding craftsmanship and design have been preserved in the ninth century graves of Tune, Oseberg and Gokstad, all in Norway. The Gokstad vessel is the finest of these, 23 metres long and over 5 metres broad amidships, made of oak with deck, mast and oars in pine. It was clinker-built, the planks of the hull being lashed to the ribs by roots of spruce. The mast carried a single woollen sail, and there were oars for inshore manoeuvring and adverse weather. A modern reconstruction of the Gokstad ship crossed the Atlantic in the late nineteenth century, often touching speeds of ten or eleven knots.

Other objects from Viking Europe show the high quality of their craftsmanship. Large quantities of silver and a sizeable stock of gold were available to artists working in a tradition which reached back to the Roman centuries. Magnificent jewellery and other personal ornaments are found in many areas of Viking influence, especially from the ninth and early tenth centuries. Their artifacts are easily recognized for their craftsmen were surprisingly little touched by influences from other parts of Europe at this time, even from the neighbouring empire of the Franks. Fine work was also carried out in stone and wood. Memorial stones were carved for the illustrious dead, with intricate designs, human and mythological figures, and runic inscriptions. Groups of such stones were set up in royal or aristocratic cemeteries at Ringerike (Norway) and Jelling (Denmark), both sites giving their names to distinctive styles of ornament. Skilled carving in wood is found in a wide range of surviving objects, from a furniture post in the form of a fabulous animal-head in the Oseberg ship to the wooden doorway to a church at Urnes (Norway), which gives a name to the latest Viking ornamental style, of the eleventh and twelfth centuries.

Much is known about the religion of the Viking peoples from the store of myths and sagas which survive from the later stages of northern paganism. These reveal a world in which the virtues of the warrior and the man of action were considered as paramount, the struggle against death and the powers of darkness as endless. Four powerful gods, among others, were worshipped by the Vikings: Odin, the god of battle and of inspiration; Thor, god of the sky and of the community; Freyr and his sister Freyja, gods of fertility and prosperity. The origins of these deities and the world they inhabited were ancient, lying far back in the early Germanic tribal world. It was a world rich in symbols, of bridges, caves and journeys through air, all of them links between this earth and the next world. There were terrifying creatures, too: giants, elves, dragons, serpents and other monsters. And yet it was not a world devoid of hope. Courage and steadfastness still could triumph and ensure a man's fame. Moderation was seen as a great virtue, surprisingly, in view of the Viking reputation for excess of all kinds.

Although their popular image is that of destructive and bloodthirsty raiders, which many of them were, Vikings were mostly concerned with farming and life on the land, and with trade, often over immense distances and in a wide variety of goods. Their entrepreneurial achievements were their most distinctive contribution to early mediaeval Europe and in turn these helped to stimulate other developments, in urban life and in craftsmanship. The Viking achievement was thus many-sided and the impact of these northern adventurers was felt on many aspects of human affairs over a wide sweep of Europe and beyond. Their descendants, too, are to be found not only in the Scandinavian homelands, but in the many countries of Europe and the New World in which they settled.

See: Belgium, Denmark, France, Germany, Holland, Iceland, Ireland, Norway, Russia, Spain, Sweden, Ukraine, United Kingdom

The Vlachs

In Romania, Albania, Yugoslavia and north-western Greece a people speaking a language derived from Latin survives from antiquity. They are commonly termed Vlachs (*Volokh* in the Slav language, *Koutzovlachs* in Greek), though they usually call themselves Aromani or Romani. It is not clear how many exist today, but they may number more than half a million. They are settled mainly in Romania, Moldavia and Walachia (which means land of the Vlachs), though another group lives in northern Greece, Albania and southern Yugoslavia. Precisely how these Latin-speakers were established in these regions is a matter for dispute, but the most likely explanation is that they were directly descended from the Roman population of Dacia and other Danube provinces displaced in the migrations which took place from the third to the sixth centuries.

Vlachs were known to the Byzantine world, but they formed no political unit. They did, however, play a major role in the foundation of the Second Bulgar Empire in the late twelfth century. Thereafter, they largely disappeared from view until the nineteenth century.
See: Albania, Bulgaria, Greece, Romania, Yugoslavia

The Welsh

The Celts of western Britain retained their identity and culture after the end of Roman Britain and the Germanic migrations that followed. The name 'Welsh' was applied to the British in Wales and Cornwall by the Anglo-Saxons (from their word *wealh*) and survives in the modern names Wales and Welsh. Welsh society after AD 400 was, as it had been earlier, tribal and Wales was occupied by numerous small tribal groups that were frequently at war among themselves. Virtually no immigration from Germanic England occurred and the boundary earthwork drawn by Offa of Mercia at the end of the eighth century between his kingdom and the Welsh for long marked the frontier between the two countries. Much of the earthwork still survives today.

Within Wales, no political unity was established until the ninth century, when Rhodri the Great brought the major peoples together to combat the Scandinavian threat. After 900 the rule of Hywel Dda continued this unifying work, his main achievement being an important code of law. After 1066 the Normans attacked lowland south Wales and swept away the small princedoms there. In the north, however, Welsh resistance was maintained by a sequence of determined rulers until the thirteenth century. Even after English control was completed by Edward I late in that century, there were serious revolts, the most effective being that of Owen Glyndwr (Glendower) early in the fifteenth century. The victory of Henry Tudor, himself of Welsh descent, at Bosworth in 1485 brought Wales firmly into the orbit of English power and in 1536 the principality of Wales was formally assimilated into the kingdom of England.

Welsh culture was far from extinguished by the political union and it remains a living force today. Music has played a vital role within Welsh society for centuries, while the Welsh language, which is descended from British Celtic with influences from Latin and from English, is still spoken by about one in five of the modern population. The greatest concentration of Welsh-speakers is in the north. There is an important and sophisticated literature which has enjoyed an unbroken history from the sixth century AD, from tales such as those of *The Mabinogion* to poetry and drama in modern Welsh.

See: United Kingdom

The Countries of Europe

The Foundations of Modern Europe

Towards the end of the third century AD, the Roman Empire, which had brought peace and stability to vast areas of Europe, began its slow decline. The centuries that followed were a time of change as people from beyond the empire's old frontiers gradually moved west and south into the Roman provinces and migrants from the east settled in central Europe. For hundreds of years Europe became a continent of shifting, often feudal kingdoms, frequently quarrelling and fighting among themselves, their societies based on essentially local loyalties.

While Europe remained a collection of disparate kingdoms, the Christian Church was a major unifying influence. Early in the fourth century, Christianity was accepted as the official religion of the Roman Empire and the collapse of Rome's western empire did not undermine the Church's fundamental strength; indeed, many of the barbarian peoples who entered the Roman world were already Christian or were soon converted and conversions continued for centuries after the fall of Rome. The Anglo-Saxons became Christian in the seventh century, the Scandinavian peoples not until 1000 or later, the Magyars around 1100. Throughout the disturbed centuries of the Dark Ages, monasteries kept learning alive and formed major focal points of social and economic activities. In the eastern Roman provinces (the Byzantine Empire) emperors promoted a strong version of Christianity which influenced the Slavs and other eastern peoples. However, the Great Schism of 1054 divided the Greek east from the Latin west, a division which still exists between the Roman Catholic Church and the Orthodox Churches of eastern Europe.

Under the authority of the Popes, the western Church developed political as well as religious power, actively supported by Charlemagne, who built the first major (but short-lived) post-Roman empire in Europe. Nearly 200 years after Charlemagne was crowned emperor of the Romans, the concept of a united Christian Europe was revived in the Holy Roman Empire, under the German emperor Otto I.

The Holy Roman Empire consisted of a number of member states with a parliament and an elected emperor. The title was not hereditary but from the end of the thirteenth century until 1806, the elected emperor was always a member of the Austrian ruling family, the Hapsburgs. The Holy Roman Empire thus became closely linked with the subject states of the Hapsburg's own extensive empire and the influence of the powerful Hapsburg family was felt in almost every European nation.

By 1000 the political map of Europe was beginning to stabilize around a number of major powers. The Byzantine Empire dominated Greece and the Balkans. In the centre was the Holy Roman Empire, with Spain, France and England in the west, the Scandinavian monarchies in the north, and Poland, Hungary and Russia in the east. Several of these powers were to survive for the next five hundred years; others were to wane or disappear altogether.

The boundaries of most individual states, however, were ever-changing and often ill-defined. Royal marriages between the ruling families of different kingdoms led to complicated disputes over inheritance and whole states passed from the rule of one royal house to another.

Throughout the mediaeval centuries Europe remained a patchwork of small states. The Church continued to be a unifying influence but gradually the authority of the Popes was undermined by corruption and the rise of Protestantism. In the east, the Turkish Islamic empire was expanding into Europe and Greek scholars who fled from Constantinople in the late fifteenth century brought a revival of interest in the Greek language. Studies of the New Testament in the original Greek highlighted how far Christianity had diverged from its roots and, in the sixteenth century, Protestant ideas spread widely. The deeply felt differences brought a century of religious wars in France and Germany, culminating in 1618 in the Thirty Years War when Catholic and Protestant rulers of independent states in the Holy Roman Empire ravaged Central Europe. In the Balkans, the Turkish Ottoman Empire continued for 400 years, and its Islamic influence for even longer: there are still Muslims in Yugoslavia and Albania, as well as European Turkey.

After the turbulent sixteenth and seventeenth centuries there followed a time when great powers dominated the scene: Russia, France, Britain, Prussia, the Hapsburg Empire. The eighteenth century was to become known as the Age of Reason, when political philosophers such as Voltaire and Rousseau spread ideas of social justice. Then, in 1789, came the French Revolution, followed by the aggressive empire of Napoleon: the face of Europe was transformed for ever. In 1810 Napoleon ruled directly or indirectly over almost the whole of continental Europe. Those states that were not within Napoleon's empire were his empire's allies; Russia successfully halted his progress to the east but only Britain, Portugal, Sweden and the Balkan states under Turkish rule remained outside his influence.

After Napoleon's defeat at Waterloo in 1815, Europe was significantly reorganized. A new revolutionary spirit spread through Europe in 1848—the Year of Revolution—and although this led to civil war in Austria, to Italy and Germany it brought a new movement towards unity. As the Turkish Ottoman Empire declined, several new nations came into being in the east.

The era of nation-states ended with the devastating European war of 1914–18. For several years before the outbreak of war the nations of

Europe had been spoiling for a fight. France and Germany were suspicious of each other's intentions; Britain and Germany were rivals at sea; the Austrian-Hungarian Empire was competing with Russia for influence in the Balkans. When the Archduke of Austria–Hungary was assassinated in Bosnia (then under Austrian rule) Austria accused Serbia of master-minding the killing while Russia and France supported Serbia against her. Allies were drawn in on both sides and the conflict became worldwide with both Japan and the United States involved. Russia's revolution in 1917 brought new divisions and, later, new alliances.

The map of Europe was drawn afresh after 1918, not always with happy results and the second and still more destructive war from 1939 to 1945 left Europe politically divided between east and west for over forty years. The break-up of Russian domination over eastern Europe and the dissolution of the Soviet Union itself, all within a few years, are a reminder that European history is subject to many dynamic processes.

The rise and fall of states is often used to chart the course of European history, but other developments often had greater impact both on nations and on the lives of ordinary people. The invention of printing, the great revival of art and learning of the Renaissance, the spread of Protestantism and the growth of industrialization, have all been fundamental influences on the development of modern Europe.

Europe, its peoples and states, have never been static. The great movements of peoples that transformed the continent between AD 200 and 600 have their counterparts in this century. Millions were displaced at the end of the Second World War; thousands of migrant workers moved to Britain from the West Indies and Asia and to prosperous northern Europe from the Mediterranean south and from Turkey. As colonies became independent, colonial citizens returned, often to unfamiliar homelands, and Jews from many countries of Europe left to start a new life in Israel. Asylum seekers from all over the world sought refuge in the west and, as famine and war increasingly devastated the Third World, a new surge of migrants began to seek a better way of life. In the final decade of the twentieth century the continent is once again poised for profound changes to its political and social structure.

Albania
Republika Shqipërisë

The Land: Albania is a rugged Mediterranean republic, on the west of the Balkan peninsula. Much of the country is very mountainous, with areas that are still today remote and inaccessible. Most settlement is concentrated in the western coastal plain where there is good farming land. The coastline is indented and its many harbours are convenient for shipping and trade from the opposite coast of Italy. It remains essentially an agricultural country, with few towns of any size and little industry.

The Language: Albanian is descended from Illyrian, an Indo-European language but the only surviving member of its language-group. There are two major dialects: Gheg in the north and Tosk in the south. Tosk is the official language of the state.

The Name: The Albanians' name for themselves is *Shqiptare*, 'Sons of eagles'. 'Albania' comes from the ancient Albani tribe who lived in the north of the region in Roman times.

Albania is the poorest and least developed of all the countries of Europe. This tiny state, invaded many times by many different peoples, has been poor and insecure since it first appeared in the records of history. The earliest settlements were probably largely confined to the coastal plain where Indo-European tribes may have arrived as early as 2000 BC, crossing the mountains from the east. Their descendants, known to the Greeks as Illyrians, established a long-lived kingdom in the region.

In the Classical Age (600–450 BC), Greek colonies were founded on the coast, and in the third century BC the Romans conquered the region, opening up the western Balkans to Roman control and occupation. Even under Roman rule, however, the area did not flourish, for the independent tribes retained their tribal system and resisted the advantages of a more advanced civilization.

Albania

Albania, the Land of the Eagle, is a country of mountains, effectively isolated from its neighbouring states inland but with a coastline that has attracted a succession of colonists. It has been inhabited since at least 2000 BC, when the Indo-European ancestors of the ancient Illyrians made the long and difficult journey across the Balkans from the western steppes. Ethnic Albanians claim descent from the Illyrians, though over the centuries Greeks, Romans, Slavs and Turks have all lived in the country. Vlachs, in the south, speak a language close to Latin and may be descended from Roman provincials driven from the Danube provinces by migrating tribes after AD 200. In recent years, economic hardship and political unrest have led to a new attempted migration as thousands of Albanians have tried to cross the Adriatic to more prosperous Italy.

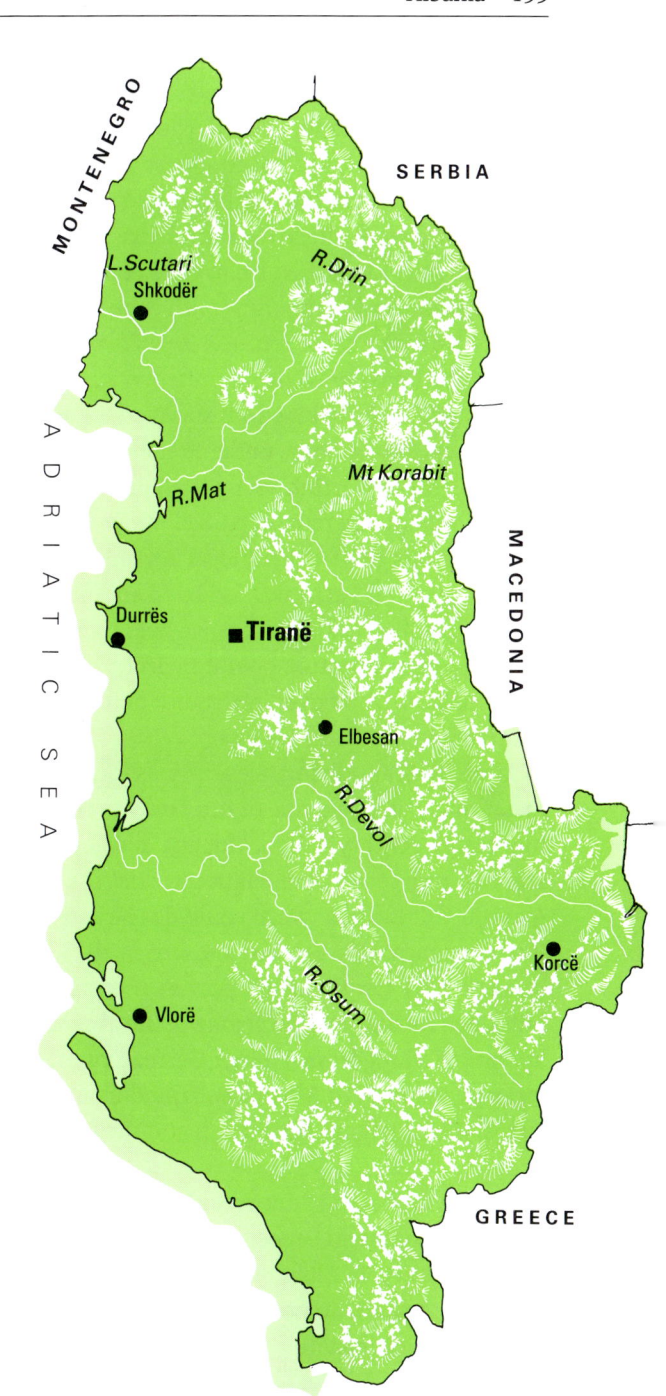

From the later sixth century AD Slav peoples settled in the Balkans but they, too, had only a limited effect on Albania. The rugged terrain provided formidable obstacles to full conquest and control, though after 800 the Serbs gained land in the north and east. Byzantine emperors were unable to exert any more effective control, except on the more accessible coastal areas. About 1100, the Norman rulers of southern Italy took possession of the coastland and in the thirteenth century Venice controlled the main ports. Late in the same century, in 1272, southern Albania and the adjacent part of northern Greece were united in a small state under Charles I of Anjou, and this little kingdom survived for about a century, until it was swept away by the Serbs under Stefan Dusan (1330–55). But Serbian power was itself soon overthrown by the Turks on the battlefield of Kosovo and most of Albania thereupon passed under Ottoman rule. There it remained, but for revolts and frequent local uprisings, until 1878. The most effective resistance to the Turks was led by Skanderbeg. From 1443 to 1468, having pushed out the Turkish forces, he held them off and resisted all their efforts to regain control, operating from his mountain-stronghold at Kruje. After his death, however, resistance faltered and by 1506, the Turks were again in possession of Albania.

After 1878, an Albanian league was formed to resist the corrupt and increasingly unstable rule of the Turks in the Balkans. In the late nineteenth century national feeling developed rapidly in Albania, stimulating a series of rebellions against the Turks. These culminated in a major revolt in 1912 which could not be suppressed. Albanian demands for independence were granted and late in 1912 the Republic of Albania was proclaimed. Later the major powers recognized Albanian independence but, since Albania had no strong political candidate of its own, they appointed a king from a minor German ruling family. He lasted only six months and in 1914 Albania collapsed into anarchy. During a period of chaos, the Austrians, the French and the Italians all occupied parts of the country.

At the close of the First World War the political future of Albania was far from clear. Italy and Greece proposed to partition the country between them but, in 1920, Albania again achieved independent status and passed from near anarchy to near tyranny under King Zog or Zogu. He operated an oppressive police-state and turned the country into a satellite of Italy.

When Zog's regime collapsed in the spring of 1939 the Italians moved in and for the next four years Albania was a puppet state under the control of Fascist Italy. After a brief German occupation from 1943 to the autumn of 1944, a Communist government was installed under Enver Hoxha, with the encouragement of Yugoslavian left-wing partisans. For four years, the country was heavily influenced by Yugoslavia, but when its northern neighbour was expelled from the Cominform by Stalin, Albania renounced all agreements with Yugoslavia and aligned itself with Soviet Russia.

Albania had little to offer Russia in either strategic or economic terms, and in any case Albania soon began to lean towards the more militant Communism of China. In 1961 diplomatic links with Russia were broken off and two years later Albania left Comecon for political and economic isolation. Political unrest broke out in the 1960s and again sporadically after 1970, but was quickly stifled. By the time that Hoxha died, the economic state of the country was extremely weak and its political system in ruins. Civil strife broke out in the south and thousands of Albanians tried to flee to Italy and Greece in 1990 and again in 1991.

The ancient ancestors of ethnic Albanians were the Illyrians, with later Greek colonists, Romans and Slav and Turkish invaders. Today, the population is divided broadly between the Ghegs of the north, mostly Sunni Muslims, and Tosks in the south, who include both Muslims and Orthodox Christians. The uncompromising terrain and unhappy political history of the land mean that in no part of Albania is life easy. National reconstruction will only be possible with help from outside.
See: Greeks, Illyrians, Romans, Serbs, Slavs, Turks, Vlachs

Austria
Republik Österreich

The Land: Much of the republic of Austria is mountainous country, encompassing and lying to the north of the eastern Alpine ranges. Between the Alps and the Danube lies a well forested upland and north of the Danube the land is hilly and wooded. The plain east of Vienna is part of the great lowland area which spreads into Hungary. The land has varied mineral resources, plentiful water and good agricultural land as well as spectacular scenery. The climate is generally favourable, with hot continental summers but cold winters.

The Language: Almost all Austrians are German-speaking. Small minorities speak Serbo-Croat, Hungarian and Slovene.

The Name: Österreich, 'the eastern realm' was used for the region in the ninth century, when it was formed to provide a firm frontier between western Europe and the Magyars. Austria is the Latin form of the German name.

Early settlement in the region is known mainly in the Danube valley and in the adjacent uplands, where the first farming communities arrived along the Danube corridor after 5000 BC and colonized the lower ground. In the mountains there is little sign of settlement until the Bronze Age, after 2000 BC. From that time, there is evidence of contacts with Italy, but the region remained remote from the main stream of cultural influence. By 600 BC, Celts had moved into the more productive regions of Austria and one of the major Celtic sites in central Europe lies at Hallstatt, where salt was mined from very early times. The Celtic chieftains who controlled this valuable resource enjoyed considerable wealth and had wide contacts to the south (with Italy) and the west (with the Rhine valley and France). Later, from the third century BC, the Celtic kingdom of Noricum was established on the middle Danube and this grew rich on its reserves of iron and on trade with Italy. It was conquered by Rome late in the first century BC and became the province of Noricum.

The Roman frontier province of Noricum occupied broadly the same territory as the later core of the state of Austria. The lowlands of Noricum were fertile with rich resources of iron and until the later third century AD, the province enjoyed a relatively peaceful existence. Christianity was introduced before AD 300 and one of the most effective defenders of the province against the later barbarians was the bishop Severin.

Noricum was invaded by the Germanic tribe of the Rugii in the fifth century, and the land was several times devastated by the Huns on their passage from east to west. Slavs and Avars settled in eastern Noricum in the sixth and seventh centuries and it was not until the eighth century that the Dukes of Bavaria were able to establish a reasonably firm control over what was by now an area divided between Germans and Slavs. The Magyars threatened from the east in the ninth century, but when they were defeated on the Lechfeld in 955, the Holy Roman Emperor Otto I created a firm frontier against them on the Danube. From this time modern Austria began to take shape.

The importance of Austria's frontier position was fully grasped by the Babenberg dynasty, which ruled the country from 976 to 1246. They exercised firm government in their own territory and kept watch over their volatile neighbours to the east. Trade and lines of communication followed the east-west route of the Danube and important monasteries were established, several of which became great pilgrim shrines (e.g. Melk, Klosterneuburg and Heiligenkreuz). In 1273 the region came under the control of the great ruling family of the Hapsburgs who steadily extended its boundaries to the east and south-east. Despite its strategic importance, Austria was still not governed as a separate kingdom.

In 1493, the ruler of Austria, Maximilian, was elected Holy Roman Emperor and he was able greatly to enlarge Austrian power. Marriage alliances with other European dynasties gave Austria a leading role in the wider world and under Maximilian and his grandson, Charles V, Austria was the most powerful state in Europe. After 1500, Austria continued to look eastward for opportunities of extending its empire. In 1526, Bohemia and Hungary were joined to Austria, forming a region on both sides of the Danube which survived as the heartland of the Austrian empire until 1918.

The Austrian empire was expanding, but was itself threatened by the growing empire of the Turks. A major invasion thrust deep into Austria in the 1520s and Vienna was besieged in 1529 but defended successfully. The rest of Europe relied on Austria to maintain a strong eastern barrier against the Ottoman Turks and that role continued until well into the late seventeenth century. As late as 1683 the Turks struck westward in force and again laid siege to Vienna, again without success.

During the sixteenth and seventeenth centuries there were internal strains within the Hapsburg empire as well as threats from outside. After the Reformation, Protestant doctrines spread rapidly through Austria, attracting a majority of the population and creating severe problems for the Catholic rulers. A reaction against the Protestants gathered strength late in the sixteenth century, leading to serious political problems. A revolt in Bohemia had to be suppressed, an event which led directly to the Thirty Years War of 1618 to 1648, in which the Catholic Austrian Hapsburgs played a major part. Catholicism was re-established in the Austrian territories in the 1620s and many Protestants were expelled.

Austria remained a great power in the eighteenth century, but had to struggle to maintain her position. Because of the Hapsburg connections with the ruling family of Spain, the country was involved in the War of the Spanish Succession in 1714. At the end of the war Austria gained Naples, Milan, Sardinia, and the Spanish Netherlands. Under the rule of Maria Theresa, after 1740, costly campaigns were waged against Spain and Bavaria and later to regain lost territory, with limited success. The empress, a staunch Roman Catholic, was more successful in her reforms of finance and administration. Soon after her death, Austria was confronted by revolutionary France and then by Napoleon. From 1792 to 1815, the country was engaged in almost continuous war, usually unsuccessfully.

Austria's favourable position in the fertile Danube valley attracted migrants from prehistoric times. Inhabited since around 5000 BC, and a centre of early Celtic settlement, it became a prosperous province of the Roman empire (Noricum). In the early centuries AD Germanic tribes and then Huns and Slavs raided and settled there but, later, under the control of the Dukes of Bavaria, it became a firm frontier region against further eastern invasions.

Heavy defeats in 1805 left the French in possession of Vienna and at the end of the year, Napoleon won a great victory over Austria and Russia at Austerlitz. The Hapsburg monarchy was all but finished and the Holy Roman Empire finally dissolved in the following year.

In 1811, Austria was virtually bankrupt. Her decline was halted by the chief minister, Metternich, who dominated central European politics for the next forty years. His skilful diplomacy ensured a future for Austria, though his strong support for the old order encountered opposition from rising nationalism in many states and contributed to the outbreak of revolution in 1848. The German state of Prussia was also now beginning to

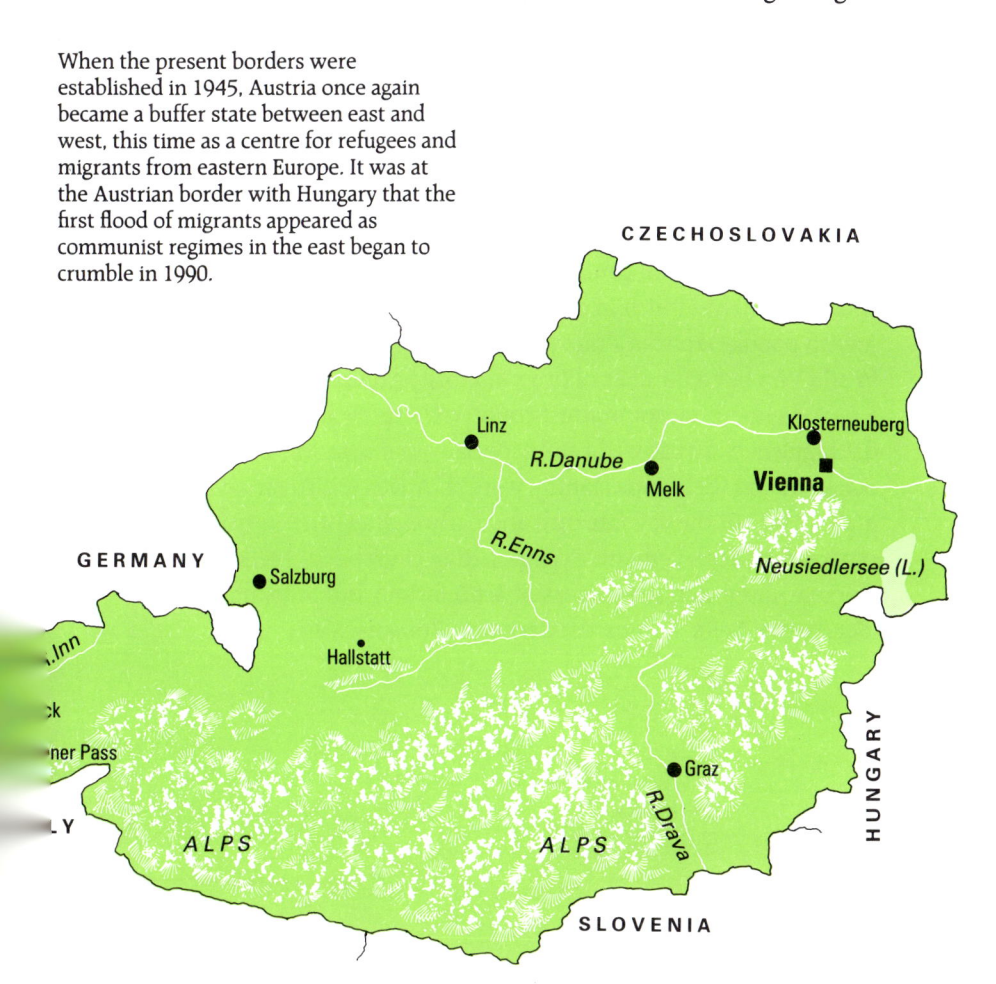

When the present borders were established in 1945, Austria once again became a buffer state between east and west, this time as a centre for refugees and migrants from eastern Europe. It was at the Austrian border with Hungary that the first flood of migrants appeared as communist regimes in the east began to crumble in 1990.

become more powerful and in 1867 the kingdoms of Austria and Hungary merged to resist this growing threat. Until the First World War, Austria-Hungary also comprised the Czech and Slovak lands, Slovenia and Croatia, Bosnia and Dalmatia, southern Poland and south-western Russia about the river Dniester. But this ramshackle structure was being energetically shaken by nationalist forces long before the Great War of 1914–18 finally brought it crashing down.

In 1918 Austria became a small independent republic, deprived of the Czech and Slovak lands, Hungary and the west Balkan territories. As an essentially German state, it naturally was a goal for Hitler's ambitions (Hitler was himself an Austrian) and in 1938 was annexed by Nazi Germany (the *Anschluss*), an event which many Austrians had desired. The republic was restored in 1945, but the occupying Allied forces remained in the country until 1955. As a condition, Austria was to remain neutral and refrain from any political link with Germany. Since 1955, there has been a marked economic resurgence, although Austria remained outside the EC.

The population is very mixed in character and descent, with Celts, Germans and Slavs all contributing; but it is overwhelmingly German-speaking and has much in common with that of Germany. The large Jewish population was almost completely destroyed during the Second World War but a number of other minority groups arrived as refugees from neighbouring communist countries. Austria has a long and distinguished artistic tradition, especially in music. Mozart, Haydn, Schubert and the Strauss family were all Austrians. Austrian Baroque architecture of the seventeenth and early eighteenth centuries is another outstanding achievement, exemplified in churches at Melk and Herzogenburg, and the palaces of Schönbrunn and Schwarzenberg.

See: Avars, Celts, Lombards, Germans, Romans, Slavs

The Baltic States
Estonia, Latvia, Lithuania

Although they are commonly grouped together and described as the Baltic States, these three countries have distinct populations with individual cultural traditions and history. Lying close together on the Baltic coast they share a common prehistory and have similar geographical characteristics.

The Land: The area of these three countries is low-lying, rolling coastal terrain with low hills and ridges formed by the glaciers of the Ice Ages. The coastline is deeply indented by the Gulf of Riga. Although forested in ancient times, most of the land has been cleared, leaving large areas of woodland only in Lithuania. Many marshes, lakes and peat-bogs lie across the region. The land is generally fertile and agriculture is important in all three republics.

The Languages: Latvian, or Lettish as it is often known, and Lithuanian are both Indo-European languages and are related to each other. Estonian is a Finno-Ugrian tongue, related to Finnish. It has two major dialects, Tallin and Tartu. Both contain borrowings from German and the Slav languages.

The Names: Estonia comes from Aestii, the name given to one of the tribes who lived in the area in Roman times and who were the predecessors of the East Prussians. Latvia and Lithuania (formerly Litva) are both derived from the Letts, early inhabitants of the region. The general name 'Balts' is a modern term and does not reflect the relationships of the people.

Hunting and foraging groups were making at least seasonal use of this eastern Baltic region by about 10,000 BC and continued to do so after farming was introduced before 3000 BC. Throughout prehistoric time, there was a slow immigration from the peoples of the western Russian plains, who were moving westward in the search for new land. An important natural resource of the eastern Baltic was the much prized amber found on the coast. This made its way by trade and exchange to Mycenaean Greece, western Europe and Britain. By the late first millennium BC, the Baltic lands were in contact with the Roman Empire, exporting amber and probably furs, and importing Roman bronze vessels, glass and coinage in exchange. The Baltic peoples at this time were also influenced by Germanic tribes to the west. The leading tribal group was the Aestii (as the Romans called them) who were in touch with the Mediterranean world at least to the fifth century AD. The great migrations after AD 400 scarcely affected this region and the Baltic peoples remained free of outside influence into the early Middle Ages and beyond.

Estonia / Eesti

The early inhabitants of Estonia, a people related to the Finns, were known to the classical world as Aestii (*Eesti* in Estonian), gatherers of the amber which lay on the eastern shore of the Baltic. Estonian language, unlike those of the neighbouring Baltic States, is Finno-Ugrian in origin, and thus related to Finnish. Like Latvia, Estonia came under the influence of the Viking settlers in Russia in the ninth century. The first moves towards statehood were made in the thirteenth century when more advanced settlers arrived, with urban ideas and organizations: the German Teutonic Knights moved into Latvia and southern Estonia and the Danes occupied the north of the country and founded the town of Tallinn. The favourable trading position of Estonia, poised between Russia and Scandinavia, attracted German merchants, and several Estonian towns became members of the Hanseatic League.

Estonia, always vulnerable to stronger neighbours, was governed in succession by Russia, then Sweden, Denmark and Poland. Sweden was more commercially and politically successful in the seventeenth century, but Russia took charge after 1700 and Estonia remained under the Tsars until 1917. The Estonians retained their sense of identity during this long period and were able to act independently to some extent, as when they abolished serfdom in 1819, long before this was achieved in Russia. Estonian national hopes were finally fulfilled after the Russian Revolution in 1917. An independent republic was recognized in 1920. Estonia looked to western Europe in its twenty years of independent life, but was absorbed into the Soviet Union in 1940 and remained a part of the USSR after German occupation ended in 1944. Along with Latvia and Lithuania, Estonia had to wait until 1991 to recover her independent status.

Estonians have more in common with the Finns than with their neighbours to the south. Emigration to Russia, the USA and Canada has been heavy and forced exile has carried others to many parts of Europe and Russia. Russians make up about a third of the present population of a million, many of them attracted by the higher living standards of the Baltic States. The distinctive national culture of the Estonians, expressed in art, literature and music, is very strong and has proved an effective agent in the preservation of nationhood.

See: Finns

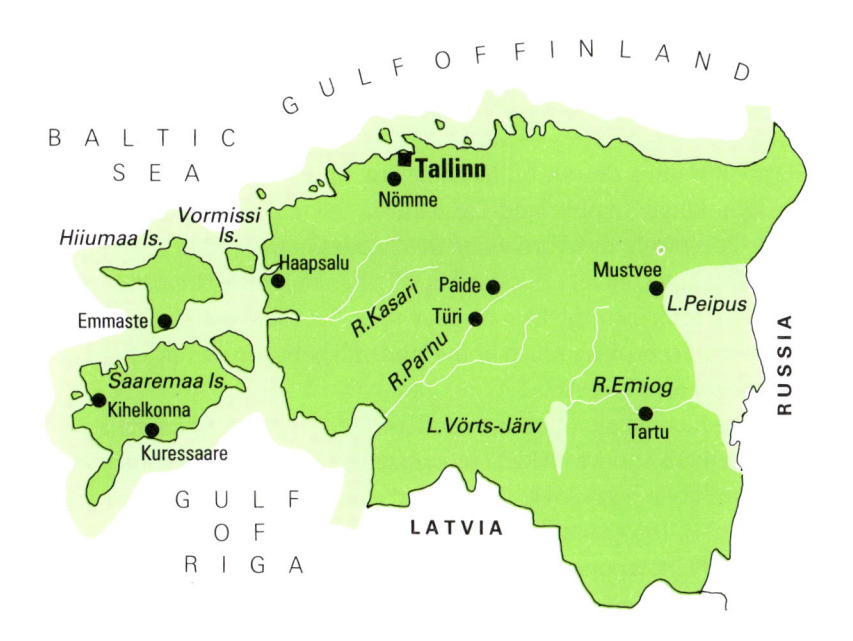

Estonia is the most northerly of the Baltic States and its people are more closely related to the Finns than to other Europeans. In the 1200s the Teutonic Knights occupied the south of the country. The Knights had fought in the Crusades and when these ended, they undertook a new campaign, to convert the people of the Baltic States to Christianity. Many Germans remained as landowners and it was not until 1919 that the land was redistributed among native Estonians.

Latvia / Latvija

Latvia is a small republic lying on the Gulf of Riga to either side of the river Dvina. Its original inhabitants, the Letts or Latvians, were related to the Lithuanians and spoke a related Indo-European language. The early tribal groups of this region were conquered by Viking invaders from Scandinavia, who settled in western Russia in the ninth century. In the early thirteenth century, the still pagan Latvian homeland was conquered by the Teutonic Knights, a semi-religious military German order who had fought in the Crusades and were dedicated to the defence of Christendom. Latvia, or Livonia as it was then called, was effectively ruled by one group of the Knights from 1207. The German connection became much more significant after 1282 when the major port of Riga joined the Hanseatic League (the great association of German commercial cities which dominated Baltic trade) and became one of the great trading centres of the Baltic Sea. Much of Latvia was governed by the joint kingdom of Poland-Lithuania in the mid sixteenth century, until the Poles were overthrown by the Swedes in the 1620s. A hundred years later, Latvia fell into Russian hands when Peter the Great ejected the Swedes and took over the Latvian provinces. But the German connection was not entirely broken, much of the land still being owned by German families from East Prussia.

After the Russian Revolution, an independent republic of Latvia was declared in 1918 and was widely recognized by 1920. Its government tried to distance Latvia from Soviet Russia and looked to western Europe for support. But in 1939 Russia was given military bases in the country, and in 1940 formally incorporated Latvia into the Soviet Union. The German occupation of 1941–4 was ended by the Red Army and Latvia was returned to Soviet rule, from which it returned to independence in 1991.

Many Latvians have emigrated from their homeland since the mid nineteenth century, to America, western Europe and Russia. Others were deported during Soviet rule. Russian immigration into Latvia has been correspondingly high, so that Russians make up about a third of the population, Latvians themselves making up barely 60%. For such a small

state, Latvia is a surprisingly urban society, with more than fifty cities or large towns. Historically the country has depended heavily on commerce in the Baltic, especially through Riga, and that is where its economic future will lie, along with closer ties to western Europe.
See: Balts, Germans

The River Dvina (or Daugava) flows through Latvia from western Russia and has long been an important highway, first for migrating peoples from the Russian steppes, who arrived some 5000 years ago, later for Viking invaders and traders moving eastwards. Well placed to dominate the Baltic trade, Riga became one of the great commercial cities of the Middle Ages, though its harbour was usually ice-bound in the winter months.

Lithuania / Lietuva

The Lithuanians are first mentioned in chronicles of the eleventh century, but existed as a separate group of peoples for several centuries before that, occupying a forested region about the river Niemen. Their language was related to that of the neighbouring Letts (Latvians), but in other respects they maintained a separate identity.

In the thirteenth century the Teutonic Knights, a German military order founded in the time of the Crusades, were based in the Vistula valley. Under the pretext of bringing Christianity to the pagan inhabitants of Prussia, they began to expand northwards, aiming in fact to establish a German state around the German colony of Riga, in Latvia. The struggle was long and bitter but by 1270 much of Prussia had been overrun by Germans. Prussia was immediately to the west of Lithuania and the threat to their own land brought the Lithuanian tribal groups together. Under the leadership of Mindaugas they were able to prevent the total conquest of the Baltic region. Shortly afterwards the Lithuanians successfully extended their territory far to the south-east into Russia. The fourteenth century saw the peak of independent Lithuanian power when the country won control of the entire basin of the Dnieper around Kiev and a new capital was founded at Vilnius. Expansion further east was halted by the Mongols in 1399.

In the west, the ruler Jagiello forged strong ties with Poland in 1385. In 1387 he accepted Roman Christianity but for long afterwards the peasants clung to their old beliefs. Jagiello shortly afterwards became ruler of Poland (under the name of Vladislav II), and for the next four centuries the two states were bound together. By 1409, Poland-Lithuania was strong enough to turn on the Teutonic Knights and defeat them at Tannenberg in East Prussia but from the early part of the following century, Lithuania began to lose her eastern lands to the Russians. Gradually, Poles began to dominate the government and the economy of both states, and by 1600 the Lithuanian part of the joint kingdom was in decline. Control of the Ukraine passed to Poland and in 1795, Russia and Prussia partitioned Lithuania and it ceased to exist as a political state. But Lithuanian culture remained alive and gathered strength after the Russian revolution of 1905 and again after 1914 when the German army occupied the country. Independence was declared in 1918 and a pro-Russian government installed in 1919.

The independent republic lasted for only two decades and throughout that time its capital Vilnius remained in Polish hands. Late in 1939 Russia again asserted its power over Lithuania and a Soviet government was installed in 1940. The German invasion of June 1941 was followed by more than three years of occupation, at the end of which Lithuania was once more returned to Soviet Russia, where it remained until 1991. Demands for independence became irresistible following the Gorbachev reforms in Russia and these have now been answered.

Ethnic Lithuanians make up about 80% of the population, the remainder being Russians and, especially around Vilnius, Poles. Large numbers of Lithuanians have emigrated to western Europe, the USA, Australia and Latin America. Possibly up to a quarter of all Lithuanians left their homeland after 1880. Many others fell victim to the brutal deportations which occurred under German and Russian occupation.
See: Balts

In the 1300s Lithuania's power stretched from Moscow to the Black Sea and when it united with Poland their combined force was able to resist the Teutonic Knights, who had occupied the neighbouring Baltic States of East Prussia, Latvia and southern Estonia. East Prussia no longer exists as a separate state but once occupied an area stretching inland from the Baltic coast, to the north of Poland. In 1945 the territory was divided between Poland and the Soviet Union and the Soviet part was renamed Kaliningrad. Since Lithuania became independent, Russia's access to the Baltic at Kaliningrad (part of the Russian Federation) has been guaranteed by treaty.

Belgium

Royaume de Belgique / Koninkrijk België

The Land: Belgium, which became an independent kingdom only in 1830, is the southern part of the low-lying delta-land bordering the North Sea and drained by the rivers Rhine, Meuse and Schelde. All this geographical region was historically known as the Netherlands, or the Low Countries, but is today divided between the independent countries of Holland, Luxembourg and Belgium. The only upland area in Belgium contains the wooded hills of the Ardennes, in the south-east. The rest of the country consists of a large alluvial plain running west from the Meuse towards the shallows of the North Sea coast. This is rich agricultural land, but since much of it in the west is below sea-level it is protected from flooding by an impressive system of canals, dykes and dams. The Belgium coast is short and exposed, with shallow seas and no good natural harbours. The chief port is Antwerp, which lies a little inland, on the lower reaches of the Scheldt. But communications across the country, both by road and waterway, are excellent. The climate is variable but mild and the well-watered land produces good crops. But industrial production is also important and Belgium has adequate reserves of coal and minerals. The country lies at the crossroads of busy European trading routes, and this strategic position has been recognized by the EC which established its administrative headquarters in Brussels.

The Language: Belgium has two official languages, French and Flemish, a Dutch dialect spoken in the north and west of the country. The French-speaking inhabitants, generally living in the south and east, are known as Walloons. A small minority near the eastern border speaks German.

The Name: Belgium was chosen when the separate state was established, looking back to the days when the Celtic Belgae occupied part of the area and to the Roman province of Gallia Belgica.

The remains of hunter-gatherer communities, dating back to 30,000 BC, have been found on the coast and in cave-sites of the Ardennes. Neolithic peoples, migrants from east of the Rhine, settled in the middle Meuse valley after 4500 BC and introduced agriculture. Their distinctive long-houses suggest an origin in central Europe. By 2000 BC the inhabitants shared in the Bronze Age culture widespread across the north-west of Europe. Around 600 BC, Celtic tribes pushed into the Netherlands, up to the west bank of the Rhine. Among these tribes were the Belgae.

When the Romans abandoned the lands of their northern empire, invading German tribes moved westwards to replace them. By AD 500 the Franks were ruling over most of the Low Countries and Germanic peoples had merged with the original Celtic population. The area remained under Frankish rule until, after the death of Charlemagne in 814, his great empire broke up and the land was divided. From the tenth century, Flanders (western Belgium) formed part of northern France, while the rest of the Low Countries passed to the German principalities.

Already, by the early Middle Ages trade played a major part in the economy of the region. An international trade in cloth was based in Flanders and Brabant and metalworkers and potters were active in the Meuse and Rhine valleys. Lively commerce made some cities large and prosperous. By 1350 Ghent was the largest city of western Europe after Paris, and Bruges attracted traders from the Baltic to the Mediterranean. The urban craftsmen and merchants grouped themselves in guilds which often exercised great power in their communities. Rivalry between cities frequently broke out into warfare, but this was usually on a small scale and did not interrupt the overall prosperity of the stronger cities.

In the late fourteenth century the provinces of the Low Countries became part of the kingdom of Burgundy and then, in 1477, passed by marriage to the Austrian Hapsburgs. The cities continued to prosper and under the Emperor Charles V, economic life blossomed as never before. Antwerp became the largest port in western Europe, shipping goods to the New World and to Africa. The wealthy merchants commissioned brilliant works of art, and the fine buildings that survive bear witness to the prosperity of the time. The peasants and the urban poor, however, received few benefits from this economic success.

Although the free cities and small states of the Low Countries were included in the Hapsburg Empire, they still acted as if they were independent. Charles V aimed at unifying them and made some progress before his abdication in 1555; but by then the theological ideas and reforms of Luther, and later of Calvin and the Anabaptists, were causing tension and division over the whole of Europe. These religious differences, and their social and political repercussions, came to a head under the next ruler of the Netherlands. Philip II, son of Charles V and King of Spain (1556–98), was a serious-minded monarch but one who did not know the Netherlands well. Opposition to him developed among the nobles and richer merchants of the Netherlands and quickly spread to the rest of the population, already in a ferment of Calvinist reforming ideas. In 1648 the Dutch were finally granted an independent Dutch republic, but the southern provinces remained with Spain until 1700, forcing many Calvinists to move to the new republic to the north, to its considerable economic benefit. Antwerp sharply declined but although commercial opportunities were lost to the north, the Spanish Netherlands, relying on patronage from the court and Church, could also boast great figures, including Van Dyck and Rubens.

The later seventeenth century saw major changes to the whole region of the Netherlands. The Spanish Netherlands lost territory to the French and what remained passed from Spain to the Austrian Hapsburgs in 1714. The tensions of the eighteenth century were heightened by growing economic strain as commercial competition in western Europe became tighter. The French Revolution accelerated the transformation of the Low Countries. The southern provinces were annexed by France in 1785, the old social order was dismantled and a new middle class arose which looked towards France. After Napoleon's defeat in 1815, both the Spanish and independent northern Netherlands were brought together in a kingdom of the United Netherlands, a constitutional monarchy under King William I. It lasted barely fifteen years. Opposition to the Dutch in the southern region could not be controlled and in 1830 a separate state of Belgium was established there under Leopold I, of the German house of Saxe-Coburg. The small state of Belgium continued as a constitutional monarchy through the nineteenth century and on to 1914, economically strong, endowed with a stable government, but militarily weak.

Belgium occupies the southern part of the Low Countries, the area drained by the Rhine, Meuse and Schelde rivers. In Roman times it formed part of the province Gallia Belgica and its Celtic inhabitants were considered the most warlike of the tribes of Gaul. Around AD 250 Franks from north of the Rhine began raiding Roman Gaul and following the valleys of the Schelde and Lys settled in the fertile land they found there. An important Frankish kingdom formed around Tournai and by 500, Franks were ruling over most of what is now Belgium and Holland. Celts and Franks merged over the centuries but Belgium's two official languages remind us of their history: the division between Flemish speakers in the north and west and French speakers (Walloons) in the south and east generally reflects the original settlement area of the Germanic Franks and the earlier Celtic Belgae.

Long before Belgium was established as an independent nation, the area had become an important centre for trade, with excellent communications both inland and from the growing port of Antwerp. But its position also made the region vulnerable to invading armies, and many battles have been fought across the lowlands of Flanders.

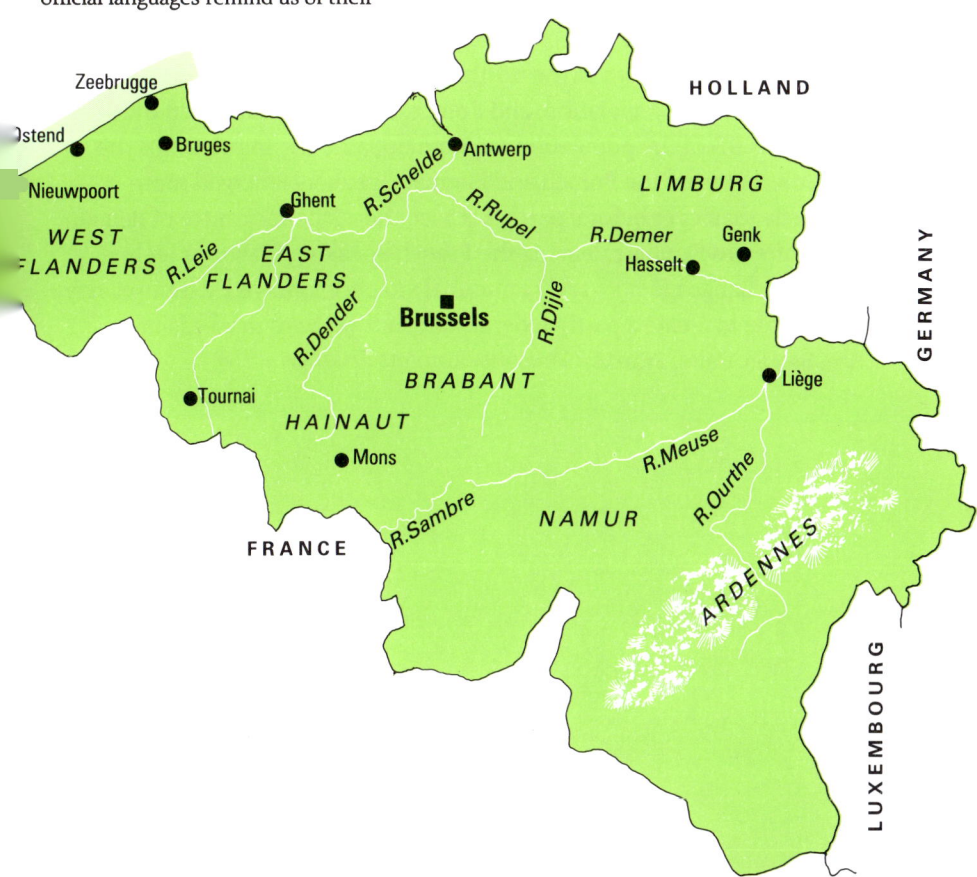

This long period of prosperous peace ended abruptly in 1914. The German armies thrust through Belgium in their attempt to smash a way into France. Four years of German occupation followed, along with massive material losses. Western Belgium suffered severely, as the opposed front lines settled down to four years of trench warfare in Flanders. In the Second World War, Belgium was again invaded, in May 1940, and endured four more years of enemy occupation. The population was largely hostile to Nazi ideology and to the aims of the Third Reich. After the war, King Leopold III, who had remained in the country in 1940, was seen by many to have compromised too readily with the invaders. He had to abdicate in 1950.

Belgium shared the growth of prosperity in Europe after 1960, but was increasingly beset by political problems going back to the origins of the state which yoked together two different peoples. The main population groups are the Flemings in the north, Dutch-speakers who make up more than half the total population, and French-speaking Walloons in the south. Formally, 90% of the population are Roman Catholics. In the 1950s the divisions between the French and Flemish-speakers emerged more distinctly than ever before, partly because the economic centre of Belgium had shifted to Flanders, leaving the French-speaking Walloons feeling resentful. Language riots and communal violence followed. Attempts have been made to create a partly federal state, not yet with marked success.
See: Belgae, Celts, Franks, Germans, Romans, Vikings

Bulgaria
Narodna Republika Bulgaria

The Land: Bulgaria falls into three well defined regions. In the north is the Danube valley and its associated plain, a fertile area of lowland. This is bounded to the south by the Balkan mountains which in turn are separated from the Rhodope mountain range by the Maritsa valley. The Rhodope mountains are high, rugged and inaccessible. The Black Sea coast forms the eastern limit of the country. Bulgaria is still a predominantly rural country, with most of the population living in villages and hamlets. Even many of the towns are mainly concerned with agricultural trades. Large cities are rare. Sofia (by far the largest) and Plovdiv are inland, and those on the coast are Varna and Burgas. Urban growth of any kind is recent. Before 1945, 75% of the population lived in the countryside and Sofia had only a quarter of a million inhabitants. The development of the Black Sea coast for tourism, especially for Russians and other eastern Europeans, has led to the familiar growth of sprawling resorts, and both Varna and Burgas have become major industrial centres.

The Language: Bulgarian is a south Slavic language, related to Macedonian, which developed into its present form after the ninth century AD. It has been much influenced by Russian in modern times and uses the Cyrillic alphabet.

The Name: The country is called after the Bulgars, who arrived in the region in AD 680 and established a strong state.

Wandering hunter-gatherer groups ranged over the lower Danube and Black Sea region between 100,000 and 40,000 BC, making use of the abundant food supplies in the rivers and the sea. From about 6000 BC agricultural settlers moved into the area from the south and south-east, to be followed around 2500 BC by the ancestors of the Thracians, with their advanced metalworking techniques. During the first millennium BC, the Thracians were powerful and successful warriors living on the northern edge of the Classical Greek world. Their chieftains were buried with costly goods and weapons, often imported from further south. Fortified settlements were built and trade was conducted over a wide area. Greek settlers and traders were attracted into the region, building colonies on the Black Sea coast. Like the rest of the northern Balkans, the area of modern Bulgaria was annexed by Rome, becoming the two provinces Moesia and Thrace.

The collapse of Roman authority on the lower Danube was a protracted affair and the emperors based at Constantinople were able to maintain a measure of control on the provinces of Moesia and Thrace until the sixth century AD. In the late fourth century, the Visigoths moved into the region but left no permanent impression on the land, nor did the raids of the Huns from the late fourth into the fifth centuries. Far more formative was the Slav invasion in the sixth and seventh centuries, for Slavs were widely spread and well established on the land before the Bulgars arrived in 680. Although the Bulgars came into the Balkans as nomads from the steppes, they seem to have settled down relatively quickly alongside the Slavs, between the Balkan mountains and the Danube, and they were recognized by the Byzantines as the masters of the region. During the eighth century, the Bulgars were slowly assimilated by the Slavs, adopting their language and much of their culture. But Christianity came late to the Bulgars, the first king to accept the faith being Boris I in 864. The missionaries Cyril and Methodius helped to spread Christianity more widely among the Bulgar people and also introduced the distinctive Cyrillic alphabet, based on Greek characters.

The high point of the first Bulgarian state was reached under King Simeon I (893–927). He had been educated at Constantinople and had great respect for Greek culture and literature, ordering the translation of many Greek works into Slavonic. After Simeon's death, the Bulgar state was faced by hostile Magyars and Russians in the north and Byzantines to the south. In 1018 Bulgaria lost its independence, remaining subject to Constantinople until 1185. When Byzantine power weakened late in the twelfth century, the Bulgars rose in revolt and established a second Bulgar kingdom. Centred at Turnovo, this reached its height under Ivan Asen II (1218–41) and for a time was the leading power in the Balkans, in religious affairs as well as in the political sphere. But Mongol attacks in 1240–1 and

To the ancient Greeks, the area that is now Bulgaria was the wild country of Thrace, home of Ares the god of war, at the northern edge of their world. In Roman times, it was within the provinces of Moesia (north of the Rhodope mountains) and Thrace. Between the Danube and the edge of the Roman empire lay the province of Dacia but this did not protect Moesia from barbarian raids and Sarmatians were allowed to settle around the Danube estuary. The wide Danube valley forms a natural route from east to west and successive migrants passed along it, finding good pasture for their cattle and abundant fish and freshwater for themselves. Some, such as the Slavs in the sixth century, settled in the land around the Black Sea while others passed further to the west. The Bulgars themselves appeared in the area in the 600s and remained to establish an influential kingdom. Though never in a majority, they remained rulers until the Turks conquered their kingdom in 1380.

major revolts by the peasants in 1277–80 weakened the Bulgar kingdom. Then, early in the fourteenth century, a greater menace approached from the east: the Turks. By 1380 the Bulgar state was under Turkish rule and remained in the Ottoman empire until late in the nineteenth century.

Placed on the route between Turkey and Central Europe, Bulgaria suffered whenever a Turkish army moved into Europe. And at all times Bulgarians were at the mercy of Turkish landowners and government officials whose activities became less humane as Ottoman power steadily declined. There were uprisings against the Turks in the early nineteenth century and in 1876 a series of revolts broke out. The atrocious reprisals taken by the Turks on the Bulgarian population forced the western powers and Russia to take action. Russia invaded the Ottoman empire in Europe in 1877 and penetrated almost to Constantinople.

A new Bulgarian state, with its own king, was created as a result of this intervention. Originally, its territories were intended to stretch from the Danube to the Aegean coast of Thrace and from the Black Sea to Lake Ohrid but these boundaries were later reduced. Turkey retained sovereignty over Bulgaria, but this was no more than a political fiction: she no longer had any practical power over the country. Russian influence, which had helped to bring about the new state, was still felt for some decades, even though the Bulgarians themselves began to develop a strong nationalist sentiment. Indeed, they now had further territorial ambitions and in the 1880s their claim to Macedonia brought them into conflict with both Serbia and Greece, both of whom were trying to expand into the northern Aegean lands.

But all three states were united in their distrust of Turkey and in 1912 formed a Balkan League to force the Turks back towards the Bosphorus. In the autumn of 1912 the League had an initial success and pushed the Turkish forces back almost to Constantinople. But the alliance soon collapsed in disagreement over Macedonia and in 1913 the Bulgarians lost heavily to the Turks in a second campaign and were forced to hand back much of the territory taken in 1912. Worse followed at the close of the First World War in which Bulgaria ranged herself with Germany and her allies against Serbia and Greece. Eastern Thrace was lost, along with access to the Aegean, and several border areas which projected into Yugoslavia.

Bulgaria played a minor role in the Second World War. Having been on poor terms with her immediate neighbours since 1919, she at first sided with Germany in the hope of regaining lost territory. When the Germans invaded Yugoslavia and Greece, much of Thrace and Macedonia was ceded to Bulgaria, but after 1945 the pre-War boundaries were restored and remain to this day.

In 1946 a republic was declared and the royal family was expelled. By 1948 Communists had come to power and the state was reconstructed. Close proximity to Russia meant that Bulgaria tended to follow the official policy of the Soviet Union. The leading figure in Bulgaria from the 1950s was Zhivkov, a devoted follower of Soviet policies, even though the economic progress of the country after the Second World War was unimpressive. Political changes in Russia in the late 1980s had their impact on Bulgaria. Zhivkov was deposed and the Communist party was separated from the state. The fall of Ceaucescu in Romania in late 1989 sparked off unrest in Bulgaria and some reforms were begun. But the future political and economic alignment of Bulgaria remains far from clear.

In the population, more than 85% are of Bulgarian stock, though some may claim Thracians as their remote ancestors. The largest minority is Turkish, a remnant of a once large community now greatly reduced by emigration since the late nineteenth century. In the late 1980s, several thousand more were required to return to Turkey. In most parts of the country there are visible reminders of earlier Turkish rule in the form of mosques and distinctive courtyard-houses. Turkish is still spoken by the remaining Bulgarian Turks. A sizeable Gypsy population exists in the east of the country, many of them settled in the towns. The other important minority is the Jews, many of whom are descended from those who left Spain in the fifteenth century and who still speak a language (Ladino) which includes many Spanish elements. A small number of Vlachs are settled in the southern hills where they make a living as herdsmen and there are also Armenians, Gagouts and Shops (descended from pre-Ottoman Turks), Greeks, descended from pre-Roman settlements on the Black Sea. The Krakachans, called Black Nomads from the colour of their tents, still live the semi-nomadic life of their ancestors from the Steppes. See: Bulgars, Greeks, Romans, Sarmatians, Slavs, Thracians, Turks, Vlachs

Czechoslovakia
Česka e Slovenská Federativni Republika

The Land: Although largely an upland country, Czechoslovakia is divided into three main regions with well defined characteristics. In the west lies the plateau of Bohemia, easily entered from the north along the Labe (Elbe) valley and thus open to settlement from Germany. The centre is occupied by the plain of Moravia and the valleys of the Morava and the Vah. Much of Slovakia in the east is mountainous and was for long almost inaccessible. Communications between the regions are poor and this has been largely responsible for divisions between the various ethnic groups within the country. Bohemia is the richest and most developed region, Slovakia the poorest. Tension between the two is still marked.

Industrial development has been greatest in Bohemia and Moravia, based particularly on iron and coal. Czechoslovakia is one of the most industrialized countries of eastern Europe, with about two-thirds of its gross national product derived from manufacturing industry, mainly iron and steel, textiles and chemicals. Agriculture, although limited by the large areas of upland and by the climate, is well developed and efficient. The climate is continental with cold winters and warm to hot summers. In mid-winter the average temperature stays below freezing for several weeks, especially in the mountainous areas. The rivers freeze for weeks on end and navigation ceases on the Danube, Vlata and Labe. The country is one of small towns, many of them mediaeval in origin, dependent upon agriculture and local industry. There are relatively few large cities, only Prague, Ostrava, Brno and Bratislava forming large centres.

The Language: Czech and Slovak are the main languages, both belonging to the West Slavic-group and mutually intelligible. Minorities speak German, Hungarian and Polish.

The Name: Cesko-Slovenska, the revised name for the country, joins the names of the two principal peoples of the republic.

The new republic of Czechoslovakia was formed at the end of the First World War, from lands which had for several hundred years been part of the Austro-Hungarian empire. The history of the area as distinct from the republic, however, goes back much further.

There is little evidence of early settlement in the uplands of Czechoslovakia, but the Bohemian plateau and the Morava valley attracted early farmers as they migrated west from the plains below the Carpathian mountains. In the Bronze Age after 2000 BC, similar types of settlement were scattered over that part of Central Europe now occupied by Austria, Hungary and Czechoslovakia. After 500 BC Celtic peoples moved into Bohemia, which takes its name from one of the tribes, the Boii. The Celts built huge fortified strongholds on hill-tops, some of which developed into small towns. After 200 BC, Germanic settlers arrived in all three parts of the region, the leading peoples being the Marcomanni and Quadi. These tribes were not conquered by Rome and their lands remained outside the Roman empire. But they maintained close trading and political contacts with the Roman world, whose northern frontier lay close to them on the Danube.

Czechs and Slovaks first came to the region in the sixth century AD, as part of the general migration of Slav peoples from the east and gradually became the dominant population, replacing the earlier Germanic tribes. The historical experience of the Czechs was notably richer than that of their partners. There was a Czech state, Bohemia, from the tenth century and for four centuries it was a flourishing and active power in central Europe. Its capital, Prague, was one of the great cities of mediaeval Europe. The kings of Bohemia held power until the sixteenth century, when the country was claimed by Austria and became part of the Austrian empire.

In the fifteenth century there had been serious religious conflict between Catholics and the Protestant followers of John Huss (Hussites, or Moravians). In the seventeenth century, the Hussites were persecuted and as many as 30,000 were expelled from the country. Later, the name Bohemian came to be applied to anyone with no settled home.

While the Czechs had a long history of independence in Bohemia, the Slovaks had little sense of national identity until after 1800, although they retained their own language and culture under the rule of both the Magyars and the Hapsburgs.

When the new republic of Czechoslovakia was formed it had been agreed in advance by the two principal peoples involved. However, they did not come together as equal partners. Both had been subject to outside rule, but the Czechs had played a leading role in the government and administration of Austria, whereas the Slovaks, though ethnically distinct in Hungary, had no particular role under Hungarian rule. It was thus inevitable that the leadership of the new state of Czechoslovakia would pass to the more experienced Czechs, who were also more numerous—nearly seven million to the two million Slovaks. Though each understood the other's language, the two peoples were kept apart by their histories and cultural inheritance.

The bounds of the new country were decided at the Paris peace conference of 1918–20 and brought together more peoples than simply Czechs and Slovaks. The Ruthenes, speaking their own language and culturally distinct from Czechs and Slovaks, were included in the east; also included were Hungarian communities on the northern edge of the Danube plain. But there was a far greater problem in Bohemia, where in the Sudetenland more than two million Germans had long been settled. It was decided to include this very substantial minority within the new state as they had never been the subjects of a German state and there was no indication that they wanted to be. A small area was annexed from Germany in northern Moravia and a larger territory from Poland about the Tesin coalfield. On the southern border an extension into the Danube plain brought in 750,000 Hungarians.

The poorest and least advanced of all the peoples of Czechoslovakia, the Ruthenes of the north-east, saw advantage in a move from Hungary. But the ethnic divisions within the rest of Czechoslovakia held considerable potential for political exploitation by neighbouring states. As the Nazis

Czechoslovakia is a federation of two republics, the Czech and the Slovak. Slav peoples first came to the area in the 500s and by the 800s the Moravian empire of western Slav peoples covered a large part of central Europe. At the beginning of the 900s, however, Magyar tribes conquered the ancestors of the Slovaks and continued to dominate them for the next 900 years. The Czechs founded their kingdom of Bohemia, which remained independent until it became part of the Austrian empire in the 1500s. The present boundaries were fixed in 1945.

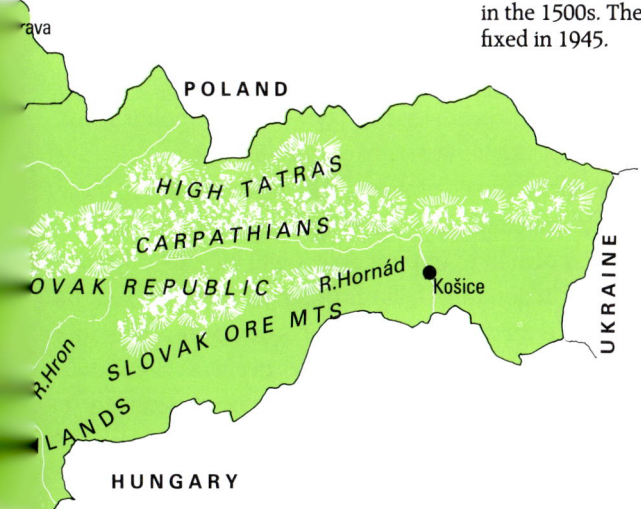

became powerful in Germany, they claimed the Sudentenland and its German inhabitants as part of their territory and eventually, under the terms of the Munich agreement of September 1938, Czechoslovakia was forced to cede the Sudetenland to Germany. Shortly afterwards, German forces occupied Prague. Bohemia and Moravia were taken over as protectorates of the Third Reich.

In the autumn of 1938 Poland seized Tesin, entirely without justification on ethnic grounds, and Hungary retrieved the lowland part of southern Slovakia. Even Ruthenia broke away from Czechoslovakia in 1938, remaining independent until the parent country was broken up by the Germans a year later.

After 1945 the country was reconstituted, following in general the territorial lines of 1920, though much of Ruthenia passed to Russia, thus giving the Soviet Union access to the Danube plain. But if Czechoslovakia were to have a lasting future as a unified country, there clearly had to be a change to the ethnic composition, which still consisted of Czechs, Slovaks, Germans and Hungarians. The problem of the Sudetenland was solved, since many of the Sudeten Germans had fled towards the end of the Second World War, and the majority of those who stayed behind were forced out. In all, three million Germans sought refuge in Germany, leaving only 160,000 behind in Bohemia. The problem of the Hungarian minority, however, was not solved, though there was an agreement between Hungary and Czechoslovakia to exchange their respective minorities. In modern Czechoslovakia more than half a million Hungarians still live in the lowland adjacent to the Danube plain.

After the Second World War, Czechoslovakia lay within the political and economic order established by Soviet Russia in eastern Europe. Liberalizing tendencies in social and economic affairs made progress in the 1960s, but were abruptly terminated after the 'Prague spring' of August 1968, when the Red Army returned to impose Soviet will by force. Twenty years later, when the contradictions and failures of Soviet policy forced the Soviet Union to relax her hold on eastern Europe, Czechoslovakia was able to establish a new democratic republic and seek closer ties with the West.

Czechs and Slovaks both trace their ancestry to the Slavs who moved into the region in the sixth century.

See: Avars, Celts, Czechs, Germans, Slavs, Slovaks

Denmark
Konigeriget Danmark

The Land: The peninsula of Denmark and the 500 or so adjacent islands form a lowland area, shaped by the final stages of the Ice Age glaciation. Most of the land is less than 30 metres above sea-level. The peninsula is narrow, so that the rivers are short; it is a landscape of small lakes, pools and peat-bogs, many now drained. The sea makes inroads upon the land, especially on the eastern side. This is a fertile country with much evidence of early settlement.
The Language: Danish is a Germanic language, belonging to the North Germanic group and related to Norwegian (with which it is mutually intelligible) and Swedish.
The Name: Danmark means literally 'territory of the Danes', *mark* being an old Germanic word for boundary. The peninsula of Jutland is thought to be named from the Jutes, a Germanic tribe who lived there in the early centuries AD.

As the ice retreated at the end of the last Ice Age, small hunter-gatherer communities spread over Denmark and the western Baltic islands, attracted not only by the virgin land but also by the riches of the sea. By 4000 BC the first farmers had arrived, cleared the land and established their settlements. The people of the later Stone Age (from about 2500 to 1800 BC) constructed a striking series of vast stone tombs where several people (perhaps warriors and their families) were buried together. From 2000 BC, an advanced Bronze Age culture developed, with skilled craftsmen producing high quality bronze weapons and other artifacts. The peoples of Denmark were in contact with both southern Scandinavia and central Europe at this time. After 500 BC, during the unrest of the Iron Age, Germanic tribal groups established communities on the mainland and especially on the islands. Contacts with the Roman empire in trade and diplomacy became increasingly important from the first century AD and continued until the fifth century. Shortly after, Danes are first mentioned in the land.

The people of early Denmark had much in common with their Scandinavian neighbours and with the early inhabitants of northern Germany. Their links with the people of southern Sweden and Norway were particularly close as the similarity of the three modern languages testify, and it was the warriors and traders of Denmark, Norway and Sweden who were together known to the rest of Europe as Vikings, 'the men of the fjord'.

After 800, the Vikings began to expand from their homelands into western Europe and the lands around the Baltic and Danes raided and settled in Holland, Russia and eastern and central Britain. For a time Danish territory extended north to central Sweden. By the tenth century, Danes were powerful enough to have established a separate kingdom and shortly after 1000 the Danish King Cnut (Canute; c. 995–1035) ruled the whole of Denmark and southern Norway as well as a large area of eastern England, known as the Danelaw. After Cnut's death the kingdom was reduced to the peninsula and islands, with part of southern Sweden.

Viking raids and explorations declined after about 950 but the tenth and eleventh centuries saw major developments within Denmark. Land was cleared, agriculture improved, new settlements were formed, and a rise in trade led to increasing wealth. Christianity spread in the tenth century, bringing Denmark more closely within the orbit of western European culture. By the twelfth century a strong monarchy was firmly re-established and Denmark was able to repel attacks by Germans from the south (especially from the commercial city of Lubeck), to subdue Estonia in the eastern Baltic, and to engage in trade deep inside Russia. However, control of trade in the Baltic was something the small north German states in the region were prepared to fight for and it was not until 1370 that the territory of Denmark was at last secure.

Once again, Danish power expanded, first taking in Norway when the royal families intermarried, and then joining Sweden in an alliance against the troublesome German states. In the Union of Kalmar, in 1397, the Danish queen, Margrethe, united Denmark, Sweden and Norway, establishing Danish authority over her weaker neighbours.

The next chapter in Denmark's history was a new struggle for control in the Baltic, especially against Sweden, which broke from the Union in 1523. And the troubles of this time were compounded by a major civil war

Denmark

Although Denmark's earliest settlements date from around 4000 BC, Danes are not mentioned by name until late Roman times. Long before this, however, their craftsmen were using bronze and many beautifully crafted artifacts have been discovered, some nearly 4000 years old. Apart from the peninsula of Jutland, Denmark consists of nearly five hundred islands, including the North Frisian Islands along its western coast, the Faeroes, Bornholm, off the tip of Sweden and Greenland, thousands of miles to the north-west.

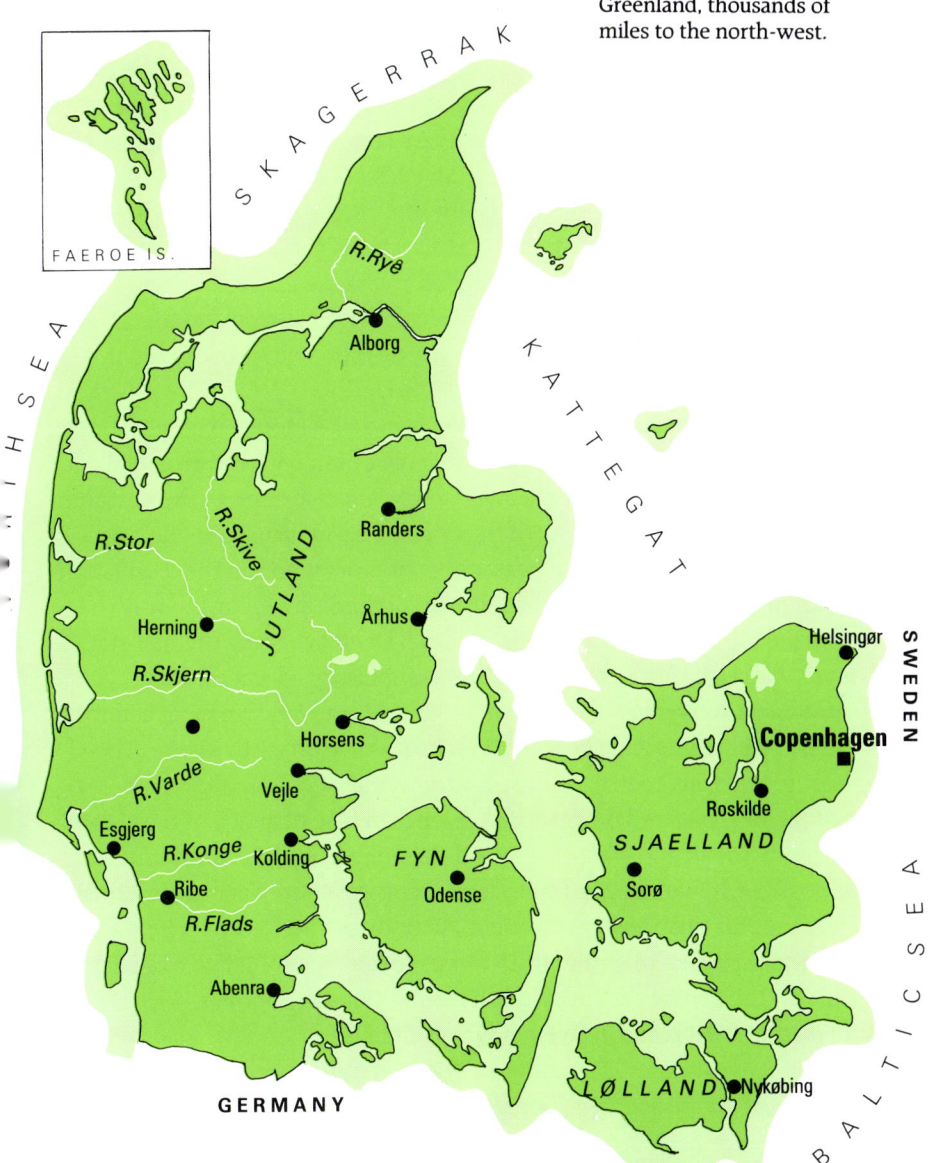

between the monarch and the aristocracy who controlled three-quarters of the land. The aristocrats eventually triumphed, though at some cost to the country as a whole. After 1550 Denmark entered into a period of prosperity, made rich by taxes levied on ships passing through the narrow channel from the North Sea into the Baltic and by exports from the wealthy estates in the south. But by the end of the century, the balance of power in Scandinavia was shifting towards Sweden. From 1618–48 Central Europe was devastated by the Thirty Years War. Denmark fought on the Protestant side, but was defeated in 1626. Later, in the 1640s, Denmark was involved in a war with Sweden. Swedes occupied the Danish islands and even Jutland, on the peninsula. By 1660, the state of Denmark was bankrupt and its land laid waste. The disastrous situation was blamed on the nobility and Frederik III used this as an excuse for establishing a period of absolute monarchy. The kingdom became more united and for the next hundred years, Denmark remained a strong monarchy—but without gaining any of the land she had lost to Sweden.

From the earlier eighteenth century Denmark's more enlightened kings began to modernize the country. Village communities were provided with a new basis for land-holding, leading to the emancipation of the peasants in the 1780s and the granting of freeholds. This in turn led to the appearance of a new class of peasant proprietors who laid the foundation for Denmark's agricultural prosperity in modern times. Slavery was abolished in overseas colonies from 1792, Denmark being the first state to do so. Early in the nineteenth century compulsory education was introduced, as were civil rights for Jews, also in advance of most countries.

The Napoleonic wars brought this progressive phase to a close. The most prosperous course for the country was armed neutrality, supporting neither side, but well prepared for defence in case of attack. A naval battle between British and Danish ships off Copenhagen in 1801 made neutrality impossible, however. The Danes later lost their entire fleet to the British and made an alliance with Napoleon, with disastrous results. The state went bankrupt in 1813, and in 1814 was forced by Sweden to exchange Norway for a small area of Swedish territory on the south Baltic coast (Pomerania). Norwegians were not consulted.

Twenty years later Denmark lost more territory when problems developed on the southern border, in the Danish-ruled duchies of Holstein and Schleswig. Control of both Holstein and Schleswig was claimed by the Federation of German States, which included the rising German state of Prussia. The first flare-up occurred in 1848. Holstein rose in revolt, seeking a free Schleswig-Holstein within the German Federation, and Denmark was plunged into civil war. The Prussian army invaded but was forced to withdraw and the first crisis passed. In 1864, Prussia and Austria declared war on Denmark over the same issue. Denmark stood alone and her forces resisted stoutly, but the outcome was total defeat. Both Schleswig and Holstein passed to Germany, taking from Denmark a quarter of her territory and two-fifths of her population. So heavy a blow might have seemed crushing, but in fact it stimulated a spirited response which brought about a strong economic recovery.

After this defeat, Denmark remained politically neutral but inevitably inclined towards the growing military and economic power of Germany. That neutrality was maintained in the First World War, though Denmark did not escape entirely unscathed. Many of her merchant ships were lost and four years of war in Europe imposed severe strains on the economy and on the working classes. After the war, in 1920 the people of Schleswig voted for the return of the northern part of the province to Denmark; otherwise the borders remained unchanged.

As the Nazis rose to power in Germany from 1933, Denmark tried to hold to a neutral position and accepted a non-aggression pact with Hitler in 1939. But in April 1940 the Germans invaded Denmark and forced a surrender. The Danish war-time government managed to prevent the worst excesses of Nazi rule, notably the transportation of Jews, though there were inevitable strains between the national leaders and the underground movement. Occupation lasted until May 1945.

The population of the country is largely homogeneous, being almost wholly ethnic Danes. Greenland has been integral to the state of Denmark since 1951, though it enjoys a large measure of autonomy. The Faeroe Islands have been Danish since 1380 and autonomous since 1947. Very few Greenlanders and Faroese have taken advantage of their Danish citizenship to settle in Denmark. There are small German, Polish and Jewish minorities, and in the last few decades guest workers from Pakistan, Iran, Turkey and Yugoslavia have arrived in some numbers.
See: Danes, Germans, Jutes, Vikings

Finland
Suomen Tasavalta / Republiken Finland

The Land: The surface of Finland is an ancient shield of granite, heavily worn down and indented by the sea. Very many small islands lie immediately offshore. The landscape has been much affected by successive Ice Ages, the glaciations leaving behind thousands of lakes and pools. Nearly 10% of the land is covered by water. Northern Finland lies north of the Arctic Circle and thus has long, severe winters and brief summers of two months.

The Language: Finnish is a Finno-Ugrian language, belonging to the same group as Hungarian and Estonian. Its origins lie with the people who entered Finland from the steppes to the east after 100 BC. About 8% of the population speak Swedish as their first language.

The Name: The Finns' own name for their country and language is *Suomi* (meaning People). Finland was the name used by the Swedes.

From about 7000 BC hunter-gatherers began to enter Finland during the summer months, later staying throughout the year. They found rich reserves of game and fur-bearing animals. Later hunting groups and settlers arrived after 5000 BC from the Russian steppes. The prehistoric ancestors of the Finns may have emerged some time after 100 BC and slowly developed a more stable and settled life, especially in the south. Three groups may be distinguished: the Suomalaiset, the Karelians and Tavastians. People speaking the Finnish language migrated to Finland from Estonia and Russia in the early centuries AD.

As an independent country Finland has had a short history, since December 1917, but the area has been recognized as the land of the Finnish people since at least AD 1000. In the late twelfth century Sweden, with the blessing of the Pope, began a lengthy Crusade against the pagan

Finland

The ancestors of the Lapps may have been the first inhabitants of Finland, hunters who moved north in the summer, following the migrating herds of animals. Finnish speakers crossed from Russia and Estonia around AD 100, probably driving the Lapps further north as they began to hunt and trap along the rivers. Unrelated to either Slavs or Germanic tribes, the Finns probably came from the great northern plains to the west of the Urals but very little is known about their ancestry. Only their language indicates that they did not belong to the prehistoric Indo-European tribes who spread through the rest of Europe.

Finns. The Swedes, who arrived as armed missionaries, stayed on in the newly-converted Christian land as colonizers, and for the next five hundred years Finland was a dependency of Sweden. But Finland was, on the whole, governed with a light hand. The Finns retained a large measure of freedom in local affairs. Their language, customs and culture lived on. Inevitably, there were frictions which led from time to time to quarrels and minor rebellions. But Finland was a large land. Oppressed or disappointed Finns were always free to escape to the vast interior spaces of the undeveloped country where their lives were quite undisturbed by Swedish regulation.

Sweden, for its part, looked on Finland as a more or less autonomous province which provided some economic benefit and a useful number of good soldiers. In particular, with the passage of time, Finland became important to Sweden as a buffer-zone lying between its own ambitions to the east and the powerful resistance and counter-attack from Russia. By the eighteenth century Sweden was in decline, Russia was rising, and Finland was a disputed territory between them. In 1721, on the death of Charles XII of Sweden, Russia took the south-east corner of Finland. In 1743, by the Treaty of Turku, Russia gained another large slice of Finnish territory. In 1809 Finland was annexed to Tsarist Russia as a self-governing Grand Duchy and so it remained until the Russian revolution of October 1917. A feeling of Finnish nationalism had grown in the later nineteenth century and independence was declared very soon after the Russian revolution, in December 1917.

The immediate result, however, was tragic. A war followed which was both a war of liberation from Russia and a civil conflict, when some Finns sided with Russia. Finland emerged as a nation, but had only twenty years of independence before Soviet Russia invaded the country late in 1939. The Finns resisted with great courage and resourcefulness against the much larger Red Army and Russia was finally induced to come to terms in March 1940. Under the peace-treaty, Finland lost the southern part of the province of Karelia and the Hango peninsula. Finland then turned to Nazi Germany for protection, but later declared herself neutral when Russia took over the republics of Estonia, Latvia and Lithuania, and Germany invaded Russia, in June 1941. A Russian attempt to invade Finland in the summer of 1944 was halted at Vyborg after heavy casualties on both sides and an armistice was signed. The war had been costly to Finland, in lives lost, damage during the invasions, and in war reparations demanded by Russia when it was over. But the country emerged without great loss of territory, except in the east and along the northern corridor to the Arctic Ocean.

Finland maintained friendly relations with the Soviet Union, not without difficulty, after 1945. But she steadily developed closer links with the other Nordic countries, both in the political and economic spheres. There has been a marked diminution of Communist influence since 1970, but socialist ideals have always been strong. The multiplicity of political parties has made the formation of governments difficult. Coalition cabinets are normal, often with civil servants occupying some of the posts.

Finland is the fifth largest state in Europe, but its population density is low and it ranks as one of the smallest in number of inhabitants. The people are almost exclusively Finnish and Swedish. Since 1945 there has been virtually no immigration due to official controls, while there has been a steady stream of Finnish emigration to Sweden. In the north the Lapp minority maintains a precarious existence, but probably no more than 20,000 remain. Finland is an overwhelmingly Protestant country, 90% of the population belonging to the Evangelical Lutheran Church.
See: Finns, Lapps, Swedes

France
La République Française

The Land: France is a land of enormous contrasts in geography and landscape, ranging from broad, flat plains in the north and west to the heights of the Alps in the south-east and the Pyrenees in the south. Most of the upland lies in the east and centre (the Massif Central). Nearly two-thirds of the land is occupied by plains and broad valleys, often productive and with a climate favourable to agriculture, France's main resource. Although France is a fertile land, it is surprisingly thinly populated and there are few very large urban centres. The great rivers of France (Rhone, Garonne, Meuse, Seine, Loire and Marne) have contributed greatly to its economic development since the Roman period, providing good communications and efficient means of transport.

The Language: French is a Romance language, rooted in Latin but with many influences from elsewhere, including Greek. Modern French is based on the dialect spoken in the area of Paris and the Ile-de-France in the Middle Ages. Breton, a Celtic language related to Welsh and Cornish, is widely spoken in Brittany. The ancient pre-Indo-European language of the Basques is still current in the south-west, while in Provence, Provencal or Occitan, a Romance tongue predating modern French is widespread. A million German-speakers live in Alsace and Lorraine; Flemish is still used in the north-east corner and dialects of Italian are spoken in the French Alps and in Corsica. Catalan speakers are found in the eastern Pyrenees.

The Name: France is the Norman, mediaeval version of Francia, in turn derived from the Franks, the Germanic people who took over the region at the end of Roman rule. Gaul, the Latin *Gallia*, was the territory of the western Celtic tribes.

France has a very long history of human settlement, extending back at least 500,000 years. Neanderthal man occupied both caves and open sites in central France, for example in the famous caves at Le Mouster in the Dordogne. Later Palaeolithic remains are particularly rich and important: settlement sites and superb cave paintings and rock-engravings (e.g. at Lascaux and Font-de-Gaume) date from the period 30,000 to 8000 BC. New farming peoples entered the land from the east and south-east after 5000 BC. Their megalithic tombs and standing stones (e.g. at Carnac) are among the most remarkable monuments of prehistoric Europe. Metalworkers were active from 2500 BC and there may have been further immigration from the east. Celtic peoples had occupied much of the area that became France by the sixth century BC and a well defined tribal structure developed. Greek colonies were established in the Mediterranean south (including Marseilles, Antibes and Nice) and these were important centres for trade. The Celtic chieftains of the centre and the east imported luxury goods from the Mediterranean world, including fine Greek pottery and Etruscan metalwork.

The roots of present-day France lie in the area of land known as Gallia (Gaul) in Roman times. Between 58 and 52 BC the tribes who occupied central and northern Gaul, which included central and northern France, Belgium and Germany up to the Rhine, were conquered in a series of brilliant campaigns by Julius Caesar and thereafter governed by Rome for four and a half centuries. The Romans did not interfere with the tribal structure of the Celts but established Roman cities at the existing tribal centres to provide focal points of administration. Gaul was much too extensive to be organized as a single province. The Mediterranean south (Gallia Narbonensis) had already been a province of Rome for more than half a century before Caesar's time. The remainder was in due course organized as three provinces: Belgica in the north, Lugdunensis in the centre and Aquitania in the west. The extreme east and north, bordering the Rhine, were later separated off as two further provinces and occupied by substantial numbers of Roman troops to guard against barbarian incursions. The natural resources of Gaul were exploited from the beginning and the land became one of the richest areas of the Roman west. The Latin language was widely used among the educated and among provincial administrators but did not replace Celtic in the north and west. A literary culture of some distinction flourished in the late fourth and fifth centuries AD in the south, despite the steady decline of Roman power at this time.

Geographically, ancient Gaul provides the framework for later France but in cultural and political terms the growth of Germanic kingdoms in the post-Roman centuries was much more important for the French. The Visigoths who settled in Aquitaine and the Burgundian kingdom in the east had little lasting effect but the Franks in the north and centre brought the peoples of Gaul together and laid the foundation of France.

By the middle of the sixth century, the Franks were the undisputed masters of Gaul. The Frankish king Clovis (Chlodovech) had unified northern Gaul and conquered the Visigoths in the south-west and the Burgundians in the east. Frankish rule also extended east of the Rhine into central Germany and towards the Alps, where they defeated the Alamanni. Although the Frankish kingdom was the leading power of western Europe by 600, its internal dissension held it back from further conquests and from exercising a unifying role, until a new ruling family which emerged in the eighth century provided stability. Under Charles Martel and Charlemagne, Frankish power was pushed further east and north, against the Slavs and Saxons. Charlemagne's conquests, his Christian evangelism and his firm government gave some justification for his claim to be the successor of the Roman emperors: on Christmas Day 800 he was enthroned in Rome as emperor.

The empire of Charlemagne, though not by any means confined to Francia, represented an attempt at recreating the most powerful empire in world history to that time, the empire of Rome. From the Channel and the Atlantic to central Europe and into Italy, the emperor of this new Rome dominated his realm with as much authority as Augustus or Hadrian. Or so he thought. His empire proved to be fragile and shortly after Charlemagne's death it shattered into pieces. But during its short life it had done much to revive interest in Latin learning and literature, Roman architecture and art, and had provided a powerful stimulus to the renewed development of urban life and to long-distance commerce and craftsmanship.

After Charlemagne's death in 814 came divisions and decline, though his

Some of the oldest inhabited sites in Europe have been found in France. Neanderthalers lived in the Dordogne some 500,000 years ago and the cave paintings at Lascaux and Font-de-Gaume were made by people living there at least 10,000 years ago. When the Romans came they found Celtic tribes such as the Gauls and the Belgae well established and the province of Gallia (Gaul) became one of Rome's most valuable assets. As Rome declined, new tribes moved into the rich territories: Visigoths settled in Aquitaine, Germanic Burgundians in the east, while Alans, Vandals and Suevi all moved westwards into Gaul. Saxons attacked from northern Germany from the 300s but it was the Franks who, around 600 established themselves as undisputed rulers and were the true founders of modern France.

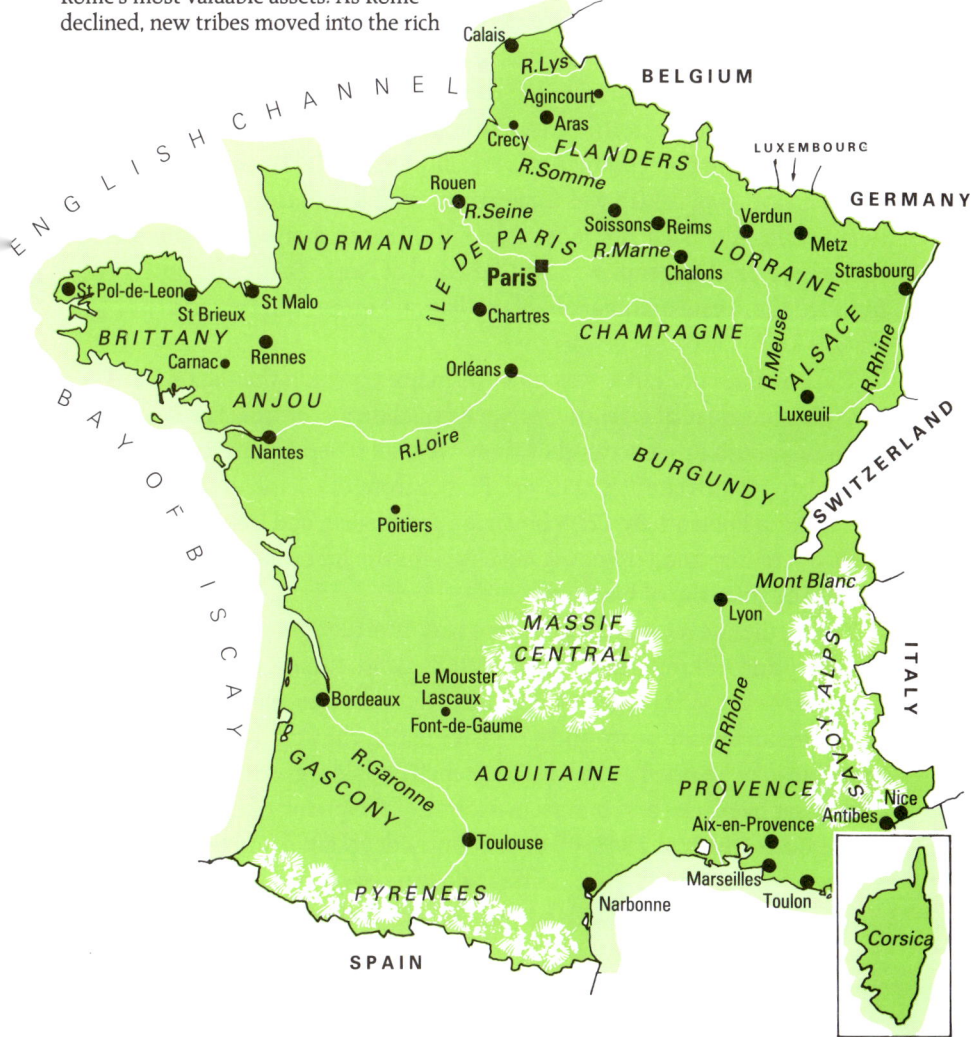

descendants continued to rule until the later tenth century. In the period from 850 to 1200, the region was divided up among numerous smaller rulers and the kings of France were compelled to seek alliances with the many princes, dukes and other leaders of such areas as Anjou, Burgundy, Brittany, Flanders, Champagne, Aquitaine, Gascony and Provence. Normandy was ceded to a Viking force under Rollo in 911 (and in 1066 its duke, William of Normandy, successfully invaded England) and there were also many other lesser lordships and territories over which the king had to try to exercise at least a measure of control.

In 987 the French monarchy was set on a new path when Hugh Capet, the duke of Francia, was elected to the kingship. His domain included Paris, Orleans and the fertile area of the Beauce, and from this modest base the power of the French kings was steadily enlarged. The position of Paris as the major royal centre was finally confirmed late in the twelfth century, when Philip Augustus, the most able of the French monarchs, constructed the Louvre palace, completed the Cathedral of Notre Dame and, in 1200, founded the greatest university of mediaeval Europe, the University of Paris.

The kingdom of France was now the major power in the region but considerable areas of territory remained outside its control. The Duchy of Burgundy, Goth Provence and Brittany were all independent entities while in the late twelfth century, western France from the Seine to the Pyrenees belonged to England. By 1214, however, the English had lost most of their French territory and Philip Augustus was for the first time in control of more land than any of his vassals.

The further development of France was interrupted by the long period of rivalry and intermittent conflict with England, commonly known as the Hundred Years' War (1338–1453). The early successes fell to the English and, after an uneasy peace and a decisive battle, the kingdoms of England and France were briefly united. The French people were at their lowest ebb, beset by plague and famine (a quarter of the population may have died in the Black Death of 1348–9), their country devastated and their towns in ruins. Yet within thirty years, a miraculous recovery had been achieved. This was partly because England was preoccupied and weakened by civil war but another factor was the extraordinary intervention of Joan of Arc, a peasant girl from the Meuse valley in eastern France. Led by her voices and visions, in 1429 she persuaded the king to allow her to join the force which raised the siege of Orleans and then accompanied him to Reims and a triumphant coronation. French morale was raised, but in the next year Joan was captured by Burgundian troops and sold to the English who burnt her as a witch and heretic. Her intervention had turned the tide of success in France's favour and in 1436 the French king retook Paris. By 1453 the long sequence of wars was over and with it the English hold on France.

England now abandoned all claim to French lands except for Calais and when, by about 1500, Burgundy, Provence and Brittany were all joined to the kingdom, modern France had taken shape. Only Alsace-Lorraine and Savoy remained outside the French king's control. At this same time, France came under the influence of the revival of classical learning, mainly by contact with the Italian cities. Paris was transformed into a city fit for a royal court and the nobility, attracted to the new centre of culture and power, quickly lost their independent habits. The nation-state was now secure. The rapid spread of printing encouraged the rise of French as a written language, replacing Latin in the sixteenth century and creating the vehicle for a magnificent and varied literature in the seventeenth. But political strength could not insulate France from the religious tumult of the sixteenth century. The general revolt against the power of the Roman Catholic Church and its many abuses spread into southern France, especially into Aquitaine and the central uplands. Long years of religious struggle followed before Catholics triumphed under Louis XIV. Many protestant Huguenots were compelled to flee, to Germany, Britain and America. Unity was gained, but with considerable loss in talented and energetic members of the French community. Partly as a result, from the late seventeenth into the eighteenth century, France became more isolated than she need have been.

Geographically, the final aim of French monarchs, to extend their eastern frontier to the Rhine, was accomplished by the end of the seventeenth century, when the three bishoprics of Metz, Verdun and Toul were acquired, to be followed by Alsace and Lorraine. Much of the eighteenth century was notable only for its degree of stagnation. Agriculture continued almost unchanged, overseas commerce was slight, the beginnings of industrialization barely visible. The effects of periodic war with England were destructive, but not so severe as to threaten total disaster. The revolutionary cataclysm of 1789 was not predicted before it struck and its effects were magnified, in France and abroad, by its suddenness. Its causes, however, lay in the corruption and mismanagement of preceding years.

The long reign of Louis XV (1715–74) had been disastrous for the people of France. Wars abroad were both costly and unsuccessful, the royal court was profligate with revenues collected from the middle and lower social ranks and many of the peasantry languished in a state not far removed from servility and starvation. By the 1770s, French debts were mountainous and there was no sign of any attempt by the monarch and his ministers to alter policy. From 1787 the nobles and clergy came under increasing financial pressure, adding to the ferment. In May 1789 the States-General declared itself the National Assembly and demanded a constitution for France. The Revolution had begun.

The National Assembly remoulded French institutions, abolished old feudal rights, declared the Rights of Man, and framed a constitution in which a limited monarchy still had a place. This was constructive change, carried through at great speed. But it was accompanied by mob-violence in 1789 and followed by a regime of terror which claimed victims from all social groups. The Revolution laid not only the foundations of modern France, but also those of modern liberal ideas, including human rights. But from 1792 the Revolution moved inexorably towards foreign wars and dictatorship. A republic was declared, the king deposed and killed. The Jacobin dictatorship of Robespierre unleashed a new wave of terror in 1792–4 and paved the way for the military dictatorship of Napoleon Bonaparte. His brilliant victories on land against Austria and Prussia brought most of western Europe under French control, but the British fleet was still master of the seas, as the victories of the Nile, Copenhagen and Trafalgar made clear.

In 1810 Napoleon's power was at its zenith, his empire and its allies extending to the borders of Russia and Ottoman Turkey. Only two years later, his invasion of Russia ended in catastrophic failure and his allies and subject peoples began to slip away or rise in revolt. Two more years and the emperor had to abdicate. His return in 1815 was a brilliant final gamble, which might have succeeded had he not faced a united allied army under Wellington. After Waterloo, in 1815, the monarchy was restored, not by ardent royalists but by disappointed Bonapartists, and the king's ministers were men who had served Napoleon. But the great days were over and Napoleon's broken empire left behind more problems than glory.

The first phase of the restored monarchy ended in insurrection and the flight of the king in 1830. The second phase was marked by social turbulence which broke forth in 1848 and brought Napoleon III to the throne of the Second Empire in 1852. Both at home and increasingly overseas, Napoleon III struggled to exercise control but rarely succeeded. The power of a united Germany under Bismarck's skilled and determined direction posed a threat that could not be ignored. War came in 1870. A German army invaded France and Paris was under siege. When it fell in January 1871, the war was clearly lost and with it the monarchy.

The defeat of France in 1870 marked a major change in the balance of power in Europe. France lost not only Alsace and Lorraine but also much international prestige. Alliances had to be sought against Germany and were secured with Russia in 1890 and with Britain in 1904. When European rivalries came to a head in 1914, France was still a great power with a strong army but she was ill-prepared for the destructive war which now engulfed her. French military tactics, locked in nineteenth-century traditions, almost lost the war in the first few months as the Germans burst through Belgium and came within reach of Paris, only to be beaten off in the decisive battle of the Marne. As the fighting settled down into the futile waste of static trench-warfare, France became ever more dependent upon Britain and the USA for the means to continue the war, much of her industry being lost to the Germans or immobilized in the war zone. Her greatest resource was now her infantry and she expanded it without stint, especially in the defence of Verdun in 1916. By November 1918, France was all but exhausted, her losses of 1.5 million men being the heaviest of all the warring nations. Her recovery after 1918 was understandably slow and her fear of invasion from Germany was still strong. The reconstruction of France had to be paid for and it was paid for by the French, a heavy burden borne particularly by the middle class. But France came out from the economic crises of 1929–31 stronger than most of the other great powers, with large reserves of gold, with productive agriculture that enabled her to be in most respects self-sufficient and with increasingly healthy trade.

The Great War, however, had left very deep scars on the French. In the 1930s, faced with the Nazi threat, the country had no will to rearm. When World War II came, neither the government nor the army was strongly committed to fight. When the Germans invaded the Low Countries and France in May 1940, the French were at a serious disadvantage in tanks and aircraft. Within weeks France was compelled to withdraw from the fighting, leaving 1.5 million prisoners in German hands and German armies on the Channel and Atlantic coasts. Many Frenchmen fled to England and North Africa to continue the struggle from there in the Free French forces. The four years of German occupation brought their own trauma, compounded by collaboration in official and other circles. The liberation of France by the Allies in 1944 did not immediately dispel the bitterness which had built up over the previous four years.

After the war, recovery had just begun when France's hold on her overseas possessions was severely shaken. First, in Indochina, a military disaster at Dien-Bien-Phu in 1954 released Vietnam from French control and then, in Algeria, a savage war of independence was fought from 1954 to 1962. When a political settlement was agreed, many of the settler-families were compelled to move to France leaving all their possessions behind them.

Compensation for the loss of empire came from the rising economic prosperity of France within the EEC and its correspondingly important political role within a changing Europe. After the long sequence of unstable governments of the 1950s, the regimes of De Gaulle, Pompidou, Giscard d'Estaing and Mitterand provided France with her longest period of secure administration and economic growth in modern times. Her new and relaxed relationship with her long-time enemy, Germany, is one of the strengths of the European Community in the 1990s.

Compared with Britain and Germany, France is not a densely populated country; a high proportion of its inhabitants still live in the countryside and in small towns. Large cities are few and Paris is very much larger than all the rest. Despite their immense pride in being French, the people are very mixed in ethnic terms. The Germanic Frankish stock was long ago absorbed, as were the Burgundian, Visigothic and later Norse elements in their respective regions of France. Brittany, however, has remained a recognizably Celtic part of France, with a widely spoken Celtic language, and the Basque region in the south-west retains a distinct population which has not been wholly assimilated into the greater unity of France. The eastern lands close to the Rhine have naturally received many settlers from Germany, while Alsace and Lorraine still preserve more than a trace of their earlier history as German possessions. Italians have also migrated to France in considerable numbers, especially into Provence and the larger northern cities. Poles found refuge in France during the nineteenth century and again in the 1940s. French Algerians who had never lived in France were compelled to settle in the mother-country and in the past twenty years large numbers of African immigrants from Algeria and Morocco have flooded into Marseilles and Paris in search of a more secure life, bringing social and religious problems with them.

See: Alans, Basques, Belgae, Bretons, Burgundians, Celts, Franks, Gauls, Goths, Ligurians, Normans, Romans, Saxons, Suevi, Vandals

Germany
Bundesrepublik Deutschland

The Land: In many senses the modern republic of Germany occupies the central position in Europe. Geographically and economically it dominates the entire continent, forming an essential link between east and west. It shares a border with nine other states, more points of contact than any other country. The main features of Germany are the North German plain, drained by the three rivers Weser, Elbe and Oder, the central uplands (the Mittelgebirge) including the Harz mountains and the Thuringian forest, and the southern Highlands leading to the Bavarian Alps. The ancient forest cover has been largely removed, but vast areas of more recently planted forest (about 30% of the total land surface) exist in the centre and east. The population is massed in the Rhine valley, the Ruhr region and central east Germany. Many other regions are thinly populated. The major rivers provide outstandingly effective lines of communication, especially the Rhine and Elbe. In general, the climate is of the type known as continental, with fairly low rainfall, but with seasonal extremes of temperature increasing towards the east.

The Language: The Germanic languages, of which three groups once existed, are Indo-European in origin. Modern German developed from *Hochdeutsch* (Old High German) from the sixth century AD onward. It had been influenced by the Latin used in monasteries in the Middle Ages, and there has been much later borrowing from French and latterly from English. Dialects are strong all over Germany, several (e.g., Bavarian) having the status of regional languages.

The Name: *Deutschland*, the German name for their country, means simply 'land of the people'.

Hunter-gatherer communities extended over many parts of Germany after 10,000 BC. Agriculture spread from the south-east by 4000 BC and was well developed on the areas of light soil (*loess*). In the Bronze Age, from 1800 BC, pre-German tribes, well-placed in the centre of Europe, shared in the cultural and technological transformation which affected all regions, from the North Sea to the Carpathians. Although the modern state of Germany was a creation of the mid nineteenth century, the Germanic peoples have possessed a distinct identity for well over two thousand years. First mentioned by Classical writers in the first century BC as a group of warlike tribes of northern Europe, Germans had already emerged as a distinctive population by around 500 BC, living north of the Celts and west of the nomadic peoples, occupying the north European plain and southern Scandinavia. The Celts occupied much of central Germany and the south-west after 600 BC, but were steadily pushed out by Germanic expansion after 100 BC. Germanic tribes invaded southern Europe late in the second century BC, and the Germans were viewed as a dangerous threat to the security of the Roman empire. Roman campaigns against them ended in ignominious failure in AD 9 and the territory of the Germanic peoples remained outside the borders of the empire, though German life could not avoid Roman influence in cultural, social and political affairs.

During the third century AD the great migrations of Germanic tribes began. Larger groupings of people came into existence (Alamanni, Franks, Goths and Saxons) and began to attack and later settle within the Roman provinces. One of Europe's greatest tranformations was completed in the fifth and sixth centuries, when migrant Germans moved into almost every part of Europe, establishing transient kingdoms and a number of more enduring states. Within what was to become Germany, the most important of these tribes were the Saxons and Frisians in the north, the Thuringians further south, the Alamanni or Suevi (Schwabians) in the south-west and the Bavarians in the south. Later in the seventh and eighth centuries, the Franks extended their power east of the Rhine, towards the borderlands of the Slavic tribes on the Elbe.

There was no unity about this early Germany. By the tenth century the Germans were broadly divided into five large duchies: Franconia, Saxony, Schwabia, Bavaria and Thuringia. These were the powers that formed the first German monarchy which held off the Slavs, Magyars and invaders from the east. The kingdom did not last long. By 1075 its strength had been sapped by weakness within and by growing hostility from the Papacy. Over the next two centuries Germany declined to a condition close to anarchy. And yet during this very time German peasants, labourers, craftsmen and merchants were bringing about the three greatest achievements of mediaeval Germany: the clearance of waste land, the development of towns, and the colonization of the eastern lands. The clearance of the waste land was made necessary by a rise in population and the consequent demand for land on which to grow food. The process gathered momentum after 1000 and reached a peak between 1100 and 1250. Many of the place names of modern Germany bear witness to the work of those who cleared the forests and built the new farms and hamlets: -*feld* (field), -*holz* (wood), -*roth* (to clear). The need for more land was also one of the reasons why Germans began to colonize eastern Europe, though this was seen as a Christian crusade to convert and civilize the Slavs. By 1100 the Bavarians had settled in the Ostmark, roughly Austria. Further north, Germans moved eastwards from the Elbe in the twelfth century, and after 1200 German settlers were tilling the land in the Oder valley. Much further east, in what became East Prussia, colonization came after military conquest by the Teutonic Knights (a military-religious order of chivalry, founded in the twelfth century at the time of the Crusades) and was accompanied by the conversion of the still heathen Prussians. Other Germans spread to the Baltic coast of Mecklenburg and Pomerania. In the eastern European lands German settlers often formed islands amid a predominantly Slav population, preserving their German langauge and culture until the twentieth century. This was the case with the Germans who settled in Bohemia and Moravia.

Germany today is a federation of sixteen provinces (the Länder), its boundaries established after the 1939-45 war and confirmed when East and West Germany were reunited in 1990. The first Germanic tribes were far from united. According to Julius Caesar, they were divided into more than forty independent and warlike states, each made up of several different, often quarrelsome tribes. In larger groupings, some migrated into almost every part of Europe in the 400s and 500s, but others, including Saxons, Frisians, Thuringians and Bavarians remained in sufficient numbers to found the first Germanic kingdom.

Germany

The towns of northern and central Germany were also of enormous significance in the social and economic development of Europe, fostering a middle class of burghers who helped to break down the feudal relationships of European society. In the disturbed conditions after 1250, towns banded together in leagues to protect their interests. The most formidable of these was the League of the Hansa cities—Lübeck, Hamburg, Bremen and Cologne—which grew rich on trade with the Baltic, the Low Countries and Britain. This period of economic growth had ended by 1350 and was followed by stagnation, though not marked decline, in an age of many minor states, free cities and a small number of larger powers.

In 1517 Martin Luther, a priest and scholar at Wittenberg University, attacked the Church's use of papal indulgences and altered this stable, structured world dramatically. His attack sparked a reaction against the many abuses of the Church, from papal interference to immorality among the lesser clergy. Luther found abundant support not only among the common people (he came from a peasant family) but also among the princes and learned men at their courts. Luther's work in another direction had an impact almost as profound. His translation of the New Testament and later of the Old Testament into German, published in 1534, not only made the Bible accessible to a wide readership, but also provided the foundation for the German language as spoken by educated people in modern Germany. But not all the results of Luther's doctrines were of benefit to everyone. The peasants, oppressed by landowners and nobles, rose in revolt in 1524–5, with Luther's call for freedom ringing in their ears, only to be denounced by Luther himself. The rising was savagely put down and the living conditions of most peasants remained wretched for the next two centuries.

The Protestant Reformation hardly affected the political map of Germany. Germany was still a mosaic of little powers, and when a determined attempt to unite them was made, by the Emperor Ferdinand in 1618, the result was a catastrophe for the people of Germany. The Thirty Years War fought between the central European powers brought untold misery and deprivation to most parts of Germany. Power was fragmented, religious differences combined with dynastic and political ambition to cause chaos as mercenary armies devastated the land. The Peace of Westphalia, which brought the chaos to an end in 1648, marked a low point of German history. The German emperor was a forlorn figure, his ancient crown merely a tawdry ornament of the Austrian Hapsburgs. Swedes were in control of the lower Oder, Danes of the Elbe. The French grip on Alsace and the neighbouring territories was confirmed, and both Switzerland and the Netherlands gained their independence. Germany had sunk low, but the princes remained in control and their outlook changed hardly at all. Great Baroque palaces and fine town houses went up all over Germany in the late seventeenth and eighteenth centuries, as ruler emulated ruler. They ruled, in their petty courts, with absolute authority. The administration, often of a high order, was firmly in their hands. The old independent towns now lost their power and influence to the princes. Several minor towns became important simply because they were the capitals of princes, for instance Stuttgart, Düsseldorf and Berlin. Some of the more energetic and acquisitive princes stimulated industry and trade: porcelain at Meissen and Dresden, glass at Hanover, iron in Silesia and the Ruhr, woodworking in the Black Forest. These activities were to form the basis for Germany's industrial transformation in the nineteenth century.

While most of Germany was torn by religious and dynastic quarrels, in the north the state of Brandenburg-Prussia began its rise to pre-eminence. In 1701 the ruling house of the Hohenzollerns was allowed to take the title of king and did so under Frederick I. This rather primitive state, occupying one of the poorer parts of Germany, vigorously defended its frontier position, quickly dominating the eastern Germans and spreading its influence to the more cultured west. Frederick the Great (1740–86) greatly enlarged the boundaries of Prussia and made it a serious rival to Austria as the strongest German power. The state was turned into an efficient administrative machine, its engine being a powerful standing army, still a rarity in Europe at the time. The interests of the state were made supreme over those of the citizens, an omen for a later stage of German history.

The French Revolution which threw a long shadow over the whole of Europe, quickly upset the delicate balance of the petty German states. The minor principalities in the Rhineland were absorbed into France. Even Prussia could not resist Napoleon's power. But the defeat of Napoleon in 1815 gave Prussia another chance to consolidate her position and to seek out a leading, unifying role in German politics. Under Prussian leadership, German economic power was dramatically enlarged after the 1830s. The removal of trade barriers and improvements in transport brought small principalities together. War also proved a useful instrument in unifying the nation. Under Bismarck, Prussia, with Austria, took Schleswig and Holstein from Denmark in 1864. Prussia then fell upon Austria and excluded her from the German confederation. The unity of the country was finally sealed by the Prussian war with France in 1870, a rapid success which told the world that Germany had arrived as a world power. The ruler of Prussia, Wilhelm I, was hailed as emperor (*Kaiser*) of the confident and properous new state. Industrial development continued at an unparalleled pace and the population greatly increased. Agriculture did not progress so rapidly, but by 1914 Germany was the most formidable power in continental Europe, and France, Russia and Britain were bound to seek ways to check her advance. The great powers drifted into war in 1914, though conflict was inevitable sooner or later. No-one appreciated how destructive it would turn out to be.

For Germany and the German people the war of 1914–18 was disastrous. Two million lost their lives, Communist revolution threatened the break-up of the state in 1918–19 and the economy was wrecked, first by war, then by raging inflation early in the 1920s. Under the Treaty of Versailles, Germany lost an eighth of her territory and a tenth of her population. Alsace-Lorraine was returned to France, North Schleswig to Denmark, Malmédy to Belgium and part of Upper Silesia to Poland. Economic recovery resumed from the mid 1920s but the Versailles treaty had created enormous resentment among Germans and this was skilfully exploited by nationalist groups, especially the Nazi party under Adolf Hitler. By 1931, the Nazis had greatly extended their power base in many parts of Germany. Hitler became Chancellor and then President in 1933. By means of nationalist appeal, brilliant propaganda and naked violence, the Nazi leaders forged a state which sought to dominate Europe, and particularly eastern Europe, by military conquest followed by German settlement—the *Drang nach Osten* (literally, the 'push to the east').

Other European powers held back from confrontation, and indeed appeased Hitler's Germany, for as long as possible. By 1939 all hope of a peaceful settlement of German demands was gone. The second and decisive stage of the great European conflict began in 1940 when Hitler attacked Denmark, Norway, the Low Countries and France, winning amazingly quick victories. Britain held out against him, though conquest of the British Isles was in any case not Hitler's prime aim. His domination of Europe was now almost complete, and his success might have been assured had he not attacked Russia in June 1941, following his master-plan for conquest in the east. The largest and most costly campaign in world history ensued from 1941 to 1944, and marked the turning-point for Hitler's Reich. The massive defeat at Stalingrad in 1943 was followed by the Russian advance towards the old borders of Germany and, in June 1944, by the allied invasion of France across the Channel. Russian armies entered Berlin in April 1945 and Hitler committed suicide. The Reich that was to have lasted a thousand years had endured for only twelve.

The suffering it brought to the subject peoples and to the Germans themselves is impossible to quantify. Between 5.5 and 7 million Jews had been exterminated, along with untold numbers of gypsies, Slavs and other groups—perhaps 10 million in all. Millions of others had been forced into slave-camps and either died there or suffered the most harrowing conditions. These victims included many ethnic Germans who opposed the regime. The suffering of the German people as a whole in the latter stages of the war was appalling, under allied bombing and especially under the hideous reprisals of the Red Army as it swept westward. The suffering did not end in 1945. Twelve million Germans were forced westward from Poland and Russia and other eastern territories, often to a Germany they had never seen. Most of the major cities lay in ruins, the economy was smashed and starvation rife. Beside these stark facts, the mere loss of territory seemed hardly significant. But Germany lost much of the territory it had held until 1939, especially to Poland and Russia. By 1949 it had become two states, the Russian zone of occupation becoming the German Democratic Republic with its capital in East Berlin, the western *Länder* (provinces) being united in the German Federal Republic with its capital at Bonn. Berlin was itself divided, the western part of the city remaining within the Federal Republic. The worsening of relations between Russia and the western powers in the late 1940s hardened the boundaries of the two states, even at one stage in 1948 threatening a new war. Hitler's great, unified Reich for the Germans appeared to have disintegrated into a land permanently divided between east and west.

The experience of the east and west Germans after 1945 was very different. In the east, stagnation in the economy was followed by rapid decline from the 1970s. In the west, the ruined land was restored with astonishing despatch, and from the mid-1950s an economic boom took many of its people to new heights of prosperity. By the later 1960s, West Germany was a major economic force. But the Cold War between capitalist west and communist east still kept Germany divided. Then, after 1985, the Gorbachev reforms in Russia and the mounting economic and political crisis in eastern Europe suddenly produced a changing climate in which reunification was possible. In the autumn of 1989, the Berlin wall was demolished and the border thrown open. Formal reunification followed in 1990. Great problems remain to reconcile the eastern *Länder* with a western way of life. But Germany is restored as one of the pillars of the new Europe.

The ethnic mixture of Germany is diverse, even within the Germanic stock, with the result that regional feeling is still very strong. The traditionally German population, tall, fair-haired and blue-eyed, is found mainly in the north. Slav and other populations have long been resident in the east and centre; some Slav-speakers are still to be found in east Germany. The people of the Rhineland include many settlers from the Low Countries and France and there are more recent immigrants who have arrived as 'guest workers', economic refugees and asylum seekers from all over the world. Differences in temperament are still evident among the German population. The Bavarians are noted for their love of pleasure, their neighbours the Schwabians for their reserve and thrift. The Rhinelanders are much more carefree and open than the northern Germans, who tend towards dourness. But these are no more than stereotypes, and exceptions abound. Everywhere, the traditional German values of industry, organization and loyalty are still widely respected.

Since the late nineteenth century the history of Germany and its people has had an overpowering influence on the fortunes of all other European states. Following the recent reunification of east and west Germany, there is little doubt that Germany will be the dominant influence on Europe for many years to come.

See: Avars, Alamanni, Bavarians, Burgundians, Celts, Franks, Frisians, Germans, Goths, Jutes, Lombards, Romans, Saxons, Slavs, Suevi, Thuringians, Vikings

Greece
Elliniki Dimokratia

The Land: Greece and the Aegean islands are part of the limestone mass of the Balkans. Mainland Greece is essentially a peninsula from which several smaller peninsulas project, a mountainous land of steep cliffs, narrow valleys and barren rock, heavily eroded and now largely unproductive. Less than 20% is cultivable land, so that most of the country is very sparsely populated. Most of the population now lives in the lowland areas around Salonica and Athens and there has always been a tendency for the upland peoples to move to the richer lowland in search of a living. The influence of the sea upon Greece and the Greeks has always been profound. Greeks have taken to the water as traders and sailors and in the last resort, as immigrants. Land communications, by contrast, are poor, leading to isolation of many communities.

The Language: Modern Greek is very different from the Greek of Classical times. It is derived from the Byzantine Greek of the period from the sixth to the fifteenth century AD, with Turkish, Italian and French influences. After Greek independence in 1821, the language was revised after the long Turkish occupation and many earlier words were revived. Its alphabet is still based on that of the ancient Greeks.

The Name: The modern name 'Greece' is taken from the Latin word *Graecia*, which was the name used by the Romans for the land called *Hellas*, 'land of the Hellenes' by its own people.

Early Stone Age people occupied at least parts of Greece from around 50,000 BC, and remains have been recovered from both caves and open settlements. Hunter-gathering and fishing had a long history before the first farming communities arrived after 6500 BC, probably from Asia Minor across the Hellespont. These early farmers grew not only grain, but also olives and vines, and raised both sheep and goats. From 3000 BC onward advanced

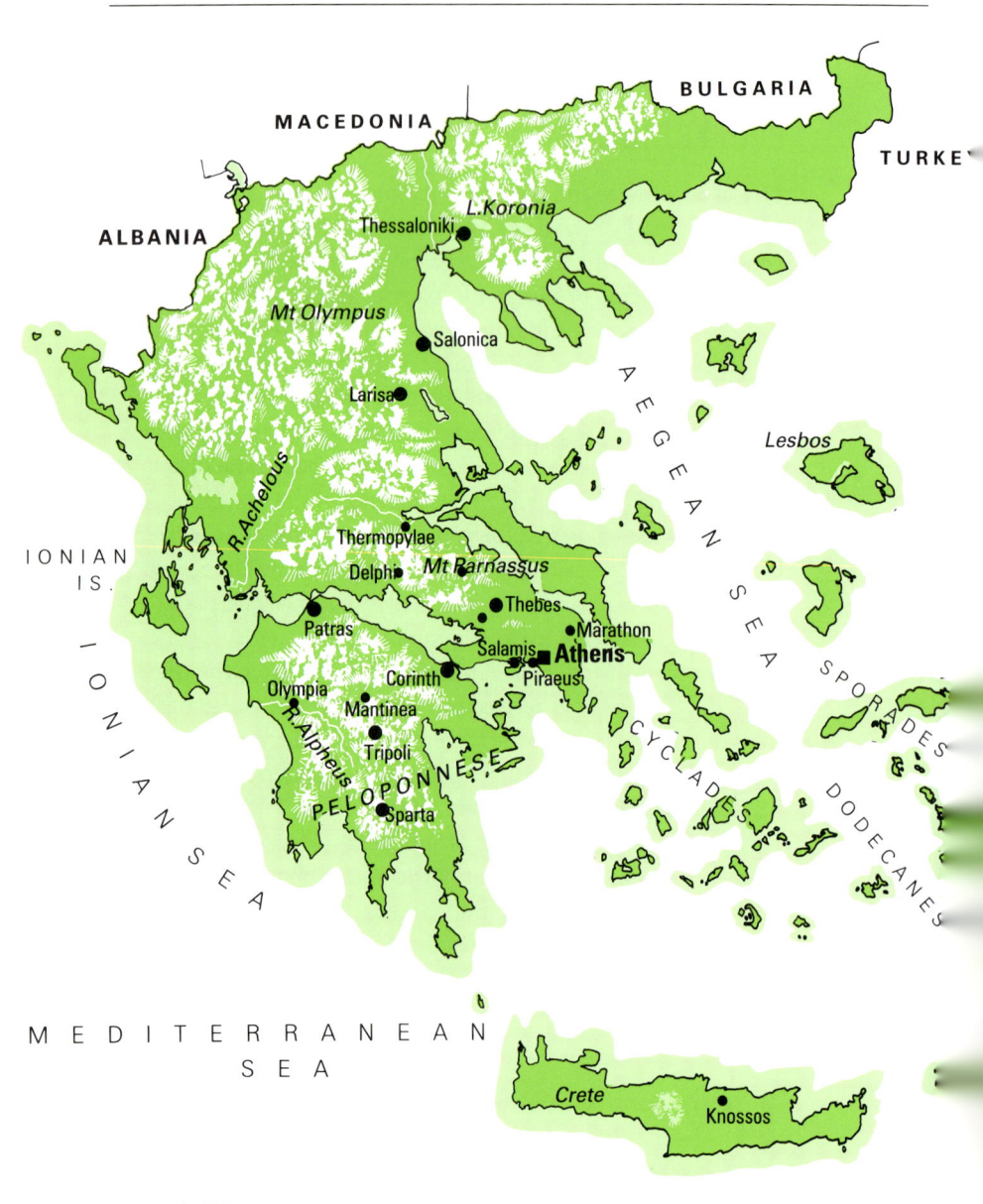

The Cretans and Greeks provide the earliest written evidence of European civilization, a civilization which stretches back some 4000 years. By the fifth and sixth centuries BC Greek artists, writers and philosophers were producing works which had an enormous influence on the development of the whole of western civilization. Athens, Corinth and Sparta were all powerful mainland city states but cultures moved onto the Aegean islands and later onto the mainland. About 2600 BC an influx of peoples entered northern Greece from Asia Minor and was followed by another from the north before 2000. In the meantime, the brilliant Minoan civilization had come into being on the island of Crete and left its mark on mainland Greece. This is often seen as the first of the great European civilizations. It was followed by the culture of the Mycenaeans, based on many small chiefdoms committed to trade and warfare as a means of accumulating wealth. The Mycenaeans flourished from 1600 to 1150 BC and are seen as the ancestors of the Greeks of Classical times. They spoke an early form of the Greek language. Before 1100 BC there was another invasion from the north, probably of northern Balkan tribes, and this ushered in the so-called Dark Ages of Greece, actually an important formative period. By 850 BC, the origins of the Greek city state were visible and this political and communal organization was later carried by Greek settlers to Asia Minor, Italy and other parts of the Mediterranean. By the late sixth century BC, the main outline of Classical Greece had taken shape. The great city-states continued to dominate the eastern Mediterranean until Philip II invaded from Macedonia. His son was Alexander the Great, whose empire extended for a time to the borders of India. By 171 BC Rome was expanding her empire into the Balkans. In 148, Macedonia became a Roman province and in 146 the sack of Corinth by a Roman general marked the end of Greek independence.

After the magnificent achievements of the Classical Age, Greece under the Romans after 150 BC, resembles a long, slow afternoon. Although politically unimportant as a Roman province, Greece, and more particularly Athens, retained her cultural significance as a centre of culture and education. Young Romans of good family were sent to Athens to learn it was in the cities of Ionia, on the coastland of modern Turkey, that many of the most famous works were created. The Romans admired the Greeks' achievements and way of life and in the western provinces, Greek culture was accepted as an ideal. When the western Roman empire declined, Greek learning was preserved in the eastern court at Constantinople.

good Greek, read the literature and sit at the feet of Greek philosophers. The history of Roman Greece was uneventful in the first two centuries AD, though the admiration of Greek culture felt by such differing emperors as Nero and Hadrian kept the fame and achievement of Greece alive. Invasion by the Goths after the middle of the third century was the first sign of turbulence to come, but for the greater part Greece suffered little from the disruption of the period of migrations which began to destroy the Roman empire. Very much more significant for later Greece was the foundation by Constantine I of his new capital of Constantinople on the Bosphorus in 324, on the site of the old Greek city of Byzantium. The new city was to serve as the focus of the eastern Roman empire, the richest part of the Roman domains, until its final conquest by the Turks in 1453.

During the centuries of Byzantine rule, Greece was economically quite sound. She took an active part in the commerce of the eastern Mediterranean and possessed industries of her own (for example, silk making at Corinth and Thebes). But from the sixth century she was increasingly attacked by Slavs and Bulgars from the north, and later by the Normans from Italy. In 1204 Crusaders from the west captured Constantinople and Greece was divided between the Byzantines and the western invaders. Large areas fell under Frankish domination in the thirteenth century and Venice retained a strong influence in those areas which offered commercial advantage. But the worst threat came from the westward march of the Turks after their great victory over the Byzantines at Manzikert in 1071. By 1400 it was clear that they would continue their advance into Europe, and Greece lay immediately in their path.

Even before the Turkish conquest, the condition of the Greeks and their land was critical. From 1200 onward the land had been devastated and its population reduced by Slav invasions from the north, by banditry and piracy, and by internal crises in Greece itself. Matters did not improve under Turkish domination. The long wars which the Turkish empire pursued with Venice and with the Slavs simply increased the insecurity of the Greeks, while large scale emigration and deportation to Asia Minor and the Aegean, along with both forced and voluntary conversion to the Islamic faith, threatened their very existence as a separate nation. Kidnapping and sale of prisoners into slavery had been a common feature of Greek life under the Byzantines. At the time of the Turkish conquest, untold thousands were taken and sold from the Peloponnese, Rhodes and Cyprus. Many passed through the international slave markets or ended up as rowers in Turkish and Venetian ships. Others were forced to settle on the land in poorly populated areas. Piracy by sea flourished around Greece under the Turks. These pirates, Christian as well as Turkish, could depopulate whole areas of countryside or entire islands. The hinterland of Athens was almost deserted for three years after one pirate raid in 1688.

The Turkish conquest of Greece had an impact on European cultural history which can scarcely have been foreseen. Byzantine scholars had preserved and transmitted the learning and literature of Classical Greece over the previous thousand years. Many now fled to Italy and elsewhere, taking that Greek tradition with them, together with books and works of art. The influence of this Greek dispersal on the Renaissance of Classical civilization, first in Italy and then in the rest of Europe, was immense.

In the late eighteenth century, the Turkish administration in Greece was becoming increasingly corrupt and lethargic while at the same time new revolutionary ideas were flowing from Europe. The French Revolution gave stimulus to a movement for independence and the armed struggle began in 1821 with a revolt in the Peloponnese. The Turks, who grossly underestimated the determination and courage of the Greeks, were almost cleared from the area. Support for the Greek cause grew in Europe, greatly aided by the influence of Lord Byron (who died in Greece in 1824) and other admirers of Greek culture. But the Turks mounted a counter-offensive and recovered much of the ground they had lost. Foreign help was needed to continue the struggle and this was forthcoming from Britain, France and Russia. From 1827 to 1829, warfare punctuated by complex diplomacy finally forced the Turkish Sultan to accept terms, the decisive blow being struck in the naval battle of Navarino in October 1827, when the Turkish and Egyptian fleets were destroyed by the combined fleet of the great powers. Otho, a young prince of Bavaria was given the throne and Greece emerged as an independent kingdom. Its boundaries were still ill-defined and they were not to be settled for several years. Athens, then little more than a large village, became the capital. Crete, however, remained under Turkish rule and was held by Turkey until 1898, finally achieving union with Greece in 1912.

The early years of the new kingdom were far from placid. There were outbreaks of violence and widespread resentment of the Bavarians at the young king's court. In 1843 a revolutionary movement demanded a constitution and the removal of the Bavarians. In 1862 a further revolt removed the king altogether and replaced him with the young heir to the Danish throne, who was to reign until 1913. Throughout these disturbed times, Greece remained a poor country, confronted by her old enemy Turkey and still seeking to enlarge her territory in the middle Balkans. War with Turkey broke out in 1897 and again the great powers had to come to the aid of Greece. When the king was assassinated in 1913, the state finances were in so appalling a condition that they had to be regulated by an international commission.

At first neutral in the European war which erupted in 1914, Greece was drawn into the conflict against Germany and her allies in 1917. Far more dangerous, however, was the old enmity with Turkey. This came to a head in 1921, when a Greek army invaded Turkey and came within 60 miles of Ankara before being defeated and forced to turn back. The Turks then counter-attacked, taking Smyrna in September 1922 and massacring many of its inhabitants. This disaster cast a long shadow over Greece for nearly twenty years. It was followed by the exchange of Greek and Turkish populations, under which many Greeks returned from Asia Minor. The population of Greece increased by 20% without any addition of territory or other resources. After this prolonged crisis the interval for recovery before World War II was brief.

Fascist Italy planned to conquer the Balkans as part of the wider strategy of domination in the Mediterranean. In September 1940, Mussolini's army invaded Greece from Albania, but then made slow progress against determined Greek resistance. Hitler sent German forces to assist the Italians early in 1941 and by June these had most of Greece and Crete under their control. Much of the mountainous areas of Greece, however, was not occupied and paid for independence with severe starvation over the next three years. Successive Greek governments collaborated with the invaders, but the resistance of the Greek people was strong and left-wing political aims were developed that were to be pursued in post-war Greece.

Although German troops left the mainland in October 1944, Greece was so shattered by the war that she was heavily dependent on external aid for years to come. The immediate post-war years were a time of great hardship. Civil strife broke out in 1946 and continued for two years, creating much bitterness. Recovery after the civil war was slow and soon other problems intruded, especially that of the future of Cyprus, where a Greek majority live in uneasy juxtaposition with a Turkish minority. Cyprus was under the control of the British and when Greece pressed for it to be released, it touched on the raw nerve of relations with Turkey. The crisis in Cyprus came to a head in 1956 and dragged on for more than two years before a diplomatic solution was reached. The troubled island again erupted in 1973, when Turkey invaded and seized the northern part of the land. Cyprus was effectively partitioned between the Greek and Turkish communities, a situation which still prevails.

Greece, meanwhile, had experienced a military coup d'état in 1967 (the Revolt of the Colonels) and remained under right-wing rule for six years. The monarchy was abolished and a republic proclaimed in 1973. But later that same year, the military government was overthrown and democracy, but not the monarchy, was restored. Serious economic problems continue to plague Greece and they have not been diminished by membership of the EEC. The countryside is being increasingly depopulated as more and more people seek employment in and near Athens. Many others leave Greece altogether, for other parts of Europe and the USA. Even the rise of mass tourism in the past twenty years has created as many problems as it has alleviated, since it is subject to severe fluctuation as other resources wax and wane.

Modern Greeks live in the countryside and in many of the cities of Classical Greece. Although for four hundred years Greece was part of the Turkish world of the Ottoman empire, many Greeks today can claim direct descent from the classical age.

See: Greeks, Thracians, Turks

Holland
Koninkrijk der Nederlanden

The Land: The kingdom of Holland, known to its own people as The Netherlands (Holland, properly speaking, refers to only one of the Dutch provinces), occupies the flat, low-lying country both to the north and south of the delta formed as the rivers Rhine and Meuse flow into the North Sea. Always Holland has had to struggle against the sea, first to keep the half-submerged land from flood and from erosion, and then to reclaim extra territory from the shallow seas by means of gigantic drainage and dam-works called 'polders'. And this unending fight against nature has formed a country with many advantages: a rich agricultural land in a temperate climate, a network of good communications particularly by water and a favourable position for trade which a seafaring people were eager to exploit.

The Language: Dutch (which is derived from the same word as the German *Deutsch*) is a West Germanic language related to the two languages Flemish and Frisian, spoken respectively in the south and the north of the Netherlands. Modern Dutch was slow in developing, being subject until the seventeenth century to many regional variations both in the spoken and the written language. It required a conscious effort of scholarship to make the language standard, and the spelling was still being simplified as late as 1946.

The Name: Holland means 'Hollow Land'. *Nederlanden*, the Dutch name, means 'Low Lands'—both referring to their flat, often flooded lands.

The historical region known as the Netherlands, or Low Countries, included not only Holland but also the present-day countries of Belgium and Luxembourg. Remains of hunter-gatherer communities have been found scattered throughout this area, and these ancient peoples were displaced by Neolithic immigrants from central Europe who introduced agriculture after 4500 BC. The Celtic invasion, around 600 BC, seems to have stopped at the Rhine. The parts of Holland north of the Rhine were occupied by Saxon tribes—the Frisii and the Batavi. In the age of Roman conquests, the empire also stopped at the Rhine, though the Romans did make expeditions beyond this line and briefly controlled the territory of the Frisii. The Saxon tribes remained the dominant people until the rise of the Frankish empire. After the death of the Frankish emperor Charlemagne in 814, Flanders (western Belgium) formed part of northern France, while the rest of the Low Countries passed into German hands.

Before the late Middle Ages, the area covered by Holland, Belgium and Luxembourg was not referred to by any one name, nor did it form any kind of political or cultural unity. The term 'Netherlands' (*Niederlande, Pays-Bas, Lage Landen*) was applied to the whole region about the mouths of the Rhine, Meuse and Scheldt, the lower Rhineland and Westphalia east of the Rhine. Later, the name was given to that area adjoining the North Sea on both sides of the Rhine which was subject to Hapsburg rule. The borders of this region did not correspond with those of either modern Holland or Belgium, neither of which yet existed as states or territories.

The people of Holland were from the early Middle Ages extremely successful traders. Frisians in the north transported goods by sea to Britain and to the Baltic lands and the larger cities became rich and properous. In the free cities, craftsmen and merchants formed powerful guilds and although there were minor wars between rival cities, these did not unduly interfere with successful commerce. In 1384 the whole region came under the rule of the Dukes of Burgundy. Philip the Good of Burgundy (1396–1467), was an effective and ambitious ruler whose courtly culture rivalled that of the French kings. The Netherlands under Burgundian rule became part of a kingdom which might have stretched from the North Sea to Burgundy itself, as some of its leaders dreamed. Instead, the Netherlands passed by marriage into the possession of the Austrian Hapsburgs in the late fifteenth century. Lying at the far edge of the Hapsburg empire, the Netherlands retained a degree of local independence and the cities continued to prosper.

In the sixteenth century, two historical developments began to trouble the prosperous life of the Netherlands. First, the attempt of the Hapsburg Emperor Charles V to organize and to unify his large, sprawling empire led to a tightening of imperial control on the Netherlands. Then the religious upheavals of the Reformation caused an enmity between the Catholic emperor and the people of the Netherlands who, especially in the north of the region, had in general gone over to the new doctrines of the Protestant reformers. And when Philip II, king of Spain and completely identified with the ideal of Spanish Catholicism, succeeded his father Charles in 1556, the rift between monarch and citizens in the Netherlands became very serious. Philip imposed the Catholic Inquisition and a Spanish standing army upon the Netherlands, both of which caused horror and indignation in a people traditionally used to a large degree of freedom.

William the Silent, prince of Orange, took up the cause of that traditional liberty and began the long struggle against Spanish rule. In 1568 the Dutch came out in open revolt against their Spanish king and this rebellion was followed by others in 1576. The resultant struggle went on for nearly eighty years, but in 1648 the independent Dutch republic was finally created. Calvinists from the southern provinces (which remained with Spain) fled to the north to escape persecution and contributed to the astonishing growth of Amsterdam in the early seventeenth century. Trade was not confined to Europe. The Dutch East India Company established trading posts (and ultimately colonies) in the Far East and Dutch sea power became the most formidable in Europe. The economic expansion of the Dutch republic followed into the eighteenth century, creating for Holland a strong political position. Out of this success there was born a distinctive Dutch art, in which Rembrandt, Hals, Vermeer and Steen are only the best known names in a large company. The skills of Dutch hydraulic engineers were also perfected in the seventeenth century, as major schemes of land reclamation were carried out. The further development of these in later times was to add large areas to Holland's land surface, especially in the area of the Zuyder Zee.

The later seventeenth century saw major changes to the Dutch Netherlands. The Protestant Republic took sides with English Protestants who were resisting their Catholic King James II and a Dutch Duke, William III of Orange, accepted the English throne in 1689. There were, however, trade wars with both England and France and, as competition in western Europe became tighter, there was growing economic strain. Those who had created the wealth of earlier days withdrew to enjoy their estates and

More than two-thirds of the land area of Holland lies below sea level and was once part of the sea bed. Reclaimed by ingenious drainage and engineering schemes, it is now productive agricultural land, the polders. The only uplands lie in the south. Saxons, Franks and Frisians are the main ancestors of the Dutch people, the Frisians having lived on the marshy coastlands and islands since prehistoric times.

government stagnated. Even before the Netherlands were engulfed in the tide of revolution from 1789 onward, there were signs of dissatisfaction and disorder. The French Revolution accelerated the transformation of the Low Countries, especially in the south, where the provinces were annexed by France in 1785. Napoleon invaded the Dutch Republic in 1795 but it was not annexed until 1810, so that there was little time for the modernization of the social order according to the ideas of Napoleon.

After Napoleon's defeat both the southern and northern Netherlands were brought together in a kingdom of the United Netherlands, but after only fifteen years the new state of Belgium broke away. The small state of Holland continued as a constitutional monarchy until 1914, still economically strong and stable but with very limited military strength.

Holland remained neutral in 1914–18 and was little affected economically until late in the war though the country was occupied for four years. During World War II the population resisted strongly and suffered severely in the years 1940–45. Holland lost a third of its gross national product and the people endured immense hardship, especially in the 'hunger winter' of 1944–5. Almost all the Jewish population (90,000 people) were deported.

Holland enjoyed the growth of prosperity in Europe after 1960 and was a founder member of the EEC.

The people of the Netherlands are naturally mixed in origin, but there is a recognizable core of original stock. The basis of the Dutch population is composed of the Germanic peoples, Frisians, Saxons, Franks and others. But there has been much immigration from the later Middle Ages by Jews, French Huguenots, Portuguese, Swiss and Austrians. In modern times, and especially since 1950, many immigrants have been received from former Dutch possessions in Indonesia. The record of integrating these new arrivals in Holland has been impressive. As a whole, the population is more or less equally divided between Roman Catholics and Protestants, though the proportion of those with no religious allegiance is high.

See: Franks, Frisians, Germans, Romans, Saxons, Vikings

Hungary

Magyar Köztársaság

The Land: Hungary, a landlocked country in the middle of Europe, spreads across the wide basins of the Danube and Tisza. Hemmed in to north and west by the Carpathians and the Alps, the land falls away eastwards towards the large open spaces of the Hungarian plains. The climate is varied, but inclined to extremes of summer heat and bitter winter cold. In winter even the major rivers freeze very frequently and hinder navigation. Before the bridge across the Danube was built in 1848, the cities of Buda and Pest were usually cut off from each other for weeks at a time in mid-winter.

The Language: Hungarian, a member of the small and isolated Finno-Ugric group of languages, was brought with the Magyar invaders in the ninth century. Although the vocabulary includes many words of Bulgar-Turkish origin, Hungarian is not related to the language of any of the surrounding peoples. It is related to Finnish and Estonian, but today these two branches of Finno-Ugric are not mutually intelligible.

The Name: 'Hungary' (or similar variants) is used only by foreigners. The inhabitants call themselves Magyars, taking their name, and also the names for their country and language, from their ancestral Magyar peoples.

Of all the countries of Europe, Hungary has the strongest claim to recognition as a nation-state. The population of this small country on the middle Danube is remarkably homogeneous: ethnic minorities exist but not in significant numbers. The identification of the Hungarian people with the land they inhabit is as close as it can be.

The first hunter-gatherers moved from the east, attracted by the good lands of the Danube valley. Farming communities were established in Hungary between 6000 and 5000 BC, migrating there from the northern Balkans or Asia Minor. Later prehistoric communities flowed along the

Danube corridor, bringing cultural influences from the Aegean and Black Sea. But peoples also moved into the land from the west, especially the Celts from the third century BC. To the north of the Danube, Germanic groups (including the Quadi and Marcomanni) were settled by the first century BC. Roman armies moved into this region early in the first century AD and conquered the local tribes. The territory was then absorbed into the Roman province of Pannonia. When Roman power waned in the early fifth century, several migrating peoples moved to the middle Danube area including the Goths, Gepids, Rugii and later the Huns and Lombards. This produced a very mixed culture which survived until the Magyar invasion at the end of the ninth century.

The Magyar tribes who were the ancestors of modern Hungarians came from the east and rapidly spread over the Danube plain, quickly subduing the mainly Slav population that lived there. In the tenth century they were converted to Christianity. At first they wavered between the Eastern Orthodox and the Western or Roman forms of Christianity, but King Stephen, who had established a unified Hungarian kingdom by AD 1000, ensured the triumph of Western Christianity.

For the next six centuries, the state of Hungary was one of the most secure in central Europe, though its bounds altered over this period, reflecting changing relations with neighbouring peoples. The Magyars dominated the Slovaks, northern Croatians and the groups settled in western Transylvania. But the Magyars, themselves originally invaders from the east, now stood in the path of further waves of westward migration and conquest. Eventually they fell victim to Turkish invasion early in the sixteenth century.

After taking the stronghold of Belgrade in 1521, the Turks swept northward, defeating the Hungarian army and killing the king, occupying Buda and thrusting west as far as Vienna. Austria was able to hold them back on the Bakony hills and Hungarian resistance remained alive in the east of the country throughout a hundred and fifty years of Turkish rule.

Hungary, once part of the Roman province of Pannonia, lies in the wide valleys of the Danube and Tisza rivers, with the high mountains of the Alps and the Carpathians forming natural barriers to the north and west. The first migrants probably came from the east, along the Danube valley, but Celts travelled there from the west and Germanic tribes arrived in the area from their northern homelands. The Magyars, who gave their name to the modern country, were Finno-Ugric people from around the Upper Volga River, relations of Finns and Estonians. They came first as fierce, horseback raiders, taking what they could by force and striking west as far as the Rhine before founding a permanent kingdom on the Danube plain.

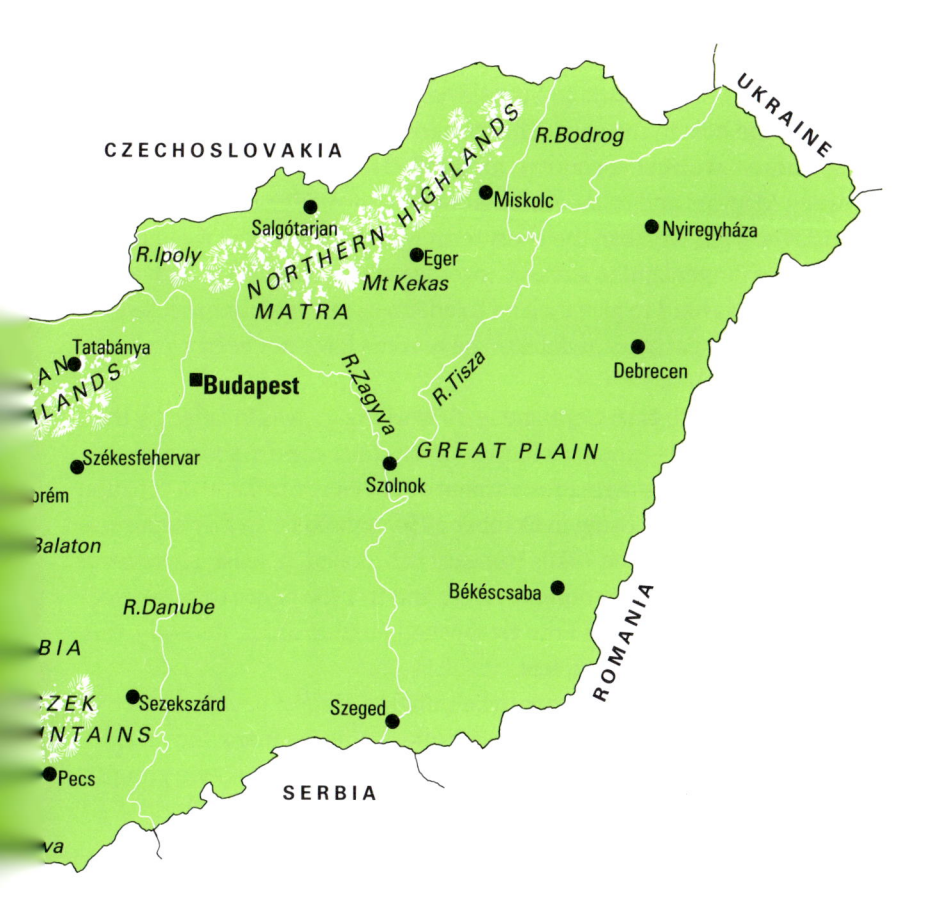

Turkish power passed its peak and a Turkish army was pushed back from Vienna in 1683. Three years later Buda was re-taken by the Hungarians. In 1718 Hungary was free of Turks but now came under rule from Austria.

In 1866 Austria was defeated in a catastrophic war with Prussia and the Hungarian state again became an independent political unit with its own government and capital at Budapest. But it remained part of the Austrian empire, the emperor including 'King of Hungary' among his titles.

At this time Hungary was roughly the same size as the mediaeval Magyar state, excluding Dalmatia and Bosnia to the south. But it was reduced by much more than half when The Austrian-Hungarian empire collapsed at the end of the First World War. Under the terms of the Trianon treaty, Hungary lost substantial areas of her territory: Transylvania passed to Romania, Slovakia to the new state of Czechoslovakia and Croatia to Yugoslavia, reducing Hungary to the Danube plain and the hills to the west. The western border of the new Hungary caused unrest within the country, for it failed to provide a clear separation between Magyars and other ethnic groups, particularly on the frontier with Yugoslavia. Even worse in the short term was the loss of the western province of Burgenland to Austria, together with a population of over 200,000. It was hard to give up land to enemies: much harder to lose it to allies who were partners in defeat. The borders have not been significantly altered since 1920.

After siding with Nazi Germany in 1939, Hungary was invaded by the Russian army in 1944 and passed into Communist control soon after the end of the War. But growing resentment at Soviet control and occupation burst forth in a major rising in October 1956, only to be swiftly suppressed by armed force. Since the 1970s Hungary has looked increasingly towards western Europe for her economic future and in 1986 began to break free from state Communism and the established Russian order. Recently, this divorce has been made complete.

Ethnically, Hungary is still overwhelmingly a Magyar country. Some 95% of the population are Magyar, the minorities being Germans, Slovaks, Romanians, Jews and Gypsies, though very many of the last two groups were killed by Nazi occupiers towards the end of the Second World War. See: Avars, Celts, Gepids, Germans, Goths, Huns, Lombards, Magyars, Romans, Slovaks

Iceland
Lydveldid Island

The Land: Iceland is a tableland, relatively young in geological terms and greatly altered by the erosive action of glaciers. It is still subject to volcanic activity, about 200 volcanoes being recorded on the island. It is also very rich in hot springs and vents which send out hot gases. Earthquakes are frequent but not usually very damaging. The central area is uninhabited and the bulk of the population lives in the south where the best farming land exists. The climate is sub-arctic, modified by the surrounding ocean. Rainfall is heavy, feeding many lakes and rivers. Almost three-quarters of the island has no continuous cover of vegetation.

The Language: Icelandic belongs to the North Germanic group of languages, being derived from Old Norse and still preserving many elements of that language. It is closely related to western Norwegian dialects.

The Name: The Old Norse word *iss*, meaning ice, gave the bleak, uninhabited island its name in the ninth century.

There is no evidence of human settlement in Iceland before the arrival of Norse and other settlers in the later ninth century. Tradition has it that Irish monks came and went shortly before AD 800. Sixty years later, a few Scandinavian seamen, driven by contrary winds, visited the island, and one of them, a Viking called Floki, tried to settle. A bitter winter drove him home with stories of this country he named Iceland. Despite these tales of hardship, others followed him. In 874 the Norwegian Ingolf Arnarson settled the first homestead at the place now called Reykjavik. The traditional tales are neither proved nor disproved by other forms of evidence but it is certain that about 870 groups from Norway in particular, but also from the adjacent Nordic lands and the Norse areas of Britain, began to colonize the island, the site of Reykjavik being an early choice for settlement. The early Norse settlers were able to develop an economy that was by no means poor. They found a land well suited to the grazing of cattle and sheep, and fish and marine mammals were abundant. Within half a century, the whole island was settled.

The *Landnamabok*, a Book of Settlement compiled around 1200, gave the full histories of the first 400 immigrant families, most of whom came from Norway, with some Swedes, and a good sprinkling of those from 'west of the sea'—that is, from Britain and Ireland. Among all nations, Iceland has the most detailed history of its people, from the first inhabitant to the latest baby born today.

From the tenth century until the mid thirteenth, the Icelanders were to all intents independent, having their own assembly and law courts. There was no single focus of power, the leading figures in the community being the *godar*, priest-chieftains who supervised groups of farmers and organized worship of the gods. Christianity first arrived late in the tenth century when the king of Norway, Olaf I, sent missionaries to Iceland. The country was quickly converted but the *godar* retained their political role, while some of them were ordained as priests and built churches. The people accepted Christianity, but they practised a rather tolerant faith which covered, but did not blot out, a deeper layer of pagan tradition.

In the twelfth century the writing of the great Icelandic sagas was begun, a major literary achievement of these settlers on the fringe of the European world and a priceless source of information on the exploration of the northern seas and life in the lands around them. The famous historical work, the *Heimskringla*, written by Snorri Sturluson in the thirteenth century, is still living history to the people of Iceland.

About 1250 a fierce struggle for power was conducted by the most powerful *godar*, possibly reflecting mounting pressure on resources. In the end, by 1264, the chieftains and their followers were induced to swear allegiance to the king of Norway, thus bringing Icelandic independence to a close until the twentieth century. But although the island was a possession of Norway, it was in practice separately governed and many of its traditions survived intact. Fishing became its staple economic activity, dried fish being exported to Norway and sold to English merchants. Later, Germans involved themselves in the trade. But settlers from Europe were very few in number, in the Middle Ages and later. Country and climate could not support many people and the population was always small.

Iceland

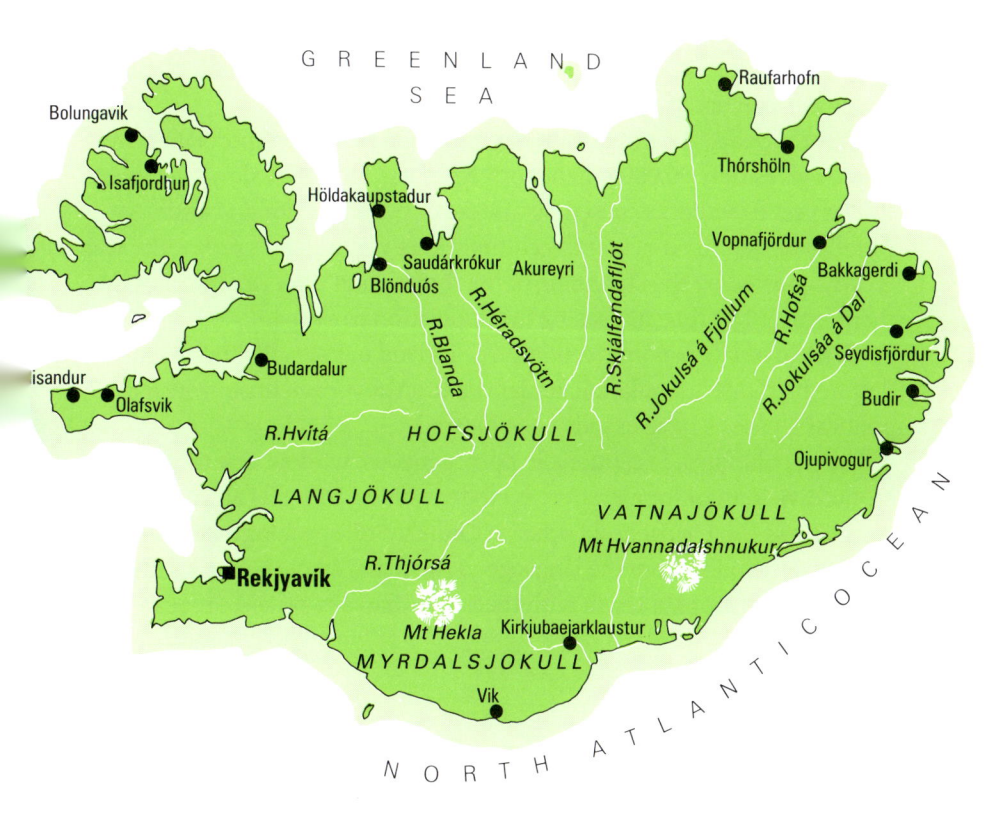

Iceland lies just south of the Arctic Circle, an island rising from the great underwater mountain range, the mid-Atlantic Ridge. Because of its strange mixture of active volcanoes, glaciers and hot springs, early Viking explorers called it the Land of Ice and Fire and it was not until 874 that a permanent settlement was established there. According to the Old Norse Sagas, it was Icelandic Vikings who, in the tenth century, crossed to Greenland and first discovered the existence of North America.

Famine and epidemics—such as the Black Death in 1402–4—sometimes reduced the numbers alarmingly. When Denmark absorbed the kingdom of Norway in the fourteenth century, it tightened its grip on Iceland and exercised a monopoly on its trade. The administration of the island, however, was left largely in Icelandic hands. So matters rested until the earlier nineteenth century, when an emerging nationalism on the island made itself felt, though at that stage having modest aims. In 1840, an Assembly (*Althing*) was restored, but it possessed little real power until 1874. In 1904, Iceland was given home rule and in 1944 the island declared itself a republic by breaking its constitutional ties with Denmark, then still under German occupation.

Over the years, the population has remained small: the thorough census of 1703 gives only 50,000 inhabitants. Numbers increased slowly but were still subject to setbacks caused by disease or by emigration to North America during the nineteenth century. However, Iceland's prosperity was greatly boosted by the stationing of first British and then American troops there from 1940, thus increasing the population to over 120,000. Since 1945, the overall economic condition of Iceland has steadily improved, despite high rates of inflation, under coalition governments in which the political divisions have usually been blurred.

The population is exceptionally homogeneous, without any racial or ethnic divisions, or immigration in modern times. Virtually all are formally members of the Evangelical Lutheran Church. Still speaking a language directly descended from the language of the majority of the early settlers, Icelanders are more in touch with their past than any other European nation.

See: Vikings

Ireland
Eire / Poblacht Na hEireann

The Land: The republic of Ireland occupies all but the north-eastern corner of the most westerly large island in the group generally known as the British Isles. The six counties of Ulster, in that north-eastern corner, still form part of Great Britain.

The island of Ireland consists of a central lowland, much eroded by glaciation and containing many lakes, pools and peat-bogs, surrounded by old mountain ranges close to the coast. The coastline is long, with many small bays and harbours. Many rocky islands lie offshore. The climate is very wet and mild.

The Language: Irish (Erse) is a Celtic language of ancient origin with a long and important literary tradition. The first official language of the state is Irish, English ranking second. Irish is closely related to Scots Gaelic and was widely spoken until the disastrous 1840s, after which time its use declined until active measures were taken in 1922 to introduce it to schools. Its use as a vernacular is now mainly confined to small areas in the west, but it is widely understood and its literature widely read.

The Name: Ireland is the anglicized version of Eire, in turn derived from the name of one of the three ancient goddesses of the land, Eriu or Erin.

Ireland was first colonized by Mesolithic hunter-gatherers from about 7000 BC onwards. The first agricultural communities developed from 3000 BC, their most striking visible monuments being great megalithic tombs in the north. Among later examples of these are the majestic passage graves of New Grange and Knowth. There is much debate on the extent of external influences on Ireland throughout its prehistory. Probably some immigration occurred after 2000 BC, bringing in new methods of metalworking and fresh traditions of burial. The late Bronze Age has yielded work of fine craftsmanship in gold and bronze.

Celtic people established themselves in Ireland, probably as a warrior nobility from about 600–500 BC. They brought with them a new language and a new social structure and Ireland has remained a recognizably Celtic community since that date, despite subsequent invasions and settlement by Vikings, Normans and the English. Although known to the Roman world as Hibernia, the island was not absorbed into the Roman empire nor was it more than superficially touched by Roman material civilization. By the later Roman period, the inhabitants of Ireland (probably especially northern Ireland) were called the Scotti. This people, whose life and culture was obscure, raided in the west and north of Britain and later settled in the north, in the land now named Scotland after them.

One of their raids early in the fifth century carried off a young boy from Britain. He spent six years in slavery in Ireland and later, after some years of wanderings, returned to the island, having in the meantime become a Christian. He spread the faith throughout the country. This was St Patrick, the most famous figure in Irish history, though born a Briton, not an Irishman. Even before Patrick's ministry there were Christians in Ireland, but Patrick's work of conversion greatly extended Christianity and laid the foundations for the most remarkable phase of Irish history, the age of Celtic monasticism and missionary activity. Before 600, Irish Christians became missionaries to the pagan peoples of northern Britain and western Europe. About 563, the Irishman Colum Cille, or Columba, founded the monastery of Iona off western Scotland and carried Celtic Christianity to much of the north. On the European mainland in the late sixth and early seventh centuries, the energetic and individualistic Columbanus was responsible for several monastic foundations, especially Bobbio in Italy and Luxeuil in Gaul, but came into conflict with Frankish rulers and the local bishops.

After the first flow of missionary zeal, the work of scholarship began. Irish monasteries became major centres of learning and art. Irish scholars carried their learning to the European mainland in the ninth century and Irish schools attracted churchmen and lay scholars from Britain and France. Superb manuscripts in the clear script known as Insular were imitated in Anglo-Saxon England and in western European monasteries, frequently with magnificently ornamented initial letters and page-margins. The greatest of the illuminated books of early Europe is the Irish manuscript known as the *Book of Kells*, dating from the late eighth or early ninth century. By the year 750, Ireland had become one of the great intellectual and artistic centres of Europe.

At the end of the eighth century, the island was drawn into a much more turbulent world. In 795 the first Viking attacks fell on Ireland and over the next half-century these invaders consolidated their hold, making

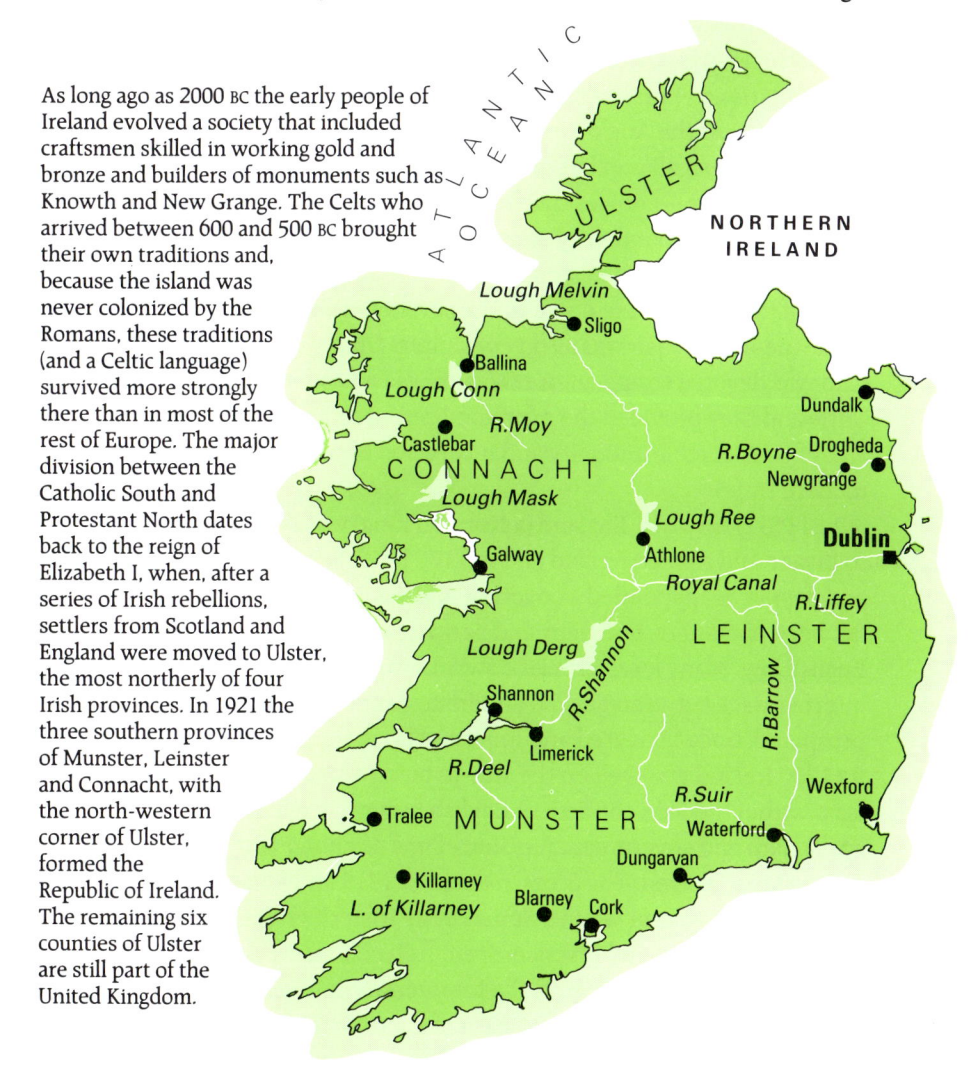

As long ago as 2000 BC the early people of Ireland evolved a society that included craftsmen skilled in working gold and bronze and builders of monuments such as Knowth and New Grange. The Celts who arrived between 600 and 500 BC brought their own traditions and, because the island was never colonized by the Romans, these traditions (and a Celtic language) survived more strongly there than in most of the rest of Europe. The major division between the Catholic South and Protestant North dates back to the reign of Elizabeth I, when, after a series of Irish rebellions, settlers from Scotland and England were moved to Ulster, the most northerly of four Irish provinces. In 1921 the three southern provinces of Munster, Leinster and Connacht, with the north-western corner of Ulster, formed the Republic of Ireland. The remaining six counties of Ulster are still part of the United Kingdom.

Dublin one of their major centres for commerce. By 920 the Vikings had taken control of Limerick and Waterford and their trading network covered the western seas. But they were not able to exert power over all of Ireland. In 1014 their defeat at Clontarf ended their domination of Ireland, though their hold on commerce was still strong. Irish society and institutions survived the Viking settlement largely intact. Provincial kings held on to their power, thus preventing the growth of any unified state or realm. High kings existed but had little power over lesser chieftains. This fragmentation of political power was a considerable drawback in the struggle against the Anglo-Normans from the tenth century onward.

Outside the small number of towns and trading-places, Irish society remained simple—families dwelling in individual settlements or *raths*, a few buildings surrounded by an earth bank and perhaps a palisade. More permanent settlements in stone,—*cashels*—also existed in great numbers, some of them still in use down to the seventeenth century. The economy of the mediaeval Irish was also very simple. Only a small proportion of the land was devoted to agriculture. Wealth was measured in numbers of cattle and they provided the main food resource. This economic system was of considerable antiquity and it survived in parts of Ireland down to modern times.

In 1155 Henry II of England (a Norman king) was authorized by the Pope to invade and subdue Ireland and in 1172 he claimed his rights over land and people. He appointed a governor and established an administration, a network of manors, boroughs and parishes on the English model, and English law. Many local Irish landowners were dispossessed, but intermarriage between English and Irish was not uncommon. Agriculture prospered, trade increased and imported luxuries arrived for the first time. By 1200 Ireland was well on the way to being a stable anglicized society at least within the Pale, the area of English influence, which had its own Parliament and governmental system. Only a century later this promising picture lay shattered. The Scots invaded in 1315 and caused widespread damage, disorder and famine. Some of the Irish chieftains still resisted the English settlement, and revenues from Ireland sharply declined. Warfare broke out in many localities in the fourteenth century and matters were made even worse by the Black Death of about 1350. Increasingly, English government became restricted to a defended area in the east around

Dublin. Elsewhere, the Anglo-Irish nobles preserved English authority, after a fashion, by using armed retinues.

By 1450 Ireland was thus divided between the English and Gaelic (Irish) worlds. The north and west were broadly Gaelic (Irish), fragmented into numerous minor lordships. The south and east were a relatively anglicized and stable part of the English domain. Gradually, after a series of Irish revolts, the soldiers of Elizabeth I forced Ireland to submit to English rule; English law and customs began to spread. A few years later, settlers from lowland Scotland and England were moved into Ulster, tenants and labourers being sent as well as landlords. This was the origin of the strong Protestant tradition in Northern Ireland, while in the south the native population remained Roman Catholic. The Reformation of the mid-sixteenth century was crucial for the further course of Irish history. Irish Catholics were quite prepared to accept a diminution of papal power, but the abolition of the Mass and other doctrinal changes were bitterly opposed. The arrival of English settlers not only brought loyal Protestants to Ireland but also marked the beginning of anglicization and the deepening of the divide between the prosperous Anglo-Irish landed and merchant classes and the Catholic majority, who were mostly poor and in many cases destitute.

The precarious peace in Ireland lasted for forty years. In 1641 the Irish Catholics rebelled and massacred many Protestants, beginning in Ulster. In 1649 Cromwell's army put down Irish resistance with appalling brutality, destroying the garrison at Drogheda and massacring many at Wexford, events which passed into Irish folk-memory. Further reinforcement of the Protestant landowning interest came when the English King James II, ejected from England, found refuge in Ireland, only to be soundly defeated at the Battle of the Boyne in 1690. Ireland was now irredeemably divided between Protestant and Catholic, between a foreign landholding class and a native peasant population. The French Revolution stimulated the rapid growth of radical republican ideas and rebellion in 1798 had to be promptly put down. Thereafter, British policy aimed at union between England and Ireland, which was achieved in 1800, though most of the Catholics remained resistant.

The great mass of the Irish people were largely unaffected by these developments. What did affect them was a 70% increase in population between 1790 and 1840, without any fundamental improvement to the economy of the land. By the 1840s, a third of the population lived largely on potatoes and when the crops failed in 1846–8 the countryside was gripped by a horrifying famine in which 800,000 died of starvation and malnutrition, while a further million or more emigrated, mostly to the USA. The population declined further after the famine and this allowed the growth of a peasant-proprietor class, generally conservative and nationalist in sentiment. That nationalism continued to grow in the late nineteenth century as political influence steadily passed to the Catholic majority, except in Ulster. The opportunity to strike at the established order came in the middle of the First World War.

The Easter Rising of 1916 in the centre of Dublin led to a determined Irish nationalism in which Sinn Fein ('Ourselves') played a leading role, demanding an Irish Republic independent of Britain. The immediate consequence was the Anglo-Irish war of 1919–21 in which the Irish Republican Army (IRA) led by Michael Collins fought a guerilla war against British troops and irregulars. In 1921 the twenty-six counties of southern Ireland became the Irish Free State, still within the British empire, a move which plunged southern Ireland into civil war and the north into sectarian anarchy. An uneasy peace was restored in 1923 and Northern Ireland passed under the control of the Unionist Party—firmly committed to British rule—until 1968, while the Irish Free State withdrew from the British empire and Commonwealth, remained neutral in the Second World War and eventually declared itself a republic in 1949. The northern provinces remained part of the United Kingdom under British rule but the nationalist dream of a united Ireland is still alive, fiercely resisted by the Protestant majority in the north.

The successive invaders of Ireland have been absorbed very successfully and the modern population is fairly homogenous, especially away from the larger towns. Immigration has been far less significant than emigration to Britain and, above all, to the USA. The population was virtually halved by the famine of the late 1840s and the subsequent migration to America. The movement to Britain has been over a longer timescale, but has been considerable, leaving large Irish communities in Glasgow, Liverpool, Birmingham and London.

See: Celts, Irish, Normans, Scotti, Vikings

Italy
Repubblica Italiana

The Land: The long spine of land which contains the peninsula of Italy and the island of Sicily reaches from the Alps in the north to not far short of Africa in the south. The central areas are mainly upland and mountainous but there are also extensive areas of plains and these are economically important, especially around the Po valley, Campania, Latium and Foggia. Strategically, Italy is ideally placed to dominate the Mediterranean and the peoples of Italy have often done so in her long history.

The Language: Italian as a vernacular language emerged from the twelfth century. There are many dialects, the south being very different from the north. Modern Italian is based on the dialect spoken around Florence. German (in the Alto Adige), Slovene (around Trieste), Greek and Albanian are spoken by minorities.

The Name: Italia was the Roman name for the peninsula.

Early hunting and foraging groups were active in Italy at least 250,000 years ago and from the late stages of the Ice Age, about 16,000 BC, many settlements of Palaeolithic humans have been found. After the final retreat of the ice about 14,000 years ago, more settled climatic conditions brought more immigrants to the peninsula and about 5000 BC the beginnings of agriculture are recorded. The use of metals in the Bronze Age, about 2000 BC, accelerated the clearance of the forests and settlement rapidly expanded over the next few centuries. Communications by sea were not difficult within the Mediterranean and contacts were established with neighbouring lands and the Mediterranean islands. The Aegean world, especially the Mycenaean culture of Greece, left its impact on Italy. Later, Greek colonial cities were founded in southern Italy and Sicily, some of them destined to become great cities in their own right (Syracuse, Messina, Naples). The native peoples of Italy, notably the Etruscans, also made dramatic advances in urban settlement, commerce and art after 600 BC. The rise of Rome at this time owed much to their influence and to that of the Greeks. Northern Italy was invaded and widely settled by the Celts in the fifth century BC.

The early history of Italy is largely the history of Rome, which was founded, according to tradition, in 753 BC. From the fifth century BC, Rome slowly extended her rule over the other tribes of the peninsula. At that time, Italy was occupied by many different peoples at many different stages of development, ranging from the tribal societies of the Celtic Gauls and Ligurians in the north to the advanced, urban cultures of the Etruscans in the centre and the Greeks in the south. In the mountains of the Appennines, pastoral communities followed ways of life that had been established for many centuries before the rise of Rome. This great diversity of culture continued under Roman rule. Certain regions, especially the fertile plain of the Po, rapidly adjusted to Roman administration and a strongly urban culture flourished there. But many areas were far less affected by the Roman way of life. The south, in particular, remained strongly Greek in culture and outlook and failed to gain much economic benefit from the Roman peace (the *Pax Romana*) which brought prosperity to many parts of Rome's great empire.

Rome herself was, of course, the dominating presence in Italy, though to survive materially, the city had to import much from outside, especially grain from Egypt. The history of the peninsula under Rome was uneventful and relatively calm: Rome's wars were fought elsewhere, enlarging the empire and protecting its borders. Generally, Italy was secure from external attack until the fifth century AD. Agriculture prospered in the more fertile regions and the richer families invested much of their wealth in developing their landed estates. Industrial development was far less significant but pottery was produced, metals were worked and marble cut

> When Venetia joined the kingdom of Italy in 1868, the country was united under a single government for the first time since the Ostrogoths overthrew the western Roman empire in 476. For most of the centuries between, Italy had been a kingdom of small states, subject to invasions and the rule of foreign powers.

Italy

A considerable area, stretching from Rome, through Umbria and Tuscany to Bologna, formed the Papal States under the control of the Church in Rome. Today, this is reduced to the independent state of Vatican City. The only other independent region is the tiny republic of San Marino.

and polished at the famous quarries of Carrara. But the unity of Italy depended on Roman genius for organization and civil administration and when the Roman empire began to disintegrate, the Italian homeland also became fragmented. The emperors had to spend more time with the armies in the outer provinces and Rome itself was no longer important as the imperial capital. In AD 330 the emperors' court moved to Constantinople to rule the remaining eastern empire, which continued to flourish for centuries.

From the early fifth century, Italy was a target for barbarian invasion, being still a rich land and the seat of imperial power. In 410, the Visigoths seized Rome briefly, sacked it and then moved on. The Vandals invaded from Africa in 455 and sacked the city. The Huns passed through the north but did not settle.

The first Germanic people to enter Italy in numbers and remain there were the Ostrogoths, who invaded from the north-east in 488 and founded a strong kingdom there. Their leader, Theoderic, had his chief stronghold at Ravenna, though his power extended southward to Rome and Naples. He admired and preserved much of what remained of Roman law and institutions but after his death in 526, the condition of Italy deteriorated rapidly. Justinian, the emperor of the surviving eastern Roman empire sent an army to reconquer Italy and a period of savage and devastating warfare between Goths and Byzantines followed. Not long afterwards, in 568, the Lombards invaded Italy from the north-east and quickly established themselves in the north, with two dependent duchies in the south, at Benevento and Spoleto. They remained the masters of Italy until after 700.

The pope persuaded the Franks to attack the Lombards and between 751 and 773 the Frankish kings Pepin, then Charlemagne overthrew the Lombards and handed control of their territories to the pope. Charlemagne could thus present himself as the protector of the papal states and claim authority over a large part of Italy. After his death, there followed an anarchic period of 150 years. Italy broke up into many small states, often at loggerheads with each other. The northern lands were attacked by the Magyars and others, Arabs raided the south and the power of the popes weakened. This time of chaos was ended by Otto I of Germany who entered Italy in 963 and took the title of Holy Roman Emperor. For a time, orderly government was restored, but it did not last. From the eleventh century to the middle of the thirteenth, the popes and a succession of German rulers struggled for dominance. Eventually, the popes prevailed, even against the superior strength of the German rulers, because they had the support of the many cities who resisted foreign rule.

From early in the eleventh century, groups of Normans gradually conquered southern Italy and Sicily, later producing a remarkable cosmopolitan culture, supported by rich and successful trade. Economic growth in the north was also marked in the eleventh and twelfth centuries and Genoa, Venice, Milan, Pavia and Florence all became leading commercial and political centres. These larger cities, seeking to extend their territories and protect their trade, developed into centralized city-states or communes, generally governed by rich merchants and landowning nobles. They frequently fought each other and engaged in complex diplomatic manoeuvres, plotting against the popes and against their German overlords. As the power of the German emperors weakened after 1250, so the city-states increased their influence, their territory and their wealth.

As wealth grew, so did the power of individuals or single families, such as the Visconti of Milan and later the Medici of Florence. Many cities came under the rule of despotic leaders as a result, though Venice and Florence retained their republican traditions. By the early fourteenth century, Venice was the dominant maritime trading city of Italy, controlling large areas of the eastern Mediterranean and trading as far away as China. Milan expanded her territory by acquiring the lands of several neighbouring cities. Further south, in Tuscany, Florence was the dominant force. Rome was less important, being frequently torn by civil war at this time, the nobles continually squabbling among themselves. Naples and Sicily were independent kingdoms and followed their own paths with little concern for what went on in the north.

By the middle of the fourteenth century, the peninsula could hardly have been more divided. Italian society was further devastated by the Black Death of 1348 and a number of famine years between 1340 and 1375. Venice, Florence, Genoa, Siena and Pisa were all severely affected by the plague. Possibly a third of the population of Italy died, though contemporaries thought more had perished.

A severe economic depression followed but after 1400 recovery was astonishing. It was greatly aided by banking and credit-finance (the cheque came into use in Pisa in the fourteenth century) which helped to expand trade and encouraged enterprise. The conditions were created in which scholarship and art could flourish. The rapid spread of printing greatly aided an upsurge of learning and carried it out of the monasteries into the cities and the academies of the secular world.

The critical investigations of these scholars—the humanists—provided an exciting new intellectual outlook which placed Man at the centre of nature. The rediscovery of Classical Greek and Roman culture and literature was hastened when Turks sacked Constantinople and many Greek scholars and churchmen fled to the west. The rediscovered culture contributed enormously to these developments, but there was much that was new. Very great achievements were made in the fields of painting, sculpture, architecture, science and philosophy. This Renaissance, or 'rebirth', of thought and learning reached a peak in Florence in the fifteenth century, though work of sublime quality was also carried out in almost every Italian city.

Then, in 1527, Rome was sacked by the Spaniards. Thousands of citizens were massacred and works of art were destroyed. The attack effectively marked the end of an astoundingly creative period. By then, however, the influence of the Renaissance had been felt in most other countries of western Europe.

After the splendours of the Renaissance city-states, Italy declined with startling suddenness. Once powerful states were eclipsed by invaders, especially from France and Spain and from the 1490s to the late eighteenth century, Italy was largely under foreign domination. Several Italian states developed their own political systems, among them the kingdom of Naples (ruled by the Spanish from 1503), the republic of Florence (under the control of the Medici family), the republic of Venice (governed by merchant families), the Duchy of Milan and the papal states.

France and Spain continued to fight for control of Italy during the sixteenth and seventeenth centuries, with devastating results for the Italian people. The sack of Rome in 1527 was only one episode in a long catalogue of destructive warfare in which the population of cities was greatly reduced and economic life shattered. The Spanish-dominated south fared better than the more independent city-states of the north but all areas were subject to disease and plague, which broke out again in 1576 and 1630. The cultural influence of Italy on her oppressors remained strong and most of the invaders, carrying away whatever art they could plunder, left Italy with the mark of her learning and culture.

In the eighteenth century, the dominant foreign influence in Italy was that of Austria. The Austrians occupied Naples in 1707 and Milan in 1713. Lombardy, too, came under Austrian control. Venice was now of minor political significance and the power of the papal states was much reduced. But Italy was not isolated from wider European affairs. Her place in history and her artistic achievements made the Grand Tour of Italy an essential part of the education of a young European gentleman.

After 1800, enthusiasm for nationalism was widespread in Europe, but the idea of an Italian nation covering the whole of the peninsula was slow to emerge in Italy. The Austrian rulers held the country firmly in check for as long as possible, but aspirations towards unification—the *Risorgimento*—were not to be denied. A brief revolution in 1830 was crushed but in 1848 a war of independence broke out in Sicily and spread to the mainland. Under the inspired patriotism of Guiseppe Mazzini the Italians gained several successes but the Austrians beat down the rebellious states with their superior military strength. The second phase of the struggle, now supported by the French, opened in 1859. The French soon withdrew but in 1860 Guiseppe Garibaldi invaded Sicily with an army of 1,200 men drawn from all over Italy (The Thousand). They quickly passed into southern Italy and took Naples. In March 1861, Garibaldi was able to proclaim Victor Emmanuel as 'King of Italy'. Rome, under papal control, and Venice, were still outside the kingdom but both were drawn in by 1870 and Rome became the capital of the whole country.

The later nineteenth century was a time of consolidation but Italy also joined in the search for colonial territory in Africa, briefly acquiring Ethiopia and later holding on to Tripolitania (Libya). In 1914, Italy was an ally of Germany and Austria but was not consulted about the declaration of war and remained neutral until 1915. When she entered the conflict, she joined France and Britain.

As in other countries of Europe, the immediate post-war years were politically disturbed. Fascism grew rapidly in the cities and soon spread to the countryside. A sequence of weak governments gave Mussolini his chance and in October 1922 he marched on Rome to found the first Fascist regime in Europe. In June 1940, Italy entered the Second World War on the side of Germany. The country was poorly prepared for a major war and most Italians were far from enthusiastic about a conflict with Britain and France. After a near disastrous invasion of Greece from Albania, Italian forces were mainly engaged in North Africa and in support of the German attack on Russia, in which they suffered massive casualties. When the Allies invaded Sicily in 1943 the Fascist party was rapidly ousted. Muşsolini was deposed and an armistice was agreed. In October 1943, liberated Italy declared war on Germany.

The country was now divided between the German-occupied north, where Mussolini was reinstated in charge of a puppet republic, and the Allied south. A very active resistance movement operated, with heavy losses, and there was also massive destruction in both the cities and the countryside, especially in the centre and the north.

In 1945, Italy and her economy lay in ruins. The overseas colonies were lost, but there was no great loss of territory in Europe, though Trieste was passed to Yugoslavia. The republic was reformed in 1948 and the monarchy abolished. Rapid economic growth followed, especially after 1956 in the industrial north. Italy was a founder-member of the European Community, brought into being by the Treaty of Rome in 1957, and derived great benefit from early membership. And, on the whole, the country continues to prosper despite the wide range of strong political opinion. Governments of the 1970s and 1980s tended to be coalitions, coming and going with startling frequency. But this has not prevented Italy from rising to a pre-eminent position in southern Europe. Divisions persist within the country, especially between the impoverished south and the industrial north. This has led to mass emigration to the northern cities and to the USA.

See: Burgundians, Etruscans, Franks, Gauls, Goths, Greeks, Ligurians, Lombards, Normans, Romans, Sabines, Samnites, Sicels, Vandals, Thuringians

Luxembourg
Grand-Duché de Luxembourg

The Land: The Grand Duchy of Luxembourg is the smallest sovereign state in Europe. To the north, bordering Belgium, are the foothills of the Ardennes while the south stretches towards the valleys of the rivers Saar and Mosel. The greater part of the population is centred in the city of Luxembourg (the only city of any size) and in the southern area of the duchy. The siting of the Secretariat of the European Parliament in Luxembourg, along with several other international organizations, has greatly stimulated the growth of the city as an international centre and has begun to alter the nature of its commercial and professional class. The countryside is still relatively unaffected by this influx, and agriculture is still very important to the state.

The Language: Although French and German have been official languages since 1830, most of the people converse in their own dialect, Letzeburgisch, given official status in 1939.

The Name: Luxembourg is derived from *Lucilinburhuc*, the name of an old fortification overlooking the river Alzette.

The territory that is now the Grand Duchy of Luxembourg formed part of the Roman province of Gallia Belgica and was later settled by the Franks and absorbed into the empire of Charlemagne. Luxembourg's political history began in 963, when Siegfried, the Count of the Ardennes, purchased the site of the old fortification of *Lucilinburhuc*. The territory expanded westward to the Moselle and Sauer rivers, and then included the valley of the river Clerve to the north.

In the late eleventh century, the title of Count of Luxembourg was assumed by the ruler of the little domain. Luxembourg passed to the house of Namur in the mid-twelfth century and its rulers enlarged the state by dynastic marriages. In 1308, the ruler of Luxembourg rose to high prominence, being elected Henry VII, Holy Roman Emperor. Henry's son John, who succeeded him and also became king of Bohemia, is still honoured as a national hero. Though blind, he died in the battle of Crecy in 1346, fighting against the English. His son, Charles, also became Holy Roman Emperor and raised the state to the rank of Duchy in 1354. Eventually, Luxembourg passed to the possession of Philip the Good of Burgundy in 1443 and then to the Hapsburgs in 1477.

Because of its position between the Netherlands, Germany and France, Luxembourg suffered much from the passage of rival armies in the sixteenth and seventeenth centuries. Briefly held by France in the late seventeenth century, the Duchy passed to Spain in 1697 and then to Austria in 1714. France again annexed Luxembourg in 1795, after a long siege of the city, and made it a department. But the Congress of Vienna in 1815 transferred Luxembourg from French control to William I of the Netherlands, having given the land the status of Grand Duchy.

This association with the House of Orange did not last long. In 1830 the Belgian revolution stirred up revolt in Luxembourg against William, and the embryonic Belgian government claimed the Grand Duchy as part of their new Belgium. A few years later, in 1839, much of Luxembourg did pass to Belgium, but the arrangement proved short-lived. A conference of the Great Powers in London in 1867 ruled that Luxembourg should be an independent state with guaranteed neutrality.

The vulnerability of the Grand Duchy to its powerful neighbours, however, could not be legislated away. At the outbreak of the First World War, German troops entered Luxembourg and remained in occupation throughout hostilities. Again in 1940, German forces invaded and remained until September 1944, during which time Hitler laid plans to incorporate the Grand Duchy into the Third Reich. After these years of troubles, Luxembourg became prosperous in the 1950s. The steel industry provided an important manufacturing base and the service side of the economy was enormously stimulated by a rapid growth in banking. Along with Holland and Belgium, Luxembourg gained, and still enjoys, great benefit from membership of the EC.

The people of Luxembourg have a strong sense of their political and cultural independence and are fairly homogeneous in their ethnic character, though foreign workers have arrived from southern Europe in recent years. The majority are Roman Catholic.

See: Belgae, Celts, Franks

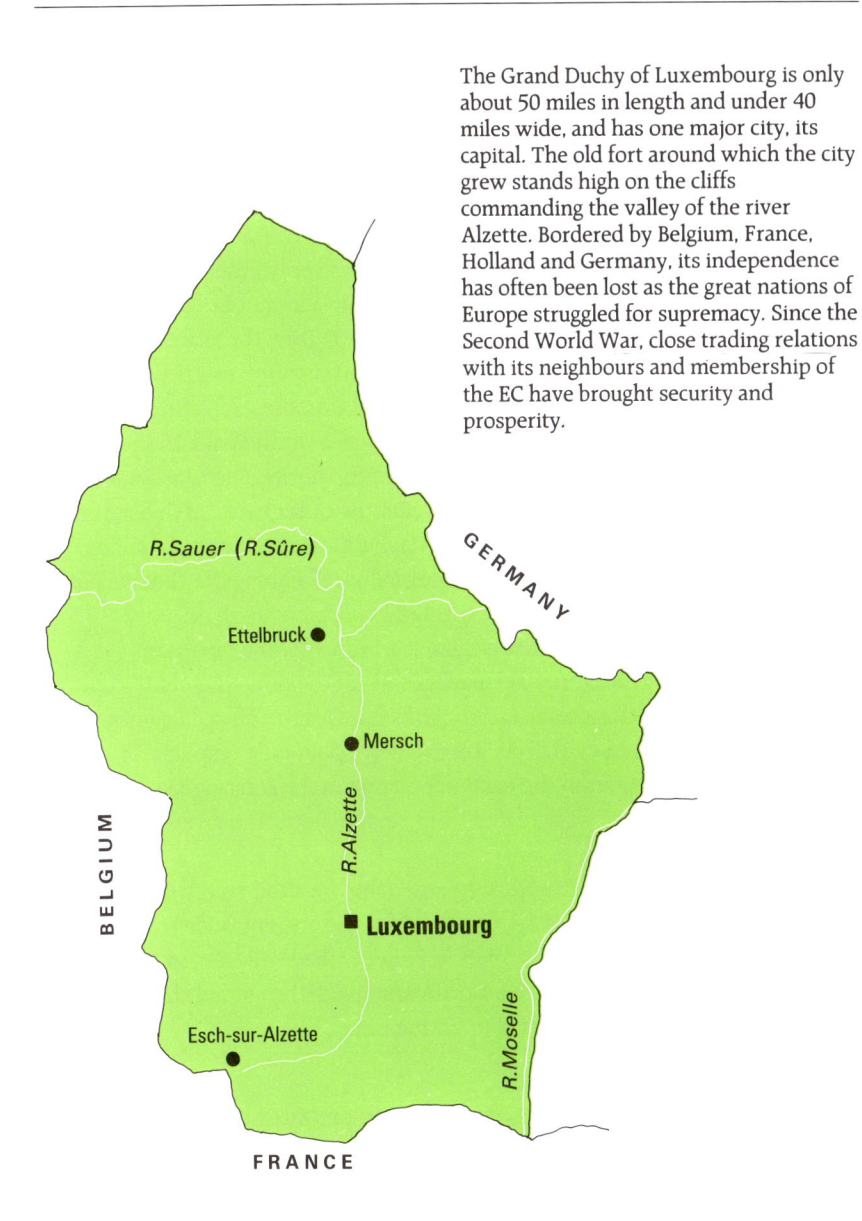

Luxembourg

The Grand Duchy of Luxembourg is only about 50 miles in length and under 40 miles wide, and has one major city, its capital. The old fort around which the city grew stands high on the cliffs commanding the valley of the river Alzette. Bordered by Belgium, France, Holland and Germany, its independence has often been lost as the great nations of Europe struggled for supremacy. Since the Second World War, close trading relations with its neighbours and membership of the EC have brought security and prosperity.

Norway

Kongeriket Norge

The Land: The land of Norway lies on the western side of the Scandinavian peninsula. Behind its deeply indented coastline is a fertile strip of land, then barren, mountainous tablelands, separated by deep, narrow valleys. During the last Ice Age the whole area was completely covered with ice, to a depth of over 1 kilometre. Norway extends well into the Arctic Circle and over the whole country winters are long and cold. In the far north, the sun never rises above the horizon between mid-November and late January. On the other hand, in midsummer there is almost continuous daylight. Off the coast, the Gulf Stream brings warmer water inshore, making the climate less harsh than might be expected in such northerly regions.

The Language: Norwegian is a branch of the northern Germanic family of languages. Until the mid nineteenth century one written language, the *Riksmal* was the official language, but several rural dialects were widely spoken. In response to pressure from the rural population, a spoken language, the *Landsmal*, was created from rural dialects and given official recognition.

The Name: The Norwegians' name for their country, *Norge*, means 'North Way', the name for the ancient trade route running from west of Oslo Fjord to the White Sea in the north. Another early name, Nordmannaland, the land of the northmen, was used in Viking times.

The land that is now Norway probably became inhabitable some 14,000 thousand years ago, when the forests had returned and the climate had warmed sufficiently to allow animals and settlers to move northwards. All evidence of pre-Ice Age habitation was destroyed by the scouring glaciers which covered the land, but the first archaeological evidence shows that people were living in coastal settlements at least 12,000 years ago. The first settlers were probably hunters and fishermen, but there is early evidence of agriculture on the west coast as far north as Trondelay.

These were Germanic people, related to the tribes of north Germany and to the people living in Denmark and Sweden at the same time. Only one sizeable early immigration of people of a different racial origin is known: a number of settlers seem to have arrived from the south and south-east, soon after 2000 BC, introducing a darker, shorter strain into the population, characteristics still seen in present-day inhabitants of the south coast.

Little is known about the lives and character of the people of Norway before about the fifth century AD. This was the time when the great migrations of people were taking place throughout Europe, but seem to have left the people of the northlands largely unaffected. From this time onwards, however, we know that boat-building skills were developed and, since many people depended wholly on the sea for their food, their seamanship and navigational skills were developing at the same time. Trade, too, was becoming established along the North Way and with the neighbouring Swedish kingdom.

Until the ninth century, Norway was divided among a number of small chiefdoms, dominated by warrior-lords similar to those of Denmark, Sweden and northern Germany. After 872 the independent warlords were gradually overcome by Harold I (the Fairhaired) from his base around the Oslo Fjord. In the next two centuries the kingdom became stronger. Christianity was firmly established towards the end of the tenth century, when Olaf Tryggvason was baptized in England. His successor, Olaf II, was recognized as a saint.

Everyone has heard of the Vikings, the Scandinavian raiders and explorers who invaded and harassed Europe between about 800 and 1000. Norwegians were among the first of the Viking raiders and for around 200 years contributed heavily to Viking raids and explorations in the Baltic, North Sea and Atlantic. Norwegian Vikings settled in Ireland, northern Britain, Iceland and Greenland, and through France to the Mediterranean. The people who came to be known as Normans in France and gave their name to Normandy, were Viking invaders. Many Scandinavian place names survive both in Normandy and the British Isles and Rollo, the Viking leader of the Nordic army which settled in Normandy may have

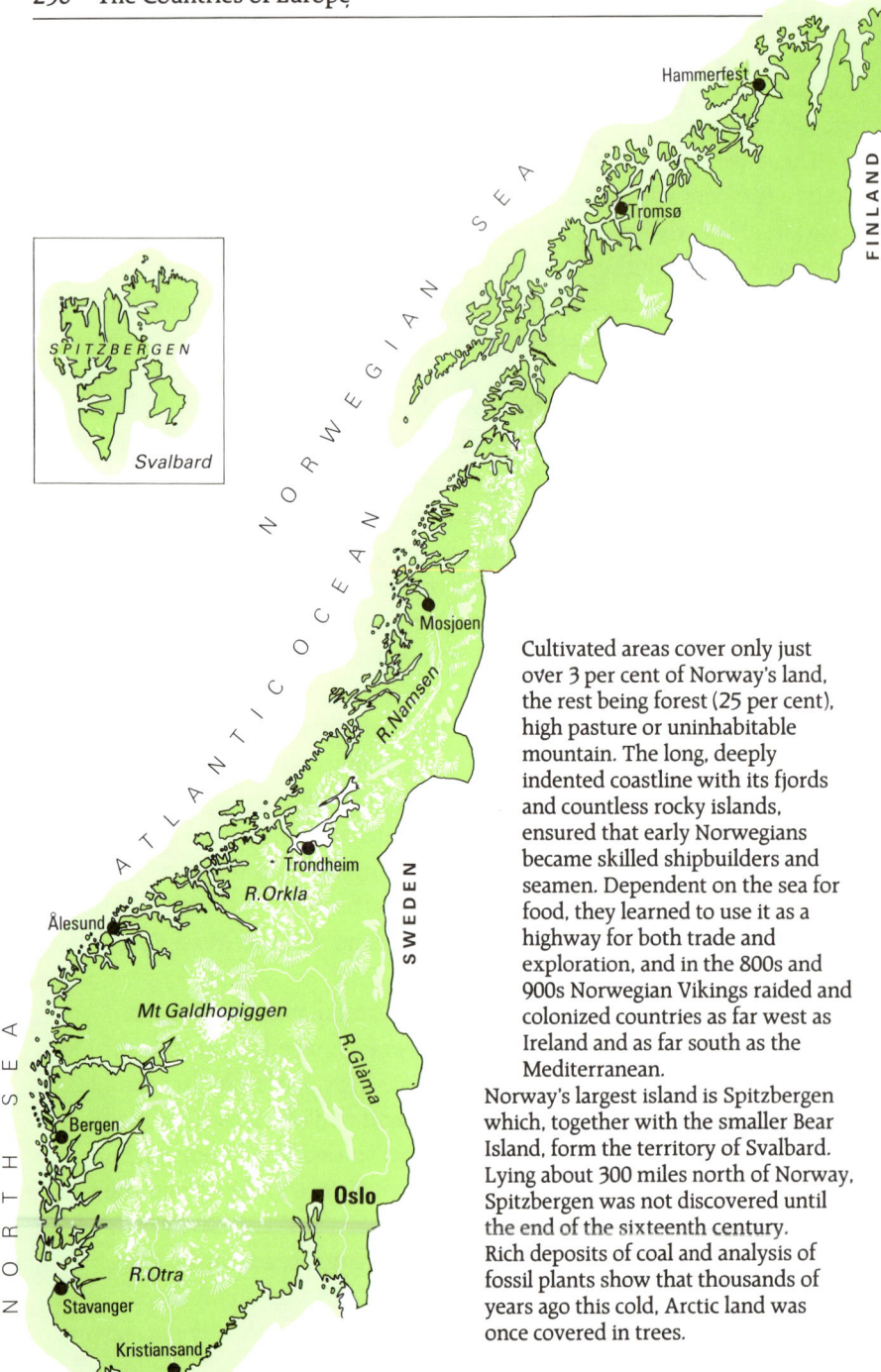

Cultivated areas cover only just over 3 per cent of Norway's land, the rest being forest (25 per cent), high pasture or uninhabitable mountain. The long, deeply indented coastline with its fjords and countless rocky islands, ensured that early Norwegians became skilled shipbuilders and seamen. Dependent on the sea for food, they learned to use it as a highway for both trade and exploration, and in the 800s and 900s Norwegian Vikings raided and colonized countries as far west as Ireland and as far south as the Mediterranean.

Norway's largest island is Spitzbergen which, together with the smaller Bear Island, form the territory of Svalbard. Lying about 300 miles north of Norway, Spitzbergen was not discovered until the end of the sixteenth century. Rich deposits of coal and analysis of fossil plants show that thousands of years ago this cold, Arctic land was once covered in trees.

been a Norwegian. Around 1000, a group led by Leif Erikson reached North America.

The great days of the Norwegian kingdom, under Haaken IV and Magnus VI, belonged to the thirteenth century. At its peak, around 1260, Norwegian rule covered the Scottish islands, Orkney, Shetland, the Faroes, Iceland and Greenland as well as Norway itself. A century later, Norway was badly hit by the Black Death, the great plague of 1349–50, in which possibly two-thirds of the population died, including a high proportion of the noble families, higher clergy and state servants, whose places were taken by Danes and Swedes. Casualties were so heavy that unified government of the country was lost and local areas conducted their own administration as best they could. The land became fragmented and poverty-stricken. In this weakened state, Norway joined together with Denmark in the Union of Kalmar in 1397. Norway was governed from Copenhagen; revolts and resistance achieved nothing. Much of the labour force had been lost in the Black Death and the aristocracy were never able to lay foundations for new wealth and power in an essentially poor land. More resources were lost when, in 1468, the Orkneys and Shetland were pawned to Scotland to provide a dowry for the daughter of Christian I.

In 1536 Norway was proclaimed a province of Denmark, although it was allowed to keep its ancient laws and institutions. With no strong aristocracy to hinder them, a successful middle class began to exploit more systematically the land's natural resources of iron, timber and fish. Middle-class prosperity rose in the eighteenth century but politically Norway remained a Danish possession until 1814 when the Napoleonic wars brought the 400-year association to an end. Under the Treaty of Kiel the union was dissolved and Norway passed to Sweden, though with its own constitution. Development of industry and trade in the nineteenth century was accompanied by a steady rise of nationalist sentiment and after a long, virtually bloodless struggle, Norway was granted independence from Sweden in 1905 and its monarchy was re-established under Haakon VII.

Norway remained neutral in the First World War (but lost half her large merchant fleet) and attempted to do so in the Second, though there was strong anti-German feeling. The country was invaded in 1940 and occupied for the next five years. The occupation was resisted by most Norwegians, though a German-backed government under the Norwegian Quisling was established and maintained for two years.

After the war, Norway entered the most prosperous phase in her history. Oil and gas fields offshore greatly enriched the country and a large proportion of the new wealth was devoted to social programmes, education and health care.

For the last thousand years, the difficulty of earning a living in harsh, rugged country has made Norway provide many settlers to other countries. In the nineteenth century many Norwegians left the country, especially for the United States. Immigration in the twentieth century has been minor. Today, the population of around four million is largely Nordic in appearance, tall, fair-skinned and blue-eyed. A shorter, dark-haired population is found in the south, migrants from other parts of Europe. In the north about 25,000 Lapps still live, 20,000 of whom still follow their traditional way of life, herding reindeer on the Finnmark plateau.

See: Danes, Lapps, Vikings

Poland

Rzeczpospolita Polska

The Land: The land of Poland is a broad flat plain drained by the Oder and Vistula rivers and extending northward to the Baltic. Once glaciated, it has glacial moraines and innumerable small lakes and marshes. Only in the south close to the Czechoslovak border are there major mountains, the Sudety and Carpathians, though there are upland plateaus in the centre of the country. Poland has connections with the wide plains of western Russia on the east, with the Baltic lands on the north-west and with central Europe along the southern border. The only outlets to the sea lie along a short length of Baltic coast.

The Language: The Polish language belongs to the western Slavic group, along with Czech and Slovak. Several dialects were once very strong, but since 1945 the language has become more standardized.

The Name: One of the tribes of Slavs who occupied the area in the fifth century was the Polanie group. They settled around the Warta river and it was from these that Poland took its name.

After the Ice Age, groups of hunters were attracted to the Polish plains by large herds of grazing animals. The first farmers arrived from the south and south-east before 5000 BC and there followed a long, slow development of settlements until after 1000 BC. Cultural innovations came from central Europe and also from the Black Sea regions. Late in the first millennium BC, tribal groups on the Polish plains began to establish connections with a wider range of cultures in eastern Europe. Later, from the first century AD, trade brought in Roman imports to the leading members of the tribes, though Poland was never part of the Roman empire. The Goths and Gepids occupied the valley of the Vistula, while the Vandals and Burgundians were situated further south; all of these were Germanic peoples. From the late fifth century AD, Slav tribes began to penetrate Poland from the east and south, bringing a new language. Several Slav groups occupied the land.

The origins of Poland lie in the region still known as Wielkopolska, Great Poland. The Slav peoples of this area, between the Warta and Notec rivers, created a state in the mid tenth century and extended its bounds west to the Oder, south into Silesia and east across the Vistula. Later expansion was mainly to the east, into the Ukraine and Byelorussia, which Poland was able to dominate with considerable ease against poorly organized Lithuanians and Russians preoccupied with threats from the steppelands. A single dynasty ruled Poland from the tenth century until 1370, when its male line became extinct on the death of Kazimierz I. Shortly thereafter, the Polish crown passed to a prince of Lithuania, Jagiello, and he and his descendants ruled both Poland and Lithuania until 1572, for most of the time as two separate states. To the west, Poland was vulnerable both to expansion by German states and to groups of German settlers seeking new land east of the Oder. Nevertheless, in the late sixteenth century, when Poland and Lithuania merged to form one state, the new kingdom was the largest European state after Russia.

After 1600 Poland came under threat from several directions. German pressure in the west intensified and Russia began to seize territory in the east. Poland's own political structure weakened in the eighteenth century, leaving the state helplessly exposed in an age when the more powerful nations of Europe were expanding rapidly. After 1770 the neighbouring states began to pull Poland to pieces, until by 1796 it had been wholly dismembered and the country vanished from the political map. Napoleon recreated a Polish state, known as the Grand Duchy of Poland, but it had no effective political power and was mainly designed to win Polish support for the French emperor's attack on Russia. With Napoleon's defeat, this shadow of Poland's earlier greatness faded back into the empire of the Tsar. A rising against Russian control in 1830 was suppressed and all pretence of an independent Poland was abandoned until the end of the First World War.

In 1918, President Woodrow Wilson's *Fourteen Points* proposed that an independent Poland should be re-established; after the Paris settlement of 1919–20 this became reality. The boundaries of the new state raised considerable difficulties, which laid up trouble for the future. The ethnic division was far from clear-cut, both to east and west. Pomerania and Silesia were left to Germany, though both contained sizeable Polish populations. East Prussia also remained German but was now separated from the main body of Germany by a Polish corridor giving access to the sea and to the city of Danzig (Gdansk), whose predominantly German population was allowed to remain in Germany. This compromise satisfied no-one, least of all the Germans. Silesia was also a difficult problem. Here, Germans and Poles were inextricably mixed in a highly industrialized area, the Germans being usually professionals and officials, the Poles miners and

Poland's borders have changed repeatedly over the centuries as the kingdom was divided among its more powerful neighbours: Austria, Prussia and Russia. By 1796 it had completely disappeared as an independent nation. The present borders were laid down after the Second World War: eastern Poland passed to the Soviet Union, but Poland gained an area east of the Oder and Neisse Rivers which had previously been part of Germany. When Germany was reunified, this border was confirmed.

farmers. The eastern border, against Russia and Lithuania, was impossible to draw on strictly ethnic lines because of a very mixed population. The Poles took matters into their own hands in 1919 and invaded the Ukraine and Byelorussia to force the issue. Eventually, a largely arbitrary border was agreed which brought four and a half million Ukrainians and nearly a million Byelorussians into Poland.

When the Nazi regime came to power in Germany, the problems of the Polish borderlands were still unresolved. The German invasion of Poland in 1939 brought about a partition of the country between Germany and Russia along a line which left four million Poles in the Soviet Union. This boundary, with minor changes, is still the border between Poland and Russia. But Poland at the end of the Second World War gained in the west, advancing to the line formed by the Oder and western Neisse rivers and gaining East Prussia and Danzig. Some six million Germans were included within the new borders. The main Polish gains, however, were in capital investment and industrial resources. Her losses were in agricultural land but much greater was her loss of political independence. After liberation from Nazi Germany, Poland passed under the domination of Soviet Russia, from which she was released only in 1989.

Although a far from rich country, in which peasant agriculture is still important, Poland is well populated, despite the loss of millions of lives in the Second World War. Most inhabitants are Poles, almost all the large communities of Jews having been killed in the Nazi occupation and the great majority of Germans having left since 1945. The largest minorities are Ukrainians, Byelorussians and Slovaks.

One of the most powerful forces within modern Poland, probably the most powerful single force, is the Roman Catholic Church, to which the great majority of the population adhere. Although the Poles were not converted until the tenth century, they have been staunchly Catholic ever since and the Church has played a major role in forming and preserving the Polish identity in long periods of oppression. In the 1980s in particular it provided great support to the Polish people in their demand for a more representative system of government under an independent Polish leadership. The election of the first Pole as pope in 1979 was a matter of enormous pride to all the Polish Catholics.

See: Burgundians, Czechs, Goths, Slavs, Ukrainians, Vandals, Vikings

Portugal
República Portuguesa

The Land: Portugal is largely a lowland country, divided by the river Tagus into two. The northern area contains most of the higher ground, much of it over 300 metres in height, and the upland plateaus. Western Portugal looks to the Atlantic and the western parts of Europe. The southern region of the country is close to the Mediterranean world in its climate, vegetation and way of life.

The Language: Portuguese is a Romance language, derived ultimately from the Latin of the Roman Empire. Its closest relative is Galician, spoken in north-western Spain. During the Arab occupation about 600 words were incorporated into Portuguese and a number of French words have been adopted. Standard Portuguese is based on the dialect of Lisbon and its region, which emerged from the twelfth century onward. Although distinct from Spanish in grammar and vocabulary, the two are to some extent mutually intelligible.

The Name: Portuguesa comes from the territory around Portucale (now Oporto), and was first applied in the eleventh century to the kingdom established by Alfonso I.

Portugal was occupied by Palaeolithic hunter-gatherer groups, but their remains are not numerous. The Neolithic farmers who began the work of forest-clearance after about 5000 BC left much more impact on the landscape, building monumental stone tombs (*dolmens*) and hill-top settlements (*castros* or *citanias*) built in stone. Celtic settlers arrived from the north after 600 BC and both Phoenicians and Greeks established contact with communities on the southern coast. Hill-top villages became more numerous in the Iron Age after 500 BC and some remained in occupation under Roman rule. Portugal was incorporated into the Roman Empire as part of the province of Lusitania.

The first people of the land to be mentioned by Greek and Roman historians were the Lusitanians, a Celto-Iberian tribe who lived in the mountains in the middle of the country. From their Iron Age hill-top forts, for 200 years they steadily resisted Roman expansion until finally pacified around 19 BC. Then Rome reorganized its Iberian territory, making Lusitania into a large southern province stretching from the River Douro to the southern Algarve coast. For five centuries the province and its people had the benefit of Roman civilization. Celtic warriors were turned into productive farmers, fishermen and traders. They exported fish, cloth, wool, agricultural produce, tannin and dyes, and a famous breed of horses. The long years of Roman civilization gave the land the basis for its future: her language, many of her urban foundations, her major roads and a general orientation towards the western Mediterranean.

When the Roman empire collapsed in the fifth century AD, the invasion of the barbarian Germanic tribes penetrated even to this remote part of the Roman world. The Suevi moved into northern Portugal and the Visigoths to the south. The invasion of the Moors from North Africa from 711 swept the Visigoths away and for another five centuries the Christian inhabitants struggled to repossess the land from Islam. The Arab invasion had a considerable effect on rural life and agriculture: they brought irrigation and intensive farming methods, introduced citrus fruit, olives and rice. Moorish craftsmanship in wood, stone and metal profoundly affected later design and production. Portuguese sailors used Arab geography, Arab astrology and Arab charts.

By 1100 the Arabs had been driven out of the territory around Portucale and in 1139 Alfonso I established it as a separate political unit and founded the modern state. By the middle of the next century, the area that is now the Algarve had also been reclaimed from the Arabs and Portugal took on broadly the form it has today, though until around 1400, it struggled to maintain itself as an independent power against the Spanish kingdom of Castile. It was in this struggle that Portugal signed a treaty with England in 1386, beginning a long alliance which remains unbroken.

Almost as soon as peace was established, there began an extraordinarily brilliant age of expansion overseas which made Portugal a rich and formidable colonial power. The visionary Prince Henry the Navigator ceaselessly planned and sent out expeditions, seeking to take the Christian message to new lands and to combat the spread of Islam. Beginning with

Portugal

Occupying most of the west coast of the Iberian Peninsula, Portugal faces the Atlantic at the western edge of the western world. There, the land of the high Iberian plateau tilts sharply towards a coastline that is some 500 miles long. Hardly any place is more than 100 miles from the sea. Portugal's position brought early trade links with the Mediterranean countries. Later, overshadowed on land by neighbouring Spain, her explorers crossed the oceans to establish a vast trading empire that at its height reached as far as China and Japan.

the capture of Ceuta in Morocco in 1415, Portuguese explorers penetrated down the Atlantic coast of Africa, discovered the Azores and Madeira and later sailed around the southern tip of Africa into the Indian Ocean. In 1497–9 an expedition led by Vasco da Gama reached southern India, opening up a lucrative spice-trade.

A golden age of Portuguese colonization, wealth and cultural achievement had begun. Cabral reached Brazil in 1500 and twenty years later Magellan (a Portuguese working for Spain) completed the most dangerous part of the first circumnavigation of the world. By 1530, Portugal controlled a vast overseas trading empire. Only fifty years later it began to decline when, in 1580, Portugal and Spain were joined under a Spanish king. Portugal regained independence in 1640 but her power and influence had declined overseas. A catastrophic earthquake destroyed the capital, Lisbon, in 1755 but the home economy was greatly strengthened by the dictator Pombal who rebuilt the city and tried to modernize Portuguese society. Portugal's old alliance with England held firm during the Napoleonic wars although the French invaded the country on three occasions. Portuguese guerillas played an important part in Wellington's defeat of the French in the peninsula.

In the nineteenth century, Portugal became a political and cultural backwater. Brazil seceded in 1822 and Portugal itself was frequently disturbed by factional fighting. A republic was finally proclaimed in 1910 but inter-party struggles continued until a military coup brought Antonio Salazar to prominence. Prime Minister from 1932, Salazar ruled the state as a dictator until 1968, ruthlessly quashing opposition but making considerable improvements to the economy and keeping Portugal neutral in the Second World War. Parliamentary democracy was restored in 1974.
See: Iberians, Arabs, Goths, Romans, Suevi

Romania
Republica România

The Land: Romania is dominated by the striking volcanic mountains of the Carpathians which encircle the plateau of Transylvania. Around this central upland a broad half-circle of fertile plain stretches south to the Danube valley and east to the Prut and the Black Sea. Walachia, to the south, is economically the most important part of Romania while Moldavia, despite its potential fertility, is far less developed. Coal, oil and iron are all mined and crops ranging from grains to vines grow on the fertile soil of the plains. The climate, however, is extreme with cold winters and dry, scorching summers, which often make crop yields unreliable.

The Language: Romanian is basically a Romance language, derived from Latin in its structure and vocabulary. There have been later influences from Hungarian, German, Albanian and Turkish. In the nineteenth century, many words were introduced from French.

The Name: Romania means 'Land of the Romans', from whom Romanians imagine they are descended.

The prehistory of Romania is complex, the land lying as it does between the Russian steppes and the Danube valley. Early Stone Age hunters ranged over the lower Danube and the Black Sea coastal areas from at least 100,000 BC. The earliest farmers of the region had strong links with others in areas that are now Bulgaria, south Russia and Hungary. These cultures with their advanced forms of settlement and timber buildings, flourished from 6000 to 2500 BC They were succeeded by a very sophisticated Bronze Age culture, especially in Transylvania, in which the skills of craftsmen in gold and bronze reached great heights. This brilliant phase may have been ended by invasion from the steppes about 800 BC, perhaps by the Scythians. Celtic groups advanced east towards the Carpathians about 400 BC, but the most significant Iron Age culture was that of the Dacians, who created a highly organized kingdom centred in the lands below the Carpathians, after 400 BC. This kingdom was later seen as a serious threat by Rome and was finally conquered by the emperor Trajan early in the second century AD and incorporated in the Roman Empire as the province of Dacia.

Dacia lay at the very edge of the Roman empire. Beyond it were the lands of the barbarians and after the fall of the Roman empire, it was vulnerable to invasion by successive migrations. Goths, Huns, Magyars and Slavs all influenced the region. Vlachs were known to be settled there in the twelfth century but were not considered to be a political unit.

By the mid fourteenth century the region had been divided into two principalities, Moldavia, to the east and Walachia (land of the Vlachs).

Walachia was ruled for a time from Hungary but in the mid fifteenth century both principalities became part of the Turkish Ottoman empire. For the Turks, the significance of the country was as a provider of agricultural products to Constantinople (now renamed Istanbul) and western Asia Minor and there was no intensive Turkish settlement there. Turkish rule was oppressive, but Walachia and Moldavia fared better than the lands south of the Danube, being more remote from Istanbul. Native rulers administered these provinces for the Turks, the most prominent being Vlad the Impaler (1456–62), noted for hideous cruelty to his subjects, and Michael the Brave (1593–1601), who brought the two provinces together in united rule for a brief time and is still honoured as a Romanian national hero. In the seventeenth and eighteenth centuries, the Turks delegated control of the land to Greek rulers.

Although now part of a powerful empire, the two principalities were often threatened by the neighbouring European powers and in the eighteenth century, when Turkish power was on the wane, Russia, searching for a base from which to control entry to the Black Sea, began to take an active interest in the region. By the early nineteenth century, Turkey and Russia exercised joint control over the two principalities, with Russia as the dominant partner.

During this same period a sense of Romanian national identity was growing, fostered by intellectuals who saw their land and culture as a survival from the Roman empire. This was an illusory concept but it possessed great power. In 1848, the year of revolutions in much of Europe, there was a revolt against Russian control, but it failed as the mass of the

Trajan's column in Rome celebrates the Roman victory over the Dacians, who lived in what is now Romania from the fourth century BC and challenged the power of Rome in AD 85. Their kingdom became the Roman province of Dacia. The Vlachs who live in Romania today (Walachia means land of the Vlachs) may be descended from the old Roman population of the central European provinces. Romania's borders were established after the Second World War when part of the old kingdom of Moldavia passed to the Soviet Union. As the Republic of Moldova, this gained independence in 1991. Some of its historic territory, west of the River Prut, is in Romania and many Moldovans have close cultural links with their neighbours to the west.

peasantry was not drawn into the struggle. But not long afterwards, the Crimean War of 1854–6 in which Britain and France were intent on supporting the weakening Ottoman empire against Russia, led to the union of Moldavia and Walachia. Shortly afterwards the kingdom of Romania was founded. In 1861 Romania became an independent sovereign state, with its capital at Bucharest in Walachia.

Romania's first ruler was deposed in 1866 and the throne was offered to a prince of Prussia, Charles (or Carol). He was to rule Romania until 1914, a half-century of considerable economic growth and political stability.

Extensive territories were added to Romania in 1878 when the Dobrudja plain, between the Danube and the Black Sea, was ceded to it by Turkey. Much more significant was the westward extension of the country into Transylvania and the Banat. Here, in what was romantically (and erroneously) seen as the homeland of the Romanians, nearly three million Romanians lived under Hungarian rule. In an attempt to win them for their 'homeland', in 1916 Romania joined the allies and attacked the German-led Central Powers, only to meet with rapid defeat. At the end of the First World War, however, Romania was given most of the territory she had sought, acquiring with it not only Romanians but also substantial minorities of Magyars, Slovaks, Germans, Russians, Bulgars, Gypsies and Jews. Another acquisition, at the end of the War, this time from Austria, was the area of Bucovina, which reached from the Carpathians to the river Dniester in south Russia and contained a large population of Ruthenes. From a war to which she had contributed little, Romania had gained a great deal.

The experience of the country in the Second World War was much less fortunate. Romania declared war on Russia in June 1941 at the same time as Nazi Germany, and joined in the invasion of the Ukraine. Moldavia east of the Dniester was briefly annexed and then lost when the Germans retreated from Russia. In the summer of 1944 Romania was invaded by Russian armies but managed to gain back territory in Transylvania, lost to Hungary in 1940. After 1945 the earlier boundaries of Romania were confirmed and have remained intact since then.

The political history of Romania since 1945 has been complex. King Michael, who had been instrumental in taking Romania into the war against Germany in 1944, was forced to abdicate in 1947. A government combining Communists and Socialists was formed and a Romanian Peoples Republic proclaimed along Soviet lines. In the 1950s Romania moved close to Soviet Russia, but there was always an independent substratum to her foreign policies. Industrialization proceeded at a rapid pace and by the early 1970s Romania had the highest level of industrial growth of any eastern European state, though this progress took its toll on social life. In 1965 there was a significant change of leadership, when Nicolae Ceaucescu came to power. Romania had already begun to pursue policies that were not dictated by Moscow and Ceaucescu greatly developed this independent line, opening diplomatic links with West Germany in 1967 and opposing the Russian invasion of Czechoslovakia in 1968. Western European leaders courted Ceaucescu as a potential ally against Russia, but by the early 1980s it was clear that his domestic policies were becoming very severe and his own position increasingly dictatorial. Economic hardship and reaction to a harsh and destructive programme of urbanization and forced resettlement led to internal strife from 1987 and to a popular revolution late in 1989 which removed the Ceaucescu regime from power and killed its leader. Although anti-Communist sentiment was strong after the revolution, many ex-Communists were able to hold on to their posts. Free elections were held in 1990, but the political state of Romania is still far from stable and economic conditions are harsh for the great majority of its people.

The ethnic composition of Romania is complex, reflecting the ease of access from all sides, as well as the changing boundaries of the country. Romanians make up about 85% of the population, but there are influential minorities of Hungarians in the west and Germans in Transylvania, as well as Jews, Gypsies and Serbians. Vlachs, possibly including some descendents of the early population of Dacia, still survive there, speaking their own distinctive language.

See: Avars, Dacians, Goths, Gypsies, Huns, Romans, Sarmatians, Serbs, Slavs, Vlachs

Russia

Russijskaja

The Land: The main geographical feature of European Russia is the immense plain, largely below 300 metres in height, which extends from the western frontier to central Siberia. This vast expanse is cut across by the long north-south chain of the Ural mountains, rarely more than 1000 metres high and easily passable. The absence of any natural barrier explains why movement from east to west was so important a feature of early Russia and why later Russia tended to expand eastward into Asia. The only other large mountain range in the west is the Caucasus, between the Black and Caspian Seas. In the great plain there were large areas of marshland and bog, the largest being the Pripet marshes in Byelorussia (now an independent state). In the north, great expanses of tundra border the Barents Sea. The main river systems—the Volga, Don, Dniester and Dnieper, drain south into the Caspian and Black Seas.

The Language: Russian is an east Slavic language with a wide range of dialects and a complex structure. Modern literary Russian is based on the dialect of Moscow. The language is related to Ukrainian and Byelorussian, from which it diverged between 1200 and 1500. There have been many borrowings from western European languages in modern times. The Cyrillic alphabet, derived from Byzantine Greek, is used in written Russian.

The Name: Russia means 'Land of the Rus', a name apparently borrowed from the Finns, who called the people across the Baltic *Ruotsi*.

The great plain of Russia supported Palaeolithic hunters from at least the end of the last Ice Age and these wandering people continued to follow the same lifestyle in places until the historical period. Farming communities were settled in the more fertile valleys by 3000 BC, having moved northward from the Middle East. Later contacts with Iran and the Black Sea region led to the introduction of metal working and this was exploited by the steppe nomads who dominated much of western Russia after 2000 BC. The Scythians are the first to be named, by Greek writers after 500 BC. Other peoples were settled on the plain, but where they came from and who their ancestors were is not known. Germanic tribes, including the Goths and Gepids, moved into south Russia and the Ukraine in the third century AD and remained there until they were dislodged by the invading Huns in the later fourth century.

The origins of modern Russia lie in the wide plains to the west of the Urals, between the Black Sea and the Baltic. Here before the ninth century a bleak and open landscape of steppe, marsh and forest was inhabited by Slavonic peoples, nomads and remnants of other earlier cultures, largely untouched by the outside world. The Slavs had spread over western Russia from about AD 500 and nomads continued to arrive from Asia. The Avars and Magyars crossed the land on their way westward in the years before the ninth century. About the middle of the ninth century, external influence from two directions brought about a rapid change. From the north, Viking raiders swept down to the Black Sea and to Constantinople itself, leaving many of their number to settle on the great trade-routes which linked the Baltic with the trading towns of Novgorod and Kiev. From the south, Byzantine missionaries, led by Cyril and Methodius, brought Eastern Orthodox Christianity to the eastern Slavs.

For the next century a number of tribes co-existed on the western plains and then, in the late tenth century, the energetic ruler Vladimir built an important state based on the city of Kiev. He made Orthodox Christianity the official religion of his domain, an act which was to prove of immense significance, for the Russians remained Orthodox after the Great Schism of 1054 divided the Latin Church of Rome from the Byzantine Greek Orthodox. Kiev's pre-eminence lasted until the late eleventh century, but then the city came under pressure from the steppe nomads and from other newly formed towns in emerging Russia, including Moscow from about 1140. The power of Kiev was finally shattered by the Mongol invasion of 1237. Although the Mongols withdrew from the west to the lower Volga, for the next hundred years they continued to dominate the steppe around the Caspian and Black Seas, and controlled most of the states to the north, cutting them off from the political and cultural influence exerted by Constantinople and by the Slavs to the west.

When the power of the Mongols declined after 1300, the state which was best placed to take full advantage was Muscovy, with its centre at Moscow, commanding the strategic headwaters of the rivers Don and Volga. This little state grew rapidly in the fourteenth and fifteenth centuries, annexing Novgorod in 1478 and thus gaining access to the Baltic and the White Sea. Ivan III (1462–1505) declared himself to be 'Tsar of all the Russias' and also, following the capture of Constantinople by the Turks in 1453, presented Russia as the protector of the Orthodox Church. His capital, Moscow, was rebuilt by Italian architects to underline these claims: to this time belong the rebuilt Kremlin (the Fortress) and the Uspenski (Assumption) Cathedral.

The expansion of Muscovy continued under Ivan IV (the Terrible) from 1533 to 1584. In his reign the kingdom doubled in size, its power extending south-east to the Caspian Sea and north into Siberia beyond the Ural mountains. Only sixty years after the death of Ivan the Terrible, Russian rule had been pushed east almost to the Pacific and to the borders of Mongolia. This astonishingly rapid progress was possible as the broad plains, though vast, offered few natural obstacles and the peoples settled on them were not organized for war. One of the immediate prizes for those who colonized the bitter wastes of Siberia was the wealth of furs: an enormously lucrative fur-trade quickly developed to satisfy the market in Muscovy.

The growth of Russian power slowed dramatically in the early seventeenth century, when both Sweden and Poland took advantage of weak Tsarist government to seize territory in the west. But from the

Russia is the largest of the fifteen republics that make up the Russian Federation, a group which stretches from the Baltic to the Pacific Ocean and from the Arctic to the borders of China. European Russia is traditionally separated geographically from Asia by the Ural mountains, a range that has never proved a barrier to migrants from the east, or to Russian expansion into Asia. From the ninth to the thirteenth centuries, Kiev (now in Ukraine) was the centre of Russian civilization but Kiev's power was shattered by the Mongol invasion of 1237 and when the Mongols were defeated, Moscow became the centre of the growing kingdom of Muscovy. Byelorussia (or Belarus), once known as White Russia, became independent in 1991. Its mainly flat landscape includes ancient forest and marshland but it is also an important industrial centre. Long dominated by Russia, and sharing Russia's early history, Byelorussians are Slavs and speak a language related to Russian.

Russia 269

1660s, a reformed Russia began to gain attention as a major European power. This happened in the reign of Peter the Great, who came to power in 1682 when he was only nine years old. He was determined to modernize Russia and that meant reorganizing government and administration in line with western ideas, introducing up-to-date technology from Germany, France, Holland and Britain, and moving his court to the western flank of his vast empire. Peter detested Moscow and ordered the building of a great new capital on marshy land where the river Neva reached the Baltic. The city was called St Petersburg.

Although Russia was firmly established as a power in Europe by the early eighteenth century, little had changed for the vast mass of her people. Russia was a land of peasants surviving miserably, tied to their village or estate by a repressive and unshakeable social order. For 97% of Russians the conditions of life were extremely harsh and there was no prospect of improvement. This was the Russia later described by Trotsky as 'the Russia of icons and cockroaches'. It is scarcely surprising that there were revolts against such oppression, but they were usually local uprisings and were put down with savage ruthlessness. No ruler was more merciless in dealing with rebellion among serfs, or with opposition among courtiers, than Catherine the Great, the daughter of a German prince who married into the Russian royal house and herself acceded to the throne in 1761. She made important territorial gains for Russia against the Ottoman empire and Poland, from whom she gained the Ukraine and Lithuania, and she greatly strengthened the imperial army, making it an equal to its western counterparts. This was demonstrated in 1812–14 when the invasion of Russia by Napoleon's Grand Army was comprehensively defeated, with invaluable assistance from the severe Russian winter and the vast emptiness of the land.

Nineteenth century Russia made progress in industrialization, with the aid of western capital, but nothing was done to alleviate the wretched and impoverished rural population nor was the new urban workforce treated much better. By the end of the nineteenth century, all the conditions were present for a major social and political upheaval. The Russian frontiers to the south-east continued to expand towards the Himalayas and India, but at home the foundation of the tsarist regime was collapsing. Radical opposition mounted in the last twenty years of the century and in 1905 there were widespread revolts by the peasants, strikes in the cities and mutinies in the armed forces. This uprising was brutally put down and its leaders exiled. But in March 1917, protests at military defeats by Germany in the First World War and economic catastrophe erupted in a general strike and the tsar was compelled to abdicate. After some months, in which power was disputed by a number of groups, the Bolsheviks led by Vladimir Ulyanov (Lenin) seized control and established a Communist regime which signed a treaty with Germany in March 1918 ending hostilities.

The greatest European revolution since 1789 had succeeded and many believed it would not be long before its message spread to other states. But this did not occur and indeed for two years Russia was in the grip of a savage civil war, which finally ended in a Communist victory. Russia and her people were now in a serious economic condition and a massive programme of reconstruction was called for to ensure the future of the revolutionary state. The reconstruction caused hardship and suffering as savage as any brought on by war itself.

Lenin died in 1924. His place as General Secretary of the Communist party had already been taken by Josef Stalin, whose political skill and powerful but crude intelligence were to keep him in supreme power for nearly thirty years. Under the banner of 'Socialism in one country', Stalin drove his people through a social and economic revolution with a total disregard for the human suffering which this caused. In a sequence of five-year plans, he forced an underdeveloped nation to transform itself into one of the foremost industrialized countries in the world. His grandiose scheme for the collectivization of agriculture was not only a failure, but also brought about the deaths through starvation and murder of at least ten million peasants. In the 1930s Stalin also purged the Communist party, the army and the state bureaucracy of all those who were believed to harbour opposing views. Several million disappeared into labour camps in Siberia and elsewhere (the Gulag archipelago), from which most did not return.

The industrialization of Russia did, however, enable the country to resist the massive onslaught by the Nazi armies in June 1941. After early disasters, the Red Army, with the fierce backing of the Russian people, halted the German advance in 1942 and then drove the invaders back into

Germany, taking Berlin in April 1945. This sweep across eastern Europe over the ruins of the Third Reich enabled Stalin to extend Russian control over countries from the Baltic to the Balkans. A hundred million people, under nominally independent regimes, in fact followed a policy dictated by Moscow.

After Stalin died in 1953, his successors continued to strengthen Russian military power and maintained the status of a superpower which could rival America by a strict system of planning which diverted resources towards certain national goals. By the 1970s, serious economic problems, with roots in Stalin's collectivization, were evident in rural Russia. By the mid 1980s, these problems forced the Russian leaders to try more liberal policies both at home and in external relations. The far-reaching reforms of Mikhail Gorbachev, from 1985 to 1991, broadly based on *glasnost* (openness) and *perestroika* (reconstruction) set Russia on a path towards democratic government and a less restrictive economic and social order. At the same time the Soviet Union lost her hold on the states of eastern Europe.

Within the Union, several republics, including the Ukraine, the Baltic States and Georgia, began to seek total independence. Even the Federation of Russia itself, under Boris Yeltsin, wanted to be free to decide its own policy. The attempted removal of Gorbachev from power by a coup in August 1991 occurred in the midst of these complex processes, at a time when the people of Russia faced mounting economic chaos and political uncertainty. The Communist Party itself, the foundation of Russia since 1917, lost effective power in most of the republics and, at the end of 1991, the Soviet Union was formally disbanded when its republics voted for individual independence within a new Commonwealth.

Russia's population is immensely mixed; Russians themselves are Slavs and make up over 80% of the total but the Federation includes large minorities of Asiatic peoples.

See: Alans, Burgundians, Finns, Goths, Huns, Lapps, Mongols, Sarmatians, Scythians, Slavs, Ukrainians, Vikings

Spain
Estado Español

The Land: Spain occupies most of the Iberian peninsula, a huge, roughly square bloc of land at the western edge of Europe. Once joined to Africa across the narrow entrance to the Mediterranean it is linked by sea to the Mediterranean world and, to the west, looks outwards to the Atlantic Ocean and the Americas. After Switzerland, Spain is the most mountainous country in Europe. The vast upland plateau in the centre covers half the country, an arid and inhospitable region, in places virtually a desert. To the north lie the high Pyrenean and Cantabrian mountains and to the south the Sierra Nevada. The Pyrenees, in particular, for long acted as a barrier between the peninsula and the lands to the north. The Atlantic climate of the north-west is mild and wet; the central plateau suffers extremes of summer and winter temperature; but the long Mediterranean coastline is sunny and warm for much of the year.

The Languages: Castilian Spanish is the most widely spoken language. It is derived from the Latin spoken in the Roman empire with later influences from Arabic, Celtic and French. Three other languages are officially recognized in Spain: Catalan and Galician in the north, both Romance tongues, and Basque in the north-west, an ancient non-Indo-European language.

The Name: *España* is derived from the name of the Roman provinces of Hispania.

Remains of Neanderthal man have been found in several places in Spain, the earliest signs of human activity going back to at least 500,000 BC. After the last Ice Age, early Stone Age hunters spread over the entire peninsula, slowly moving northward as the ice-sheets retreated in northern Europe. These hunter-groups left striking remains behind them, most spectacularly the magnificent cave-paintings at Altamira, Pindal and elsewhere. The first farmers began primitive cultivation from 5000 BC onwards, though people continued to live by hunting and gathering for long afterwards. From about 2500 BC the sophisticated use of bronze developed. The people built hill-top settlements and buried their dead in large stone tombs. As long ago as 1000 BC, peoples from the more advanced civilizations of the eastern Mediterranean established settlements and trading posts at what was to them the very edge of the world.

The Phoenicians and Greeks who established their trading posts on the southern coast of the Iberian Peninsula were attracted by the metals and other natural resources they found there. Phoenicians settled only in the south and had little impact inland, but in the seventh century BC Greeks not only founded cities on the east and south coasts but moved into the lands of the native Iberians. The Iberians had the most advanced Iron Age culture in the region and evolved a major urban civilization which produced fine sculpture and painted pottery. Carthaginians from North Africa arrived in the sixth century, attracted by the wealth of the peninsula and, from the north, Celts crossed the Pyrenees before 450 BC and settled in the north and centre. In the third century BC, soldiers of the expanding Roman empire defeated and threw out the Carthaginian settlers in the east. Nearly two centuries were needed to complete the conquest, but Rome gained a land rich in resources of many kinds, especially metals.

The south and east of the peninsula were most profoundly affected by the Roman conquerors. Roman urban life developed from the second century BC and in the reign of Augustus several new cities for ex-legionaries were founded. The character and culture of the most advanced of these cities—among them Tarragona, Barcelona, Italica and Cordoba—was equal to those of the cities of northern Italy and southern Gaul. As well as providing a secure and prosperous life for their citizens, these cities also provided legionaries for the Roman army and servants for the imperial bureaucracy. In the late first and early second centuries two emperors, Trajan and Hadrian, came from the Spanish provinces. The fertile regions of Spain were exploited for olive-oil and vines, the seas for fish, while the mines yielded gold, silver, tin and copper. Trade flourished with wide areas of the Roman west, from Italy to Britain.

This age of progress lasted into the fourth century without serious setback, but shortly after AD 400 the barbarian invasions which were causing chaos in most of western Europe reached the Iberian peninsula.

Suevi, Alans and Vandals swept across the Pyrenees in 407. The Suevi founded a kingdom in the north west, the Alans moved west into the Roman province of Lusitania, and the Vandals settled in the south-east

Spain's Mediterranean coastlands attracted traders from at least the seventh century BC and became part of the Roman empire in the second century BC. The northern mountains and barren central plateau were less easy to colonize and the Romans met fierce resistance from the Celtic tribes there. Later invaders came from the north (Visigoths and Germanic tribes) and from the south Arabs crossed the narrow Straits of Gibraltar in 711. In the inaccessible mountains of the north-west, the Basques continued to occupy the lands they had lived in since prehistoric times. Today, both Basques and Catalans (in the north-east) are campaigning for autonomy while Gibraltar, on Spain's southernmost tip, remains British. One of Europe's smallest states, tiny independent Andorra, lies in the valleys between Spain and France.

before crossing to North Africa. Far more significant was the settlement of the Visigoths over much of Spain from the late fifth century onward. The kingdom they established was one of the longest-lived of all the Germanic kingdoms of the Dark Ages in Europe, surviving into the early eighth century.

Although the period from the Visigoths' conquest, in the fifth century, to the Arab invasion in 711 is usually referred to as 'Visigothic' Spain, the kingdom was far from being a simple Germanic tribal society. The Visigothic kings retained much of the late Roman system of administration. Roman law was respected, taxes were levied and paid, urban life of a kind continued. The Visigoths had been converted to Christianity before they entered the Roman world, though to the Arian version of the faith, which led to conflict with Catholic Christians. Although the Visigothic state was more stable than many contemporary powers, there was usually friction between the monarch and his nobles which frequently flared up into conflict. That the kingdom survived until the eighth century is probably an indication of the isolation of the region from the rest of Europe. When the next invader of the peninsula struck, Visigothic rule collapsed almost immediately.

The Arab invasion of southern Spain across the Strait of Gibraltar was the final thrust of the long westward drive of Muslim forces through North Africa during the seventh century. The Arabs won quick and decisive victories. By 718 most of the peninsula had fallen to them and a large force pushed northward into France, to be halted by Charles Martel at Poitiers in 732. Spain became a province of the Arab Caliphate, ruled by an Emir who was answerable to the governor of Africa, with which Muslim Spain was always linked. Christians who submitted to the new order could retain their laws, religion, language and lands. Persecution of both Christians and Jews was rare in Arab Spain. Most groups benefited from a rise in material prosperity, despite the fact that the first two centuries of Arab rule were far from orderly, with frequent revolts and disputes. Outright civil war was never far away.

By the tenth century, Christian states in the north of Spain were again beginning to throw off the Arab yoke and establish an identity of their own. About 1000 the Christian states were set to launch a major thrust to recapture much of Spain. The beginnings of this conflict are portrayed in the heroic exploits of El Cid, who fought first for Arab masters and later for the Christians of the Valencia region.

The reconquest took the next three centuries and was a piecemeal affair, punctuated by long periods when little progress was made. By 1300 most of the area which the Arabs had overrun in the eighth century had been won back by the kingdoms of Aragon and Castile; Arab rule was confined to the province of Granada in the south. Castile and Aragon were then united by the marriage of Ferdinand of Aragon and Isabella of Castile in 1479, and their consolidated power completed the removal of the Arabs by conquering Granada in 1492. After France, Spain was now the most powerful monarchy in Europe.

The three voyages of the Italian Cristobal Columb (Christopher Columbus) between 1492 and 1502 revealed the islands now known as the West Indies and the adjacent coast of South America. Spain established her large colonial empire in the Central and South Americas from the late fifteenth century and quickly benefited from the immense wealth which the new sources of silver, gold and other minerals it provided. By the mid sixteenth century, the military adventurers known as the *conquistadores*, often using brutal methods against the native inhabitants, had annexed much of Central and north-western South America for Spain.

A period of great prosperity and expansion followed. By a series of royal marriages, the ruler of the Netherlands inherited the throne of Spain and, as Charles V, was also elected Holy Roman Emperor, with authority over virtually the whole of central Europe, from the Netherlands to the borders of Poland. Under him and his son Philip II, Spain reached the pinnacle of her power. Philip II was a devoted administrator and a very vigorous defender of the Roman Catholic faith who pursued an anti-Protestant policy in his own domain and attempted to widen its already vast scope by foreign conquests. The most dramatic was his attempted invasion of Britain in 1588 (the Spanish Armada), which came to an ignominious end in total defeat. These were costly activities and the treasury was heavily drained by them.

Philip and his predecessors had relied upon the Inquisition from 1480 onward as a powerful weapon against Jews and other non-Catholics. Torture, execution and forced conversion were its methods of enforcing compliance. Under Torquemada, the Inquisition's most infamous director, about 100,000 trials of suspects were held and at least 2000 were executed.

The sixteenth and early seventeenth centuries were Spain's golden age but they also held the seeds of the country's downfall from the status and prestige of a major power. Philip's three successors were unable to restore Spanish wealth and influence and the country rapidly lost its leading position in western Europe as French power grew on land and British on the sea. The Spanish Netherlands and the Italian possessions were lost as a result of the War of the Spanish Succession early in the eighteenth century and Spain became a political backwater. Napoleon installed his brother Joseph on the Spanish throne in 1808, but the British and Spaniards restored the Spanish line six years later. When Napoleon's empire collapsed, the Spanish colonies in the Americas took advantage of the confusion to revolt from Spain, weakening her still further. In 1898, after a war with the USA, Spain lost her remaining territories overseas.

Neutrality was the obvious course for Spain to follow in 1914 and she was relatively little affected by that war. A republic was declared in 1931, but continuing strains began to divide the country into two broad factions, Republicans and Nationalists. Civil War finally broke out in 1936, and soon developed into one of the most savage and bitter struggles of modern times. The Nationalists under Franco were able to rely on aid from Nazi Germany and Fascist Italy and in 1939 their victory was sealed. Franco ruled Spain for the next thirty five years as a dictator.

Although formally neutral in the Second World War, Franco naturally inclined towards Germany and Italy, who had helped him before, and after the end of the war relations with the victorious powers remained for a time uneasy. When Franco's grip on power was released by ill health, the monarchy was restored in 1975 and thereafter Spain followed a relatively smooth path to democratic government. Spain joined the EEC in 1986 and made rapid economic progress in the following few years.

Today, the population comprises Catalans in the north-east, Basques in the north-west as well as Spaniards over most of the country; aspirations towards autonomy are strong among both Basques and Catalans. The former Spanish colonies in Central and South America retain much of their Spanish character, religious orientation and language.

See: Alans, Arabs, Basques, Goths, Greeks, Iberians, Jews, Romans, Suevi, Vandals, Vikings

Sweden
Konungariket Sverige

The Land: Sweden is the fourth largest country in Europe. Along most of its western border with Norway, it is mountainous, the high land sloping steadily eastward to a coastal lowland on the Baltic. Much of the land has a relatively mild but variable climate, but one-seventh of the total area lies north of the Arctic Circle where winters are dark and summer lasts only two months. Over 100,000 lakes stud the surface, two of them very large. Very extensive areas of forest exist in many parts of the country. The south is the most fertile region, but the centre and the north are rich in minerals, especially iron.
The Language: Swedish is a North Germanic language, related to Danish and Norwegian. In its modern form, its origins lie in the Viking period. Minorities speak Finnish and Lappish.
The Name: Sverige (literally 'Kingdom of the Svear') is named from the ancient Svear people.

The land was first settled about 12,000 BC by hunter groups entering by the land-bridge with the continent and subsisting off reindeer. The land bridge with Denmark was finally removed by about 5000 BC, as vast quantities of melt-water were released by the northern ice-sheet. New settlers arrived after 3000 BC and brought agriculture with them, especially to southern Sweden. In the north, hunting continued as a major source of food for centuries afterwards and reindeer-herding is still practised today by Lapps. The scattered early farming communities shared ancestral links with peoples to the south and these links were maintained in the succeeding Bronze Age from 2000 BC. A fine series of rock-engravings in Bohuslän indicates a cult of the sun and the worship of fertility deities. Bronze-working technology reached a high peak after 1000 BC, again under the influence of mainland Europe. Iron-working had begun in the north by 400 BC, but early Iron Age culture was simple, possibly because of a deterioration in climate. But from the first century AD, developing contacts with the Roman empire stimulated change. In the late first century AD, Roman writers indicate that central and southern Sweden were occupied by the Svear and Gotar, warlike tribal groups inhabiting a harsh landscape. These later prehistoric people were Germanic and spoke a Germanic language. They are recognizable as the ancestors of historical Swedes.

By 100, southern Sweden and the islands of Öland and Gotland were in profitable contact with the eastern Roman world and many hoards of gold coins from this period have been excavated. Settlement, agriculture and trade increased, especially in the south, while natural resources from further north began to be exploited.

The fifth and sixth centuries were a golden age for Sweden, as quantities of precious metal arrived from the south-east, in return for furs, agricultural products and military services. This metal was turned into fine ornaments and jewellery. Two centuries later, about 650–700, Swedes were beginning to extend their trade in the Baltic, and after 750 the expeditions of Viking raiders carried Swedes across much of western Europe and deep into Russia. Swedish traders particularly exploited the markets in western Russia, penetrating south to the Black Sea and the Caspian Sea and exchanging goods there with the Byzantines and Arabs. Swedish troops also took service in the guard of the Byzantine emperors.

The political centres of early Sweden included Old Uppsala, near the modern city, where royal burial mounds still stand, and the area of Vendel and Valsgärde. A major trading-post lay at Birka on Lake Mälaren. Christianity was relatively late in arriving, the first major mission being received in 829 and the first ruler to accept the Christian faith being Olof Scotkonung about 1000. Although the king was converted, the Swedish population resisted Christianity longer than the rest of Scandinavia, until well into the twelfth century. Adam of Bremen (late eleventh century) describes a ritual human sacrifice at Uppsala.

The early Swedish kings were elected and their authority remained precarious and dependent on their success in war. More stable conditions were created in the thirteenth century, notably under Birger Jarl, who founded the city of Stockholm to command the entrance to Lake Mälaren, annexed Finland, and brought in Germany to help in economic development. Progress was checked in 1318, when nobles revolted against the king and asserted their power to elect a ruler. In the mid fourteenth

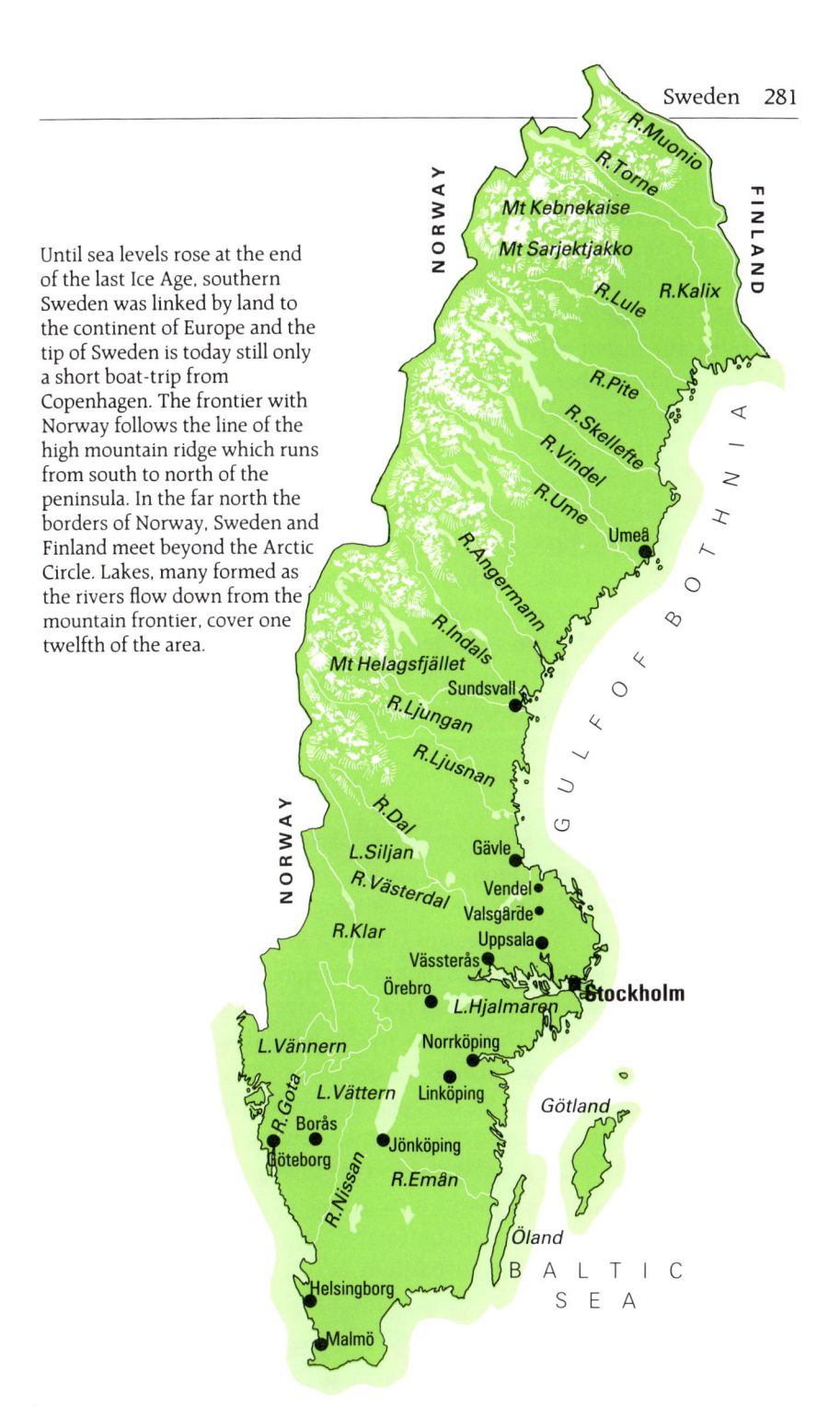

Sweden

Until sea levels rose at the end of the last Ice Age, southern Sweden was linked by land to the continent of Europe and the tip of Sweden is today still only a short boat-trip from Copenhagen. The frontier with Norway follows the line of the high mountain ridge which runs from south to north of the peninsula. In the far north the borders of Norway, Sweden and Finland meet beyond the Arctic Circle. Lakes, many formed as the rivers flow down from the mountain frontier, cover one twelfth of the area.

century came the devastation of the Black Death and the economic recession which followed it. For the next century there were continuing struggles between the kings and their leading nobles as well as bad relations with Denmark and other neighbouring powers.

In 1388 the situation was so bad that the Swedish nobles called on Margrethe, the regent of Denmark and Norway, for aid against their own king and later hailed her as the ruler of Sweden. In 1397, Margrethe's great-nephew was crowned king of Sweden, Norway and Denmark in the Union of Kalmar. Throughout the life of the Kalmar Union, Sweden and Denmark struggled for control of the three-kingdom state against a background of major social change. The first Swedish parliament, the Riksdag, convened in 1435, was the first in Europe to include peasants. The aristocracy continued to be divided, some supporting the Union, others campaigning for an independent nation. Then, in 1520, eighty-two nobles, churchmen and citizens were executed in what came to be known as the Stockholm Bloodbath, and Gustav Vasa organized a revolt against the ruling house. The revolt started with the peasants but soon attracted support among nobles and townspeople. Gustav was elected king in 1523, ending the Kalmar Union and inaugurating the long rule (to 1720) of the Vasa dynasty.

The greatest of the Vasa rulers was Gustav Adolphus (1611–32), a statesmanlike and soldierly monarch, but also an effective conciliator between the Crown and the nobility. Under him, major economic and military reforms were carried through. Gustav Adolphus was intent on extending his own influence to the continent, aiming at a Protestant alliance with the German states under his own leadership. This wider interest drew him into the Thirty Years War, in which he himself led an army into Germany in 1630 and defeated the forces of the Holy Roman Empire at Breitenfeld in 1630. He died in battle in 1632.

Under the Vasas the Swedes developed their country into a great European power, which reached its peak in the seventeenth century. Finland, Estonia and Livonia (Latvia) were at this time all Swedish possessions and Sweden aimed to control the major Baltic ports, so that it could dominate and tax the lucrative Baltic trade. This was naturally not welcome to either the Danes or the Russians, and the Swedes did not have matters all their own way. But they did effectively rule the Baltic from the

1630s to the early eighteenth century. Then their power quickly crumbled. To the east, Russia was threatening to expand into the Nordic area, and to the south, Prussia was building up her strength. In the Great Northern War (1700–9) the Russians seized all the Swedish lands in the eastern Baltic, including Finland.

Swedish power was broken and it never fully recovered. But the influence of the Swedish people in the Baltic region was still strong, especially on the social organization of Finland and Estonia. Swedish soldiers continued to serve in foreign armies, using their high quality firearms, the best in Europe, made from Swedish copper and iron. Many of the peasants came to own their farms in the eighteenth century, the nobles lost power and position and some class-barriers were removed, laying the foundation of the modern Swedish open society. Economically, however, success was limited as few innovations were made in manufacturing.

In the nineteenth century, and especially after 1860, Swedish political life was more and more occupied with internal matters. Pan-Scandinavian ideas spread in intellectual circles but led to no major results. But after 1870 Sweden strengthened her connections with Germany, forming a political alliance to balance the growing power of Russia. The country remained neutral in 1914, though this was to prove costly to Sweden's trade and merchant shipping. Neutrality was also preserved in 1939, but it came under great strain when, under duress, German troops were conveyed to Norway via Sweden in 1940 and from Norway to Finland in 1941. On the other side, after 1940 many Danes and Norwegians found refuge in Sweden before fleeing to Britain.

The Swedes are a very homogeneous population in ethnic stock, language, religion and social outlook. There has been much immigration over the centuries, from Denmark, Norway, Germany, Finland and the eastern Baltic lands, but integration has been complete. Swedes have always been great travellers and migrants, and are now encountered in every continent, especially North America and Australia, and in every country of Europe. The Lapps in the north retain their own culture and way of life, but even they speak Swedish as well as Lapp. The great majority of Swedes belong to the established state Church, the Evangelical Lutheran Church.

See: Danes, Germans, Lapps Svear, Swedes, Vikings

Switzerland
La Suisse / Die Schweiz / Svizzera

The Land: Although Switzerland is essentially the land of the Alps, which cover half of its surface, it also includes an upland plateau to the north and the broad valleys of the Aare and its tributaries, the Thur and the upper Rhine. There are several large lakes, including Lakes Geneva, Neuchâtel and Constance.
The Languages: There are three official languages: German (spoken by 70% of the population), French (by 19%) and Italian (by 10%). A small minority speak Romansch, a language based on Latin. There are several dialects of Swiss-German, some of them difficult for speakers of High German to understand.
The Name: In all three languages, the name is derived from *Schwyz*, one of the three forest cantons in the Federation.

The peoples of the Alps and the adjacent lowlands were in origin very mixed in their ethnic composition. The Celtic tribe of the Helvetii are popularly seen as ancestral to the present population of Switzerland but in fact many other groups inhabited the Alpine valleys and the plain to the north in antiquity. The high Alps were hostile to settlement by early man but the Swiss plateau and the lowlands around the lakes attracted first farmers and later Bronze Age settlers from 4000 to 1500 BC. Several Iron Age tribes occupied the regions around the Alps after 500 BC, the most important being the Helvetii in the west, and the Raeti and Vindelici in the east. All of these were Celtic peoples, noted for their warlike character. When the Helvetii tried to migrate to Gaul in 58 BC, Julius Caesar acted immediately to prevent them.

Farming was the main way of life from an early date, supplemented by booty taken in warfare and raiding. The Alpine peoples were conquered by Rome late in the first century BC and most of the Swiss Alps were incorporated into the Roman frontier province of Upper Germany, a strategically important zone which confronted the Germanic tribes to the north and controlled the all-important alpine passes leading to Italy.

When Roman rule came to an end in the fifth century, several Germanic peoples invaded the areas of good land: Alamanni settled in the northern and central Alps, Burgundians in the west and the Rugii in the east. The Ostrogoths also briefly occupied part of the eastern Alpine region. The native inhabitants were not driven out but merged with the new masters.

By the mid-seventh century the land was loosely bound up in the growing domain of the Franks, who had conquered the Alamanni. Later invasions, by Magyars and others, had no lasting effects on the Alpine lands. In 1033, what is now Switzerland became part of the Holy Roman Empire and it remained so until the late Middle Ages. It was in no sense a unified country. Geography favoured rule by a multiplicity of minor dukes and counts, dominating the peasantry of limited areas from their strongholds. Towns were few and small until the fifteenth century.

From the end of the thirteenth century, there were the beginnings of a movement towards federation among the Alpine peoples, at first among the three forest cantons of Schwyz, Url and Unterwalden and then spreading to include Lucerne and Zurich. The first federation, the Perpetual League, was a landmark in European political history. In effect it established two essential principles: the citizens' right to self-determination and the right of a community to govern itself without interference from a higher authority. Out of these principles arose the successful idea (which was strange to the Middle Ages) that a stable country could be formed out of a binding confederation between more or less independent communities which kept their local government, local traditions, and even local languages.

In spite of opposition from the Hapsburg rulers of Austria, this alliance slowly expanded and after 1400 a phase of peace and economic growth enabled the Federation to consolidate its power. The Hapsburg dynasty again tried to exert its authority, but without success, against increasingly efficient Swiss soldiers. But there were serious divisions between the cantons themselves and this lack of political cohesion slowed down the country's development. The military reputation of Swiss troops was greatly enhanced by victories against the Burgundian armies of Charles the Bold in 1476 and 1477, and then against Maximilian I in 1499. The Federation grew, 13 cantons joining it by the early sixteenth century. The Swiss Federation had won recognition as an independent political force, but it was not yet a unitary state or nation.

The religious crisis which broke out in Europe in the sixteenth century had as great an impact in Switzerland as in any part of Europe, and the country became a major centre of Protestant reform. The Church in the cantons did little to serve the people. A poor population supported an idle and often ill-educated clergy. Monasteries were rich but did nothing with their wealth. Bishops resisted all change that would affect them. The teachings of Erasmus, Zwingli and Luther were therefore welcomed, the work of Zwingli from his position at Zürich (from 1518) being particularly effective. The spread of Protestant ideas through the cantons led to armed conflict and Zwingli himself was defeated and killed in 1531. The reforms and the armed struggle continued throughout the sixteenth century, leaving the cantons divided between Catholic and Protestant and thus unable to play any effective role in political affairs for long afterwards. But there were unexpected gains as well as losses. Italian Protestants who fled to Zurich in 1555 there revived the manufacture of silk. Geneva received Huguenots from France who introduced the making of clocks. Later, French Protestants took lace manufacture into the Jura and the equally dexterous craft of watch-making.

The long tradition of Swiss neutrality began with the Thirty Years War (1618–48) and continued through the seventeenth and eighteenth centuries. There was some popular discontent during the French Revolution but it achieved little. In 1798, however, the French, under Napoleon, occupied Lausanne and the rest of the country quickly surrendered. A Helvetian Republic was proclaimed, a loose union of the cantons and a free-trade area with its own law-code and army. After the final defeat of Napoleon in 1815, Switzerland resumed its neutral stance, which it has kept ever since.

A new federal state was created in 1848 with its capital at Berne. Avoiding involvement (by a narrow margin) in the Franco-Prussian War of 1870–1, the Swiss maintained their neutrality during the First World War and, despite their common border with Germany, in 1939, though the army was mobilized to defend the frontiers if attacked. Although facing severe economic difficulties, Switzerland held out during the Second World War, receiving many refugees and escaped prisoners.

After 1945 a welfare state was created and wealth attracted to Swiss banks and other financial institutions. The little state of only six million inhabitants became one of the most prosperous parts of Europe. Despite housing the League of Nations at Geneva since 1920, Switzerland has not joined its successor, the United Nations, though it participates fully in several of its agencies.

The population is mixed by virtue of the country's history, but it reveals considerable harmony in diversity. German speakers form the majority with 70%, followed by French 19%, Italian 10% and only 1% Romansch. Other minority groups are negligible in size, but many foreign nationals reside in Switzerland for a variety of reasons and over half a million guest-workers from France, Italy and Spain were attracted there by the booming economy of the post-War years. The population is roughly equally divided between Roman Catholic and Protestant.

See: Alamanni, Burgundians, Celts, Franks, Goths

Switzerland is a federation of 26 cantons, each with its own elected parliament, its own courts (with elected judges) and its own education system. On stamps and coins the name Helvetia is used, a reminder that the Celtic tribe of Helvetii once lived in the western Alps.

Ukraine
Ykraïha

The Land: Ukraine is a vast plain to the north of the Black Sea, drained by the Dnieper and Dniester rivers. As a country, it has no natural boundaries, merging with the great plain of Russia to the north and east and with the Polish lowland to the west. The only mountainous area is a short sector of the Carpathians in the west, between Poland and Romania. Much of the plain is very fertile, its distinctive black earth producing an abundance of grain, fruit and vegetables. The flat, treeless lowland close to the Black Sea is a rich grain-growing area, though occasionally subject to severe drought. Several other areas of the country are heavily wooded. The ports on the Black Sea coast provide important outlets to the Mediterranean, western Europe and the Middle East.

The Language: Ukrainian is a Slav language, distinct from Russian and Polish but related to them. It is most widely spoken in the countryside. In the cities, Russian is as widely used as Ukrainian.

The Name: Until the sixteenth century, Ukraine was a borderland of Russia and the name *Ykraïha* means simply 'borderland'.

The greater part of Ukraine was not glaciated. Rich in both game and vegetation, it attracted Palaeolithic hunter-gatherers, some of whom formed more or less settled communities. The later prehistoric peoples were mainly nomads and found good grazing for their flocks on the gentle grasslands. The Scythians arrived from the east by 1000 BC and left behind many burial mounds. These often contained royal and noble graves containing magnificent gold and silver treasures, along with imports from the Chinese and Greek worlds. Sarmatians, Alans and Huns, all wide-ranging nomad groups, were later immigrants into the rich land. Then the wealth of the Black Sea coastlands attracted Greek colonists who founded a number of cities, including Olbia and Panticapaeum. The plentiful supplies of grain were a

Ukraine

Ukraine's rich black earth provided good grazing for the flocks and herds of prehistoric nomads and has been the home of a succession of peoples, from the Scythians with their rich gold to Goths and Huns. Vikings, following the river routes from the Baltic to the Black Sea, formed the first separate state there in the eleventh century but for centuries Ukraine was governed by stronger powers: by invading Mongols, by Lithuanians and Poles and, from the seventeenth century, by Russia. Throughout, Ukrainians managed to preserve their sense of national identity and their own language and in 1991 regained full independence within the Commonwealth of Independent States.

particular attraction for the Greeks, whose own land could not produce enough for their needs. Later, the region traded with the Roman world through the coastal cities of the Black Sea.

For many centuries Russians and Ukrainians shared the region that is now Ukraine, while various groups of nomads lived on the steppes. A separate realm was first formed there in the eleventh century when a merchant-state was created by Vikings and Slavs in the Dnieper valley, with its centre at Kiev. For a century this was one of the most influential states of eastern Europe and its network of trade reached out far, to Scandinavia, Poland, Russia and the Middle East. In 1240, however, the Mongols invaded from the east, overthrew Kiev and laid waste the plain around it. The region was slow to recover and remained vulnerable to attack from the Mongols who had moved further west.

In the late fourteenth century, the Ukraine was taken over by the Grand Duke of Lithuania and was ruled with moderation for nearly two centuries. Prosperity returned but there was no strong sense of national unity. When Lithuania was merged with Poland in 1569, the lands of the Ukraine were seized by the Polish nobility and many of the farming families were forced to become serfs on their own lands. Many fled to the Dnieper valley and there formed the military order known as the Cossacks. There were also religious differences between Poland and Ukraine. Most Ukrainians were eastern Orthodox Christians, but the Jesuits sought to impose Roman Catholicism on all Polish subjects. The result was a rebellion against Polish rule in 1648, led by the Cossacks, and for six years the Ukraine won a precarious independence. It was brought to an abrupt end when the Polish commanders called in to control Ukraine and Russian troops occupied many of the cities. Gradually, the country was drawn into Russia's control, being treated as a province of the tsar's domain and contemptuously referred to by the Russians as Little Russia.

This was the condition of the Ukraine for the next two centuries but although the tsars tried to impose the Russian way of life they had little success. After 1830, Ukrainian nationalism grew in strength, as also happened among other dependent nations in Europe, encouraged by the spread of education and political awareness in the cities. Moscow encouraged Russians to emigrate there but this failed to halt the spread of nationalism. In 1917, Lenin recognized Ukraine as a sovereign state but at the same time arranged for a Communist government to take power. For three years Ukraine fought against domination from Moscow but in 1923 she joined the Soviet Union. Some bitter years followed for Ukraine. Stalin's collectivization of agriculture led to an appalling famine in 1932–3 in which three million Ukrainians died. Then, many thousands perished in the Stalinist purges and campaign of terror. When the Germans invaded in 1941 many Ukrainians welcomed them as saviours. Disillusion soon set in and a resistance movement fought an effective guerrilla campaign which could not, however, prevent widespread destruction in the cities, oilfields and countryside. After 1945, the strict Soviet rule continued but the Ukraine was not treated too harshly because its resources of oil and grain were of great economic importance to the Soviet Union. The country possessed, in theory, the constitutional right to withdraw from the Union, maintained its own armed forces and was a founder member of the United Nations. Throughout the 1950s and 1960s, the Ukrainian Communist party was very influential in Moscow. But Ukrainian hopes of independence were still alive. After the Gorbachev reforms of the late 1980s, the chance came and in 1991 the Ukraine became an independent republic within the Commonwealth of Independent States.

The modern population is made up of Russians and Ukrainians, with Tatars in the far east of the country.

See: Alans, Huns, Russians, Sarmatians, Scythians, Ukrainians, Vikings

The United Kingdom

The Land The United Kingdom is made up of the kingdoms of England and Scotland, with Northern Ireland, the Principality of Wales, the Isle of Man and the Channel Islands. The main island of Britain, though lacking large mountains and rivers, is one of the most varied regions of Europe. Britain has a landscape of hills, plains and broad valleys, moorland, heath and forest, interspersed with large areas of good farming land. The coastline is long and varied, with many excellent harbours. The climate is generally temperate. The natural resources of Britain are abundant and account for the early development of large-scale industry. Several areas are rich in coal and iron, while off-shore resources of oil and natural gas are of great importance to the modern economy. The island as a whole is densely populated, the main concentrations being in and around London and in the west Midlands. By contrast, large areas of north-west Scotland are very thinly inhabited. Four fifths of the population lives in England.

The Language: English is very mixed in character. Fundamentally, it is a Germanic language introduced by the Anglo-Saxon invaders in the fifth and sixth centuries AD. Germanic words amount to about half of the vocabulary. But there has been heavy influence from French, Latin and Greek from the early Middle Ages to the present. The flexibility of English and its open vocabulary have helped it become one of the most widely spoken languages in the world, used by a seventh of the world population as a first or second language. Welsh is still spoken in Wales, where it is an official language.

The Name: England comes from the Angles, a Germanic tribe who came to the island in the fifth and sixth centuries. Scotland takes its name from the Scotti and Wales from *wealh*, the Anglo-Saxon name for the native Britons.

The earliest humans may have hunted and foraged seasonally in Britain about 500,000 years ago, when the island was joined as a peninsula to western Europe. At the end of the last Ice Age, sea levels rose and by about 11,000 BC, Britain was finally separated from the mainland. From about 11,000 BC, Palaeolithic hunter-gatherers were living in some areas, sheltering in caves such as Kent's Cavern in Devon and Creswell Crags in Derbyshire. By 4000 BC farming had been introduced from the continent and over the next two thousand years the early farmers transformed the landscape. They left their mark also in ritual and burial monuments, such as long barrows and causeway camps, and the great stone circles of Stonehenge and Avebury. Mining for metals began in Britain before 2000 BC, leading to further exploitation of the land and its resources, as more efficient tools were used. New immigrants from Europe probably brought some of these skills with them but there was a strongly individual strain in the prehistoric cultures of the island. Iron-using cultures were established about 600 BC and a society emerged in which warrior-chieftains ruled over and protected groups of dependants. This happened at about the time when the Celts arrived and spread through much of the island. Southern Britain was in contact with Gaul by the second century BC and some degree of immigration may have taken place at this time, especially in the upper levels of society.

When the Romans first came to the island of Britain, the largely Celtic peoples of the country were not unified in any political or cultural sense and were ill equipped to hold out against the Roman armies. Julius Caesar twice invaded south-eastern Britain, in 55 and 54 BC, and then withdrew. Over the following century, Britain remained outside the Roman world, but was increasingly linked to it by trade. In AD 43, the Emperor Claudius sent a large expeditionary force to invade Britain and over the next forty years the conquest of the island as far north as central Scotland was pursued. The limit of the Roman occupation, which at first had advanced to the southern fringe of the Scottish Highlands, was later established between Tyne and Solway, where the Emperor Hadrian ordered a wall to be built, to mark the limit of the Roman province. Hadrian's Wall marked the northern limit of Roman authority in Britain until the end of Roman rule early in the fifth century.

Roman control of the land they named Britannia was enforced by a large army, stationed mainly in the north and west. The spread of a Romanized way of life was more effective in the south and east than elsewhere, and this is where the major cities, towns and villas were built. Roman Britain was most prosperous and peaceful in the third and fourth centuries, productive enough then to export grain, textiles and metals. After AD 350, the island came under increasing threat from sea-raiders based in northern Europe—the Saxons, Franks and Frisians. The great majority of the population continued to speak Celtic, Latin being the language of the army, the law and the Church. Christianity had arrived in the fourth century, but the strength of its hold was not great. When Roman rule ended about 410, much of Roman Britain reverted to a Celtic world, conscious of its Roman past but unable to maintain the orderly society created by Rome.

By the early fifth century, Angles, Saxons and other Germanic peoples, arriving at first in the south-east in small warrior groups, steadily expanded their settlements, absorbing the British population and gradually forming the nuclei of several Anglo-Saxon kingdoms. They had come to Britain as pagans and their conversion to Christianity began in 597 when Pope Gregory sent Augustine to Kent to spread the Gospel in the island. In the west and north, large areas still remained Celtic. Wales and the south-west supported a number of minor chiefdoms. Scotland was divided between several small kingdoms, including that of the Picts in the east and Dalriada in the west. Immigration of Scotti from Ireland was later to provide a name for Scotland.

The United Kingdom includes the main island of England, Scotland and Wales, with its islands, the six counties of Northern Ireland, the Shetlands, Orkneys and Hebrides, the Isle of Man, the Isles of Scilly, and the Channel Islands of Guernsey, Jersey, Alderney and Sark. Scotland and almost half of England were ice-covered during the last Ice Age and until about 11,000 BC Britain was linked by land to western Europe. The earliest people would have come as hunters, following herds of animals in search of good summer feeding grounds. Later settlers, migrants and invaders, had to make the short crossing from western France (Celts, Romans, Normans) or the longer, more hazardous journey across the North Sea from northern Europe (Angles, Jutes, Saxons, Vikings).

The United Kingdom 295

In the ninth century, the Anglo-Saxon kingdom of England faced sudden and serious invasions from the Vikings of Scandinavia. Viking raids plagued the south and east from shortly before 800, and by 865 a large Scandinavian army was in eastern England seeking permanent settlement. From 871 English resistance was led by Alfred, king of Wessex, who won major victories against them but had to leave the invaders in control of a large area of eastern England, territory known as the Danelaw. Other Norse settlers moved into northern England in the tenth century from Ireland, so that for a time large areas of England belonged to the Scandinavian world. From 980, Viking raiding intensified and led to the installation of a sequence of Danish kings.

But another European power had ambitions to rule in England and plausible claims to do so: the Normans of France. In September 1066, Duke William of Normandy invaded and defeated the English. On Christmas Day 1066, William was crowned king of England and for the next century an Anglo-Norman monarchy ruled the island. Norman ways of administration were introduced, along with a new Norman aristocracy, but the life of the common people was little affected by the Norman conquest. The power of the Norman nobles, however, was great and posed problems for later kings. Their castles studded the land, providing local centres of security and administration. England remained linked to Normandy until 1204, but already native English characteristics were developing in the kingdom though the culture of the court and the administration were Norman French.

Under the Normans and their successors, government was increasingly centralized. A more centralized monarchy also emerged in Scotland at this time, under David I. But Wales consisted of many small chiefdoms which resisted amalgamation. Both Scotland and Wales remained independent of England, though Normans advanced into south Wales and occasionally intervened in Scotland. The next two centuries saw the development of a distinctive English monarchy with the delicate balance between the king and the feudal barons set out in the famous Magna Carta of 1215. By 1400, the English had become a nation, with their own culture and a language which served both as a vernacular and as a medium for outstanding literature. The period from 1200–1400 was far from peaceful: England was at war for most of the years 1290–1390. In 1348 the outbreak of plague known as the Black Death ravaged the population of England and Scotland, killing between a third and a half of the total. Not until the seventeenth century did the population reach the four million or so of the mid fourteenth century.

The wealth of England during this period was still its land and the great majority of the English people worked on it. Apart from producing grain and supporting animals, the most important industry of the period was based on the fine wool which was produced by large flocks of sheep. Mining of tin, iron and coal also developed, but England's growing wealth was produced by her farmers and workers in woollen textiles.

Scotland and Wales developed more slowly. The Scottish kingdom covered the area of modern Scotland by the late twelfth century and there followed a stable period under the effective kings William I and Alexander II and III. The more fertile lowlands were developed and trade began to grow with Europe. But Wales had always suffered from a lack of unified political control. By the twelfth century there were three major kingdoms: Gwynedd in the north, Powys in the south and Deheubarth in the south, along with lesser chiefdoms. Relations with Edward I of England deteriorated after 1277 and war in 1282–3 resulted in the English conquest of the north, secured by the building of the great castles of Caernarvon, Conway, Harlech and Beaumaris. Welsh resistance, however, was far from broken, and Wales was not finally united to the English crown until 1535, though parts of the country remained little altered and resisted absorption by the English.

Throughout the fourteenth and fifteenth centuries, England was still closely linked with France and English kings laid claim to extensive territory across the Channel. Intermittently, from 1338 to 1431, vastly expensive campaigns were conducted in France. The victory at Agincourt, in 1415, was the high point of English domination in France. The death of Henry V, the renewal of French nationalism and the extraordinary intervention of Joan of Arc steadily undermined the English campaign and over the next half century England lost most of her French territories.

The fifteenth century was a complex period in which both change and continuity are evident. Henry VII, after 1485, stabilized England and healed old wounds, without changing utterly the mediaeval character of the monarchy. His son and successor Henry VIII, however, was responsible for several measures which were to set the kingdom on a new path, not least the break with Rome and the creation of a climate for Protestantism. The politically uncertain reigns of Edward VI and Mary Tudor were followed by the long stability of Elizabeth I's forty four years of supreme power. Elizabeth was authoritarian and secretive but she was also slow and cautious, nearly always making sure that she ruled with popular and parliamentary consent. The Protestant Reformation was confirmed, economic progress was steady despite rising inflation, and the population of England began to increase sharply. From about two million in 1450, it had reached nearly four million by 1600.

England was still a relatively underpopulated land. Most towns were small, though growing in the sixteenth century and there were few large cities. The merchant class was on the increase as overseas trade grew and the landed gentry became an important social and political force. At the other end of the social scale, poverty also increased and was perhaps the greatest social evil of the time. Culturally, of course, the period from the sixteenth to the early seventeenth century was one of the most brilliant in British history. Although its principal figure is Shakespeare, this was also the age of Marvell, Bacon, Jonson, Spenser and More. The Renaissance came late to England, but its late flowering was a dazzling display, in literature, painting and architecture.

The death of Elizabeth, without an heir, brought the crowns of England and Scotland together in the person of James I (VI of Scotland). The decades that followed seem, on the face of it, to be one of the most turbulent in British history, for they witnessed one bloody and one peaceful revolution. The accession of Charles I in 1625 gave no hint of what was to follow within fifteen years. Charles committed a series of foolish blunders which caused open rebellion. After a wasteful civil war from 1642 to 1646, the king's forces were defeated and Charles was tried for treason and executed in 1649. For the next eleven years England was a republic with Oliver Cromwell as head of state. On his death in 1658, the support of the army and gentry for the republican Commonwealth quickly waned and in 1660 Charles II was summoned back to England and the monarchy was restored. Despite several crises, the power of the king was greatly strengthened under Charles, but then squandered by the Catholic James II in the years 1685 to 1688. His promotion of the Catholic cause led to his downfall and flight from England in 1688 and his replacement by his daughter Mary and the Dutch Protestant William of Orange in the 'Glorious Revolution'.

Support for the Stuarts was still alive in Scotland after the Union and twice erupted into revolt against England, in 1715 and 1745. Assistance from France was expected but failed to materialize and on both occasions English armies brought the movement to a close. The rising of 1745, centred on the romantic but ineffective figure of Bonnie Prince Charlie, was the last throw for the Stuarts. Its defeat was followed by oppression of the Highland Clearances, which drove many Scots to emigrate to the New World.

Already before 1745, Scotland had become a major source in European intellectual life, especially in literature and philosophy. James Boswell, David Hume and Adam Smith, and later Walter Scott, provided a distinctive Scottish contribution to the age. Scottish education had long been highly developed and Scotland boasted more ancient universities than England. There were other cultural genres which witnessed development in the eighteenth century, including Scottish folk-song, though this was later adapted for English tastes.

Throughout most of the eighteenth century, Britain enjoyed buoyant growth in her economy, population and prestige in the wider world. Agriculture was productive and kept pace with the rise in population, helped by major innovations after 1720 in machinery and crop production. Industrial growth was stimulated by an increasingly affluent society after 1750, laying the foundation for the Industrial Revolution. Those already rich became very much richer and wealth percolated down the social scale, reaching landowners and artisans alike. A strong middle class emerged and became influential in political and cultural affairs. Art, architecture and literature all flourished, as did the most English of all arts, landscape gardening. But the beginning of the Industrial Revolution was perhaps the most significant development of the time, the main impulse coming from new methods of smelting iron, the development of steam-power and the invention of new machinery for making textiles. In no other country was the drive towards industrialization so urgent and effective.

Despite the need to oppose Napoleon, which put a great burden on the economy of the country, Britain advanced steadily towards the position of the world's first industrial nation, which was achieved by the early 1800s. Social problems came in the wake of this advance, especially in the rapidly growing cities and these were to become acute by the mid nineteenth century. Impressive economic progress demanded political reform with far-reaching consequences. The Reform Act of 1832 gave the middle class a stake in government, increasing the electorate by more than 50%. In the following year, slavery was finally ended in British colonies. There was growing appreciation of the need to alleviate hardship where possible, to introduce better education, to organize public control of health and sanitation in the industrial cities. Contemporaries were aware of rapid change and 'improvement by self-help', and most took pride in British achievement.

It is impossible to separate the image of nineteenth century Britain from the image of Queen Victoria, who presided over the great days of industrial might and imperial power. That the revolutions of 1848 found no effective echo in Britain owed much to the strength of her position, as well as to firm parliamentary democracy. In her early middle years, Victoria was by no means popular and her relations with the government were strained. She was far from the grand queen empress she became. The later Victorian years saw challenges to many assumptions, political, social and cultural, but no serious questioning of the monarchy. When Victoria died in 1901, a clearly defined epoch ended, to be followed by the short Edwardian interlude before the catastrophe of the Great War of 1914–18.

The great conflict which was welcomed by so many in 1914 was a shattering experience for Britain. British society was drastically affected by the war. The old order and its certainties had gone. Much of the remaining power of the landowners was lost. The aspirations of the lower social ranks began to find a voice. A brief economic boom in the early 1920s was followed by the crash of 1929 and the succeeding depression of the 1930s. British governments after 1933 were reluctant to re-arm and confront the growing threat from Nazi Germany until it was almost too late. After the Munich agreement, Britain moved towards war with more resignation than hope. The events of 1940–1 seemed to confirm the worst fears as Nazi German power was extended over most of Europe. Hitler's assault on Russia and the American entry into the wider conflict in December 1941, assured the eventual victory over the Nazis. Britain's inestimable contribution had been to stand alone and refuse to capitulate in 1940.

The Second World War drained Britain of her remaining reserves of wealth and much of her strength. The years of reconstruction after 1945 were harsh and troublesome. Economic recovery did not make headway until after 1950. In a short time Britain lost her empire. India gained independence in 1947 and was followed in the 1950s and 1960s by many of the colonies in Africa and the Caribbean. One of the social effects of decolonization was the flow of immigrants from the former colonies into Britain after 1950, creating problems of integration which have not yet been resolved. Although Britain's world-role was greatly reduced, her ties with the Commonwealth and a deep-seated aversion in many quarters to being regarded as merely a country of Europe kept her out of the European Community until 1972. Economic prosperity in the years from 1957 to 1970 brought a marked levelling out within British society, but was followed by a steep decline in manufacturing industry and trade in the 1970s, only partly alleviated by the large revenues derived from North Sea oil and gas. The 1980s brought a further erosion of the manufacturing base in favour of a service economy, the future of which is still far from certain in an increasingly competitive European free market.

See: Angles, Britons, Celts, Danes, Frisians, Germans, Jutes, Normans, Picts, Romans, Scotti, Vikings, Welsh

Yugoslavia Bosnia-Hercegovina, Croatia Macedonia, Montenegro, Serbia, Slovenia

The Land: Yugoslavia, now bitterly divided, is a country of great geographical diversity. Much of it is high, mountainous, wooded terrain, with only a narrow coastal plain between the Dinaric Alps and the sea. Many islands lie off the Dalmatian coast. Inland, the mountains fall away to the east and around the Danube valley lies a lowland which stretches southward from the Great Hungarian Plain. This plain contains many of the larger cities, including the capital Belgrade, and is a vital agricultural resource. The borders with Albania, Greece and Bulgaria are marked by further high ranges of mountains. Within much of the country, natural communications are very poor and many regions are still isolated and difficult to reach.
The Languages: All the main languages spoken in Yugoslavia belong to the South Slavic group. The three most widespread are Serbo-Croat, Slovene and Macedonian.
The Name: Yugoslavia means 'land of the south Slavs'.

Yugoslavia is the most diverse of all the states of modern Europe in relief, climate, population and culture. Its mixture of peoples has brought serious problems since it was founded, never more so than today, when the political structure of the country has completely collapsed into civil war. As this book goes to press, the survival of the federal state in any form seems unlikely.

The remains of early humans and their artifacts have been found in the western Balkans dating to at least 200,000 years ago. Hunter-gatherer groups were active in the mountains and on the coastal lowland. From about 7000 BC the domestication of plants and animals led to a flourishing agricultural settlement over the next four thousand years, especially in the valleys of the Danube and the Save. The best known sites from that period are at Lepenski Vir and Starcevo. From about 3500 BC, northern peoples moved into the Balkans, introducing a pastoral economy and a warlike social structure. The descendants of these people were the Illyrians, a strong warrior people who controlled the mountainous lands to the north of Greece. The Greeks founded colonies on the Adriatic coast—at Zadar and Vis—and traded with the tribes of the interior. Late in the third century BC, Roman interest in the Balkans began and slowly over the next two centuries the area of Yugoslavia was absorbed in the Roman empire.

Serbs, Croats and Slovenes all belong to the group of southern Slavs who invaded the region from the sixth century onward. By the Middle Ages, both the Croats and the Serbs had established independent kingdoms. The Croats were overrun by the Magyars and then by the Turks. The large, successful and influential Serbian kingdom was also conquered by the Turks. In the long years of occupation, the subject peoples retained their Slavic nationalism and language, but there could be no hope of any independent Southern Slavic state until the Turkish empire collapsed in the mid nineteenth century. In 1878, Serbia briefly became an independent state. More wars against the Turks followed but in 1914 a Serbian revolutionary assassinated the Austrian Archduke Ferdinand. Austria-Hungary declared war on Serbia and the Great War of 1914–18, involving most of the countries of Europe, began.

A single state that would draw together the various small Slav states in the western Balkans had been discussed when Turkish power waned in the nineteenth century, but no action was taken until 1915. Then a committee of refugee Slavs from the Austro-Hungarian empire was formed to bring pressure to bear on the Allies. In 1917, agreement was reached on the establishment of a state which would include Slovenia and Dalmatia (both Austrian provinces) and Serbia and Montenegro (both independent states). The new state, first appearing under the name of the Kingdom of Serbs, Croats and Slovenes, was re-named Yugoslavia in 1929.

The state was a complex patchwork of peoples, languages, religions and cultures, and from the start there were inevitable rivalries. Apart from Slovenes, Croats and Serbs there were ten other distinct linguistic groups, the most significant being Germans, Magyars and Albanians. There were religious divisions too. Slovenes and Croats were mainly Roman Catholics, the Serbs Orthodox, while in the south there were large Muslim communities. The drawing of boundaries around this complex mass naturally presented immense difficulties. The frontier with Albania had been established on paper in 1913, but was not laid out on the ground until after 1920. On the Bulgarian border there was no clear ethnic or linguistic divide, but parts of Bulgaria were assigned to Yugoslavia on grounds of military security. The greatest problem arose in the north-west, where Yugoslavia demanded a port on the Adriatic, in a coastal area which had already been granted to Italy in 1915. An awkward compromise was reached, under which Trieste, an Italian city, remained in Italy, while Fiume went to the new state. But in 1919 the Italians took Fiume by force, leaving only its suburb and an indifferent harbour to Yugoslavia. It was later recognized as a free city.

The progress of Yugoslavia in its early years was not spectacular. By 1929 it had become a royal dictatorship under Alexander I, who created a police-state with support from Italy under Mussolini. Alexander was assassinated in 1934 and until the Second World War the political scene was darkened. The Second World War was a time of great trauma for Yugoslavia. The German invasion of April 1941 was followed by occupation and partition, Slovenia being assigned to Austria, Dalmatia and part of Croatia to Italy, part of the Danube plain to Hungary, while Bulgaria and Albania divided the southern province of Macedonia between them.

Three small protectorates remained—Croatia, Serbia and Montenegro—but even here there was serious discord. Croatia was ruled by a pro-Nazi regime which dealt harshly with its Serbian neighbours, a fact which has never been forgotten. The main resistance to the Nazi occupation came from partisans in Slovenia and Croatia, led by Josip Broz (Tito) and others. Four years of savage underground fighting, punctuated by many atrocities, left a bitter legacy for post-war Yugoslavia. The boundaries of the country were restored after 1947, Istria and the Julian Alps being assigned to Yugoslavia and Trieste returned to Italy. The restored republic was a federal structure comprising the six republics of Bosnia and Hercegovina, Croatia, Serbia, Slovenia, Macedonia and Montenegro.

After the war, the minority populations changed significantly. Most of

Yugoslavia

The Land of the South Slavs was formed in an attempt to bring together a number of small Balkan States which had in the past been independent kingdoms but which, by the middle of the nineteenth century had been under Turkish rule for some four hundred years. The uneasy grouping of six republics was restored after the Second World War and lasted, under a strong central government, until the changes in eastern Europe in 1990 brought new demands for independence. Slovenia and Croatia broke away, and a bitter civil war began between Serbia, who dominated the Federal forces, and Croatia. By March 1992 Slovenia and Croatia had both been recognized by the United Nations as independent countries and Bosnia-Hercegovina had voted for independence. But no final solution had yet been found for the remaining republics or for Serbian minorities outside Serbia.

the Germans in the north fled to west Germany. The Hungarians actually became more numerous while in the south, Albanians remained the largest ethnic minority. The Muslim community is now concentrated in Bosnia, many of its members being of Turkish origin, though as many as half may be Serbs who have converted to Islam. Albanians in the southern province of Kosovo continue to agitate against federal government as they wish to become part of Albania.

From 1945 Yugoslavia was governed by a Communist regime under Tito, but after 1948 the country increasingly diverged from official Soviet policy. An attempt at collectivization of agriculture was made but soon abandoned as unworkable. Tito's views on unemployment were realistic and many Yugoslavs were allowed to seek work in western Europe, especially in Germany. Economic difficulties mounted after the 1960s, and after Tito's death in 1980, decline and division increased, to the point where civil strife seemed inevitable, especially between Croats and Serbs. In 1990 and 1991 serious fighting broke out between the two republics. After months of international negotiation and a bitter war, Croatia was recognized by the United Nations as an independent republic. Slovenia, which was not involved in the fighting, was also recognized. In March 1992 the situation in the remaining republics was tense. Macedonia and Kosovo (a province in southern Serbia) both have close links with Albania and northern Greece; Croatia and Serbia claim parts of Bosnia-Hercegovina and Bosnia itself has voted for independence. However, the Serbian minority (up to a third of Bosnia's population) boycotted the referendum and a very large part of the former federal army is stationed on Bosnian land—and is mainly loyal to Serbia. Although a UN peacekeeping force has arrived to secure the Croatia–Serbia ceasefire, Serbians still living in Croatia are seeking a permanent recognition of their status. It seems certain that in the coming months the remains of the federal republic of Yugoslavia will be disbanded. The problem of the southern Slavs has not been resolved.
See: Celts, Croatians, Illyrians, Romans, Serbs, Slavs, Slovenes, Thracians, Turks, Vlachs.

Europe's Smallest States

Andorra / Principat d'Andorra

Surrounded on all sides by high mountains, the valleys of Andorra have been occupied since prehistoric times and have been an independent state since 819 when the son of Charlemagne made a grant of land to the Spanish bishop of Urgal. The principality covers 179 square miles (464 sq km) and lies in the central Pyrenees, on the borders of France and Spain. Since the thirteenth century it has been jointly governed by France and Spain. Today only about 30 per cent of the people are native Andorrans, 60 per cent Spanish and the rest either French or other Europeans. The official language is Catalan.

Liechtenstein / Fürstentum Liechtenstein

Between Austria and Switzerland, in the upper valley of the Rhine, is the principality of Liechtenstein (62 square miles, 160 sq km). The ancestors of its people were the Alamanni, though there were settlements throughout the Rhine valley from prehistoric times. Once ruled as two independent lordships in the Holy Roman Empire, it became a single principality in 1719. The two lordships became its two regions, the Upper and Lower Country. The official language is German but an Alamanni dialect has survived and in the Upper Country descendants of Swiss immigrants from the thirteenth century speak their own dialect.

Monaco / Principauté de Monaco

Less than a square mile (1.9 sq km) in area, the headland and hills of Monaco have been settled since the Stone Age. Greeks, Phoenicians and Romans all traded with its early peoples and, since 1297, when the ruling family of Grimaldi came to power, it has been almost continuously independent. For a short period after the French Revolution it was annexed by France and in 1815 was placed under the protection of Sardinia. But in 1861 a treaty was signed with France and independence was regained. All Monaco's land frontiers are with France and French is its official language.

San Marino / Repubblica di San Marino

According to tradition, Saint Marinus and a group of Christians escaped from persecution in Dalmatia in 301 and found refuge on the hillsides of Monte Titano in west-central Italy. The settlement developed into an independent commune and although it was surrounded by more powerful states, it remained independent. Independence was confirmed at the end of the Napoleonic Wars and again, in 1861, when Italy became a unified state. It now covers 23.5 square miles (61 sq km). The official language is Italian, though many of the inhabitants still speak a dialect descended from an earlier Celtic language.

Vatican City / Stato della Città del Vaticano

By early mediaeval times the Pope was head of the western Church and also had considerable political power. From 756 a large part of central and north western Italy formed the Papal States, stretching from Rome and parts of Tuscany through Umbria to Bologna in the north. In 1870 the Papal States became part of Italy and passed out of the Church's control but in 1929 the Vatican Palace itself became an independent state, ensuring that the head of the Catholic Church was not subject to any outside political control. Vatican City covers only 0.15 square miles (0.4 sq km) but as the centre of the Catholic Church and the residence of the Pope, it has considerable influence. The summer palace (Castel Gandolfo) is included in the Vatican's territories, which house some of the world's greatest paintings and treasures.

The European Community

When the Second World War ended in 1945, Europe was a divided and exhausted continent. As the Soviet Union began to exert its strength in eastern Europe and the Cold War began, it became more and more important for West Germany to be rehabilitated and, in particular, to be reconciled with France. It was with this aim that, in 1952, the first European Community, the European Coal and Steel Community, was proposed by Robert Schuman (the French Foreign Minister) and Jean Monnet. At first concerned only with Europe's basic industries, Schuman's community was intended to be 'a community of peaceful interests for France, Federal Germany and anyone else who wanted to join.' Its structure remains the basis of the Community today: a High Authority to act in the interests of all the member nations, not for any individual state; a Council of Ministers to represent member states, a parliamentary assembly and a court of justice.

The founder members of the Community were France, West Germany, Italy, Holland, Belgium and Luxembourg and in 1957 these six countries signed a further treaty, The Treaty of Rome. This established two new Communities—the European Economic Community (EEC) and the European Atomic Energy Community (Euratom). All three were merged in 1965. Denmark, Ireland and the United Kingdom joined in 1973, Greece in 1981 and Spain and Portugal in 1986. Turkey, Austria, Sweden, Finland, Malta and Cyprus have applied for membership and other states in Scandinavia and eastern and central Europe may join in future.

The first aim of the Community was to establish a common market and customs union, allowing the free movement of goods, services and people among the member states. It also established certain common laws and policies, including a common agricultural policy. As the Community developed, however, the need to complete the Internal Market and to get rid of barriers to trade became paramount and in 1986 the member states signed the Single European Act, the first amendment to the Rome Treaty. The completion of a large, free market was a primary goal of the Act but there are five further main objectives: the development of backward or depressed regions; co-operation on research and technology; monetary co-operation; a common social policy and a common environmental policy. The first goal, the establishment of an area without internal frontiers, comes into effect on

31 December 1992. The Community member states agreed to another amendment to the Treaty in the Dutch city of Maastricht in December 1991. This is intended to bring about European Union by linking the member states in further areas of common policy, including foreign policy and defence, as well as policing matters. Community leaders also agreed to establish economic and monetary union with a common currency at the latest by 1999. The main Community institutions are:

The European Parliament consists of 518 members (MEPs), elected by voters in each country. Members (81 from the UK) sit in groups according to their political parties. It does not make Community rules and has limited powers to oppose them. Critics of the system maintain that as the only directly elected EC institution, it should have greater democratic powers. Sessions are usually held in Strasbourg, committee meetings in Brussels. Its administrative headquarters is in Luxembourg.

The European Council, made up of the heads of government of the member states, meets at least twice a year to discuss general Community matters and joint foreign policy.

The Council, consists of ministers from the governments of each state. It approves the EC budget and takes decisions on Community matters, sometimes in co-operation with the European Parliament. It operates sometimes only unanimously but also takes decisions on certain areas of policy by majority vote.

The Commission, the Community's civil service, initiates Community policy and, as the descendant of the original High Authority, acts in the interest of the Community as a whole, without favouring any individual state. The 17 Commissioners are chosen jointly by the member states and must be strictly independent. The Commission headquarters is in Brussels.

The Court of Justice rules on all questions of Community law including on complaints by individuals who believe that Community laws have been broken in their own countries. Together with the Court of Auditors (which examines Community accounts) and the European Investment Bank, it is situated in Luxembourg.

Index

A
Abdera 137
Achaea 95
Achaeans 91
Adam of Bremen 280
Adriatic Sea 17, 30, 100, 131, 304
Aegean Sea 29, 32, 88, 92, 93, 176, 213, 237
Aenus 137
Aequi 118
Aeschylus 93
Aestii 161, 162
Aetius 62
Africa 19, 20, 38
Aggersborg 72
Agincourt 297
Aix-la-Chapelle 81
Aix-en-Provence 106
Alamanni 48–9, 77, 80, 87, 194, 203, 285
Alans 49–50, 134, 141, 275, 288
Alaric I of the Visigoths 89
Albania 100, 146, 152–5, 216, 244, 302, 303, 304, 306
Albanian language 152, 237
Albanians 101, 304
Alesia 66
Alexander the Great 32, 94, 114, 213
Alexander II of Scotland 197
Alexander III of Scotland 297
Alexander I of Yugoslavia 304
Alfonso I of Portugal 258
Alfred the Great 143, 296
Algeciras 51
Algeria 200
Alps 16, 17, 73, 223, 284
Alsace 192, 197, 199, 201, 207
Alsace-Lorraine 197, 208
Altamira 21, 273
Amerindians 22
Amsterdam 220
Anabaptists 170
Andalusia 141
Andorra 307
Angles 38, 50–1, 104, 124, 292
Anglii 86
Anglo-Saxons 146
Anjou 196
Antibes 193
Antwerp 168, 169, 170
Apennines 16, 30, 122, 123
Apulia 112
Aquitaine 55, 80, 193, 194, 196, 197
Arabs 37, 40, 51–2, 90, 113, 240, 258, 276–7, 280
Aragon 277
Arctic Ocean 16
Ardennes 168, 169
Ardiaei 101
Arezzo 74, 75
Ariovistus 85, 134
Aristophanes 93
Arius 89
Armenia 95
Armenians 177
Arno, river 73, 106
Arras 58
Artemis 76, 137
Asdings 141
Asia, migrants from 151
Asia Minor 92, 93, 95
Asparukh 61
Assyrians 102, 114
Astorge 135
Athena 93, 95
Athens 92, 93, 94, 213, 215
Atlantic Ocean 16, 142, 143
Attila the Hun 97
Augsburg 109
Augustine, St 125, 294
Augustus, Emperor 35, 60, 81, 85, 106, 274
Austerlitz 158
Austria 32, 63, 68, 106, 150–1, 156–60, 179, 180, 187, 198, 208, 224, 243, 246, 304, 306
Austria-Hungary 68, 129, 133, 151, 159, 179, 224–6, 303
Austrians 222

Avars 53, 57, 80, 106, 131, 132, 157, 267
Avebury 293

B

Babenbergs 157
Babylon 113, 114
Baghdad 139
Bajar (Avar ruler) 53
Balkan League 176
Balkans 17, 25, 26, 30, 31, 37, 39, 40, 50, 60–1, 64, 67, 68, 87, 88, 89, 90, 91, 94, 97, 100–1, 119, 129, 130, 131, 134, 137, 139, 151, 152–5, 174, 302–3
Baltic languages 45
Baltic Sea 17, 82, 135, 142, 184–6, 267, 282
Baltic States 161–7
Balts 54, 161
Barbarians 39–40
Barcelona 274
Barents Sea 266
Basque language 41–2, 273
Basques 41, 55–6, 278
Batavi 219
Batavians 121
Battle Axe people 27, 28, 33
Bavaria 57, 63, 66, 80, 158, 202, 203
Bavarians 49, 56–7, 138, 204, 210, 216
Beaker folk 24, 27, 28, 33
Bede 50, 104, 125
Belgae 57–8, 168, 169

Belgium 57, 78, 81, 168–72, 218, 219, 222, 246
Belgrade 224
Belisarius 90, 141
Benevento 240
Berbers 51, 52, 90
Berlin 207, 209, 210, 272
Berne 286
Birger Jarl 280
Birka 136, 144, 280
Bismarck, Otto von 199, 208
Black Death 196, 230, 241, 251, 282, 297
Black Sea 17, 24, 54, 64, 70, 85, 88, 92, 128, 129, 173, 174, 261, 262, 266, 267, 280, 288, 290
Bohemia 56, 63, 69, 133, 152, 158, 178, 179, 181, 182, 204
Bohuslän 279
Boii 33, 179
Boleslav I of Poland 132
Boniface, St 82
Bonn 209
Book of Kells 67
Boris (Bulgar ruler) 61
Boris I of Bulgaria 174
Bosnia 129, 139, 151, 226, 304
Bosworth 147
Boudicca 121
Boyars 60
Boyne, Battle of 235
Brabant 169
Brandenburg-Prussia 207
Bratislava 178

Brebières 79
Breitenfeld 282
Bremen 206
Breton language 43, 59, 192
Bretons 58–9
Britain 16, 36, 38, 50, 51, 57, 59–60, 64, 67, 72, 81, 101, 121, 124–7, 146–7, 151, 184, 199, 264, 292–301
Britons 59–60
Brittany 59, 196, 197, 200
Brno 178
Bronze Age 15, 24, 26–9, 32, 33, 55, 101, 109, 156, 169, 179, 183, 203, 231, 237, 261, 279, 284
Bruges 169
Bucharest 264
Bucovina 264
Budapest 226
Bug, river 143
Bulgaria 16, 96, 139, 173–7, 261, 302, 304
Bulgarian language 131, 173
Bulgars 40, 60–61, 68, 173–4, 177, 214, 264
Burgas 173
Burgenland 226
Burgundians 39, 62, 78, 138, 194, 200, 201, 210, 253, 285
Burgundy 169, 196, 197, 219
Byelorussia 254, 256, 266
Byron, Lord 215
Byzantine empire 15, 36–7, 61, 106, 113, 122, 139, 149, 150

Byzantines 68, 69, 107, 174, 214, 240, 267, 280
Byzantium 52, 95, 121, 137, 142, 214

C

Cabral, Pedro 260
Cadiz 114
Caere 73, 75, 76
Caister-by-Norwich 125
Calahorra 55
Calais 197
Caledonians 115
Calvin, John 170
Calvinists 220
Campania 73, 117, 123
Canute 72, 184
Capua 112
Carnac 193
Carnuti 33
Carol I of Romania 264
Carpathians 16, 18, 53, 70, 84, 128, 223, 261, 288
Carrara 240
Carthage 24, 114, 118–19, 141
Caspian Sea 17, 139, 266, 268, 280
Castile 258, 277
Catalan language 43, 273
Catalans 278
Catherine the Great 270
Catholicism 158, 197, 235, 256, 276, 286
Caucasian race 45
Caucasus 16, 18, 20, 30, 128, 266
Ceausescu, Nicolae 177, 265

Celtic languages 41, 43, 44, 91, 131, 294
Celts 33, 34, 63–7, 70, 73, 82, 85, 99, 106, 115, 146, 156, 179, 193, 200, 203, 224, 232, 238, 257, 261, 274, 284, 293
Ceuta 260
Chalons 58
Champagne 196
Charlemagne 53, 55, 57, 80–1, 82, 108, 127, 142, 149, 169, 194, 219, 240, 245
Charles IV, Holy Roman Emperor 69, 246
Charles V, Holy Roman Emperor 157, 169, 170, 219, 277
Charles the Bold 285
Charles Martel 51, 80, 194, 276
Charles I 298
Charles II 298
Charles I of Anjou 154
Charles II of France 112
Chartres 33, 112
Chatti 86
Cherusci 86
Childeric 78
Chiusi 73
Christianity 35, 36, 40, 52, 55, 58, 61, 62, 67, 69, 72, 79, 82, 89, 101, 103, 107, 120, 121, 125, 127, 129, 133, 135, 136, 148, 150, 157, 166, 174, 184, 224, 228, 232, 249, 267, 276, 280, 294

Cid, El 52, 277
Cimbri 85
Cirta 141
Cividale 108
Claudius, Emperor 60, 293
Clontarf 234
Clotilde 62
Clovis 62, 78–9, 194
Collins, Michael 236
Cologne 78, 79, 206
Columba, St 115, 232
Columbus, Christopher 277
Communism 155, 177, 191, 208, 226, 265, 271, 272, 291, 306
Constantine the Great 35, 36, 121, 122, 124, 214
Constantinople (Istanbul) 36, 37, 61, 90, 95, 121, 122, 139, 150, 174, 176, 214, 240, 242, 262, 267, 268
Copenhagen 186, 198, 251
Cordoba 51, 52, 274
Corinth 92, 94, 213, 214
Cornwall 146
Cossacks 140, 290
Crécy 246
Crete 16, 26, 29, 92, 110, 213, 215
Crimea 64, 90
Crimean War 264
Cro-Magnon man 20, 21
Croatia 129, 131, 159, 226, 304, 306, 309
Croats 67–8, 129, 134, 224, 303, 306

Cromwell, Oliver 235, 298
Cuthbert, St 142
Cyprus 16, 92, 217
Cyril, St 174, 267
Cyrillic alphabet 61, 173, 266
Czech language 45, 131, 178, 253
Czechoslovakia 56, 131, 133, 178–82, 226, 265
Czechs 68–9, 178–80, 182

D

Dacia 88, 146, 262, 265
Dacians 70, 85, 261
Dalmatia 101, 159, 226, 303, 304, 308
Dalriada 128, 294
Danelaw 72, 184, 296
Danes 71–2, 82, 126, 162, 183–7, 283
Danish language 44, 183, 279
Danube, river 17, 24, 38, 39, 40, 48, 50, 53, 56, 63, 64, 70, 84, 87, 88, 97, 106, 123, 124, 131, 138, 156, 157, 173, 174, 178, 179, 223, 224, 261, 302
Danzig 255, 256
Dardani 101
Dark Ages 39, 40, 148
Davi I of Scotland 296
De Gaulle, Charles 200
Decebalus 70

Deheubarth 297
Delos 93
Delphi 64, 93
Denmark 71–2, 105, 135, 142, 143, 145, 162, 183–7, 208, 230, 249, 251, 279, 282
Derby 72, 142
Dinaric range 16
Diocletian 36, 121
DNA 46, 56
Dnieper, river 16, 130, 131, 140, 143, 166, 266, 288, 290
Dniester, river 16, 130, 159, 266, 288
Don, river 16, 108, 123, 128, 143, 266
Dorchester-on-Thames 125
Dresden 207
Drogheda 235
Druids 60, 83
Dublin 102, 144, 234, 235, 236
Dunadd 127
Durham 113
Düsseldorf 207
Dutch language 44, 218
Dutch people 222
Dvina, river 143, 164

E

East Anglia 125
Ebro, river 17, 55, 56, 98
Edward the Confessor 112
Edward I 147, 297
Edward VI 298
Egypt 26, 51, 52, 64, 95

Elbe, river 17, 38, 53, 85, 106, 126, 132, 138, 202, 204
Elizabeth I 298
Elymians 130
England 38, 72, 96, 104, 105, 112–3, 142, 150, 234–6, 258, 293, 296–8
English Channel 17, 82, 87
English language 41, 42, 44, 292
Erasmus, Desidarius 286
Erik the Red 143
Essex 59, 125
Estonia 54, 76, 162–3, 184, 190, 282, 283
Estonian language 42, 77, 161, 162, 188, 223
Ethelred II 112
Etruria 73–6
Etruscans 30, 33, 73–6, 83, 117, 237, 238, 244
Eurasians 37
Euripides 93
European Community 200, 217, 222, 244, 246, 278, 301, 309
Evans, Sir Arthur 109

F
Faeroese 44
Fascism 243, 244, 278
Ferdinand II, Holy Roman Emperor 206
Ferdinand, Archduke 129, 303
Fiesole 75
Finland 16, 76–7, 105, 188–91, 282, 283
Finnish language 42, 76, 105, 162, 188, 223, 279
Finno-Ugrian languages 42, 76, 109, 161, 162, 188, 223
Finns 76–7, 188–91, 266, 272
First World War 129, 150–1, 159, 172, 176, 179, 187, 199, 208, 216, 226, 236, 252, 264, 271, 286, 300, 303
Fiume 304
Flanders 169, 172, 196, 219
Flemings 80, 172
Flemish language 168, 192, 218
Floki 227
Florence 241, 242
Font-de-Gaume 193
France 16, 30, 37, 57, 58, 66, 79, 80–1, 82, 96, 104, 112, 143, 150, 158, 170, 192–201, 208, 209, 219, 222, 240, 242, 245, 246, 278, 286
Franco, Francisco 278
Franco-Prussian War 286
Franconia 203
Franks 39, 40, 48, 49, 53, 55, 57, 59, 62, 77–81, 87, 89, 106, 107, 108, 124, 126, 138, 169, 194, 203, 219, 240, 245, 285
Frederick I of Prussia 207
Frederick the Great 207
Frederik III of Denmark 186
French language 41, 43, 59, 84, 168, 192, 284, 287
French people 196, 200–1
French Revolution 59, 170, 198, 207, 215, 222, 235, 286
Frisians 80, 81–2, 203, 218, 219, 222, 294
Fritigern 88
Fyrkat 72

G
Gaelic 43, 231
Gagouts 177
Galatia 64
Galicia 134
Galician language 257, 273
Gallia belgica 57, 168, 245
Garibaldi, Giuseppe 243
Garonne, river 152
Gascony 55, 56, 196
Gaul 33, 35, 38, 39, 48, 50, 57, 58–9, 62, 63, 67, 78, 80, 84, 85, 95, 97, 106, 119, 121, 124, 125, 126, 134, 141, 192, 193–4, 293
Gauls 82–4, 118, 238
Geneva 286, 287
Genghis Khan 111
Genoa 241
Gepids 84, 224, 253
German language 41, 178, 202, 237, 284, 287
Germanic languages 42, 44, 80, 82, 91, 98, 107, 130, 183, 202, 218, 227, 279
Germanic peoples 37, 38–9, 40, 48, 51, 54, 62, 68, 79, 81, 84–7, 124, 162, 169, 179, 194, 222, 224, 249, 250, 267
Germans 40, 85–7, 132, 182, 203–4, 209, 210, 226, 264, 265, 303, 304
Germany 29, 37, 48, 56, 57, 62, 63, 67, 81, 95, 96, 104, 109, 111, 121, 125, 126, 131, 132, 160, 164, 172, 176, 181, 184, 187, 190, 199, 200, 202–10, 226, 244, 246, 249, 254, 256, 264, 280, 283, 300
Ghegs 155
Ghent 169
Gibralter 51, 141
Giscard d'Estaing, Valéry 200
Glendower, Owen 1⸺
Gokstad 144
Gorbachev, Mikhail 272
Gotar 135
Gothic language 44, 8
Goths 84, 87, 88–91, 97, 135, 140, 203, 214, 224, 240, 253, 262
Gotland 135, 136, 280

Gournia 109
Granada 52, 104, 277
Great Northern War 283
Greece 14, 16, 26, 29, 30–2, 37, 38, 64, 88, 89, 91–5, 96, 97, 100, 110, 120, 131, 139, 146, 149, 154, 162, 176, 177, 211–7, 237, 244, 302, 306
Greek 29, 76, 91, 211, 237
Greeks 14, 33, 73, 74, 76, 91–5, 106, 137, 152, 177, 217, 257, 274, 290
Greenland 16, 143, 187
Gregory the Great 125
Gregory of Tours 79
Grimaldi 307
Guiscard, Robert 112
Gundobad 62
Gustav Adolphus 282
Gustav Vasa 282
Gwynedd 297
Gypsies 95–6, 177, 209, 226, 264, 265

H

Haakon IV of Norway 251
Haakon VII of Norway 251
Hadrian's Wall 36, 38, 293
Hallstatt 32, 33, 63, 156
Hamburg 206
Hampshire 104
Hannibal 118, 123
Hanover 207
Hanseatic League 162, 164, 206
Hapsburgs 68, 69, 133, 149, 150, 158, 170, 207, 219, 226, 246, 285
Harald Bluetooth 72
Harald Wartooth 71
Harold II 113
Harold I of Norway 249
Hastings (1066) 113
Hedeby 72, 144
Hekataeus 63
Helvetii 33, 284
Henry II 234
Henry V 297
Henry VII 147, 297
Henry VIII 297
Henry VII, Holy Roman Emperor 245
Henry the Navigator 258
Herakles 76
Hercegovina 129, 304
Hermunduri 48
Herodotus 63, 93
Hippo Regius 141
Hitler, Adolf 160, 187, 208–9, 246
Hochdorf 65
Hohenzollerns 207
Holland 72, 77, 81, 168, 184, 218–22
Holstein 187
Holy Roman Emperor 69, 150, 157, 206, 241, 245, 246, 277
Holy Roman Empire 69, 82, 149
Homer 29, 31, 92
Horace 121
Hoxha, Enver 155

Hrolf Kraki 71
Hugh Capet 196
Huguenots 197, 222, 286
Hundred Years' War 196
Hungarian language 42, 77, 156, 178, 188, 223
Hungarians 182, 265, 304
Hungary 40, 41, 53, 64, 84, 95, 96, 97, 106, 109, 111, 128, 131, 149, 150, 156, 157, 159, 179, 180, 223–6, 261, 262, 264, 304
Huns 38–9, 40, 50, 62, 84, 97–8, 111, 139, 140, 157, 174, 224, 262, 288
Hus, Jan 69
Hussites 69, 178
Hywel Dda 147

I

Iazyges 123
Iberia 26
Iberians 98–100, 274
Ice Ages 14, 17, 18, 19, 20, 22, 161, 183, 188, 248, 266, 273, 293
Iceland 16, 143, 227–30
Icelandic 44
Illyrian language 152
Illyrians 100–1, 152, 155, 303
Indo-European languages 41–5, 91, 130, 152, 164, 192, 202
Industrial Revolution 299
Ingolf Arnarson 227
Insular script 232
Iona 232
Ionia 92
Ireland 16, 64, 67, 101–2, 127, 143, 231–6, 296
Irminsul 127
Iron Age 14, 15, 30–3, 105, 123, 135, 183, 257, 261, 279, 284
Italian language 43, 44, 237, 284, 287
Italica 274
Italy 16, 30, 34, 37, 38, 39, 49, 57, 64, 73–6, 80, 82, 83, 89, 90, 92, 95, 97, 104, 106, 107, 108, 112, 114, 117, 118–20, 122, 138, 141, 154, 156, 216, 237–44, 304, 306
Ivan III of Russia 268
Ivan Asen II of Bulgaria 61, 174
Ivan the Terrible 268

J

Jagiello (Vladislav II of Poland) 166, 254
James I 298
James II 220, 235, 298
Jelling 145
Jews 102–4, 151, 177, 186, 209, 222, 226, 256, 264, 265, 277
Joan of Arc 197, 297
John of Bohemia 245

Jordanes 71
Julian, Emperor 48
Julius Caesar 35, 57, 58, 60, 83, 85, 119, 134, 193, 284, 293
Jumièges 113
Justinian, Emperor 131
Jutes 38, 104–5, 124

K
Kalmar, Union of 184, 251, 282
Karelians 77, 188
Kazimiera I of Poland 254
Kent 59, 104, 105, 125
Khazars 133
Kiel, Treaty of 251
Kiev 54, 111, 132, 133, 140, 143, 267, 290
Kirghiz 138
Klosterneuburg 157
Knossos 109, 110
Knowth 101, 231
Kosovo 129, 154
Krakachans 177
Krefeld-Gellep 79
Krim-Goths 90
Kruge 154
Krum (Bulgar ruler) 61
Kursk 54

L
La Tène 33, 64
Labe, river 178
Lacringes 141
Landsmal 248
Langobardi 86, 106
Languages 41–5
Lapp language 42, 279
Lapps 105, 253, 283
Lascaux 21, 193
Latin 76, 80, 84, 91, 131, 146, 202, 257, 261, 273, 294
Latium 73, 117, 118, 123
Latvia 54, 162, 163, 164–5, 190, 282
Lausanne 286
Le Mouster 193
League of Nations 287
Lebanon 114
Lechfeld 109, 157
Leicester 72, 142
Leif Eriksson 143, 251
Lejre 72
Lenin, V.I. 271, 290
Leopold I of Belgium 170
Leopold III of Belgium 172
Lepenski Vir 302
Lettish language 45, 161
Letts 164, 165
Letzeburgisch 245
Liburni 101
Liechtenstein 307
Liguria 119
Ligurians 106, 238
Limerick 234
Lincoln 72, 142, 144
Lincolnshire 125
Lindisfarne 142
Linear A script 110
Lippe, river 127
Lisbon 257, 260
Lithuania 54, 161, 163, 165–7, 190, 254, 256, 270, 290
Lithuanian language 45, 161, 164, 165
Lithuanians 140, 164, 165, 167, 254

Livy 121
Loire, river 126, 192
Lombards 53, 57, 84, 106–8, 138, 160, 210, 224, 240
Lombardy 39, 108, 243
Lorraine 192, 197, 199, 201
Louis XIV 197
Louis XV 198
Low Countries 37, 80, 104, 168–72, 208. *See* Belgium; Holland
Lübeck 184, 206
Lucerne 285
Lugdunensis 193
Lusatia 69
Lusitania 257–8, 275
Luther, Martin 170, 206, 286
Lutzen 282
Luxembourg 69, 87, 168, 218, 219, 245–6
Lyon 36, 66
Lys, river 78

M
Macedonia 15, 94–5, 100, 101, 119, 131, 137, 176, 177, 304, 306
Macedonian language 173, 302
Macedonians 32
Maeatae 115
Magellan, Ferdinand 260
Magna Carta 296
Magnus VI of Norway 251
Magyar language 72, 109

Magyars 40, 53, 68, 69, 108–9, 132, 133, 157, 174, 179, 204, 223, 224, 226, 240, 262, 264, 267, 285, 303
Main, river 127
Mälaren, Lake 135, 136, 144, 280
Mallia 109
Malmedy 208
Manching 66
Manchu language 44
Manzikert 214
Marathon 93
Marcomanni 86, 179, 224
Marcomannic Wars 87
Maria Theresa 158
Marius (Roman general) 85
Marne, river 192, 199
Marseilles 193, 201
Marsi 86
Martel, Charles *see* Charles Martel
Mary Tudor 298
Mary II 299
Marzabotto 74
Massif Central 192
Maximilian I, Holy Roman Emperor 157, 285
Mazzini, Giuseppe 243
McAlpin, Kenneth 115, 128
Mecklenburg 204
Medici family 241, 242
Mediterranean 15, 17, 18, 19, 24, 29, 31–2, 34, 40, 85, 95, 99, 100, 103, 113–4, 142

Megara 92
Meissen 207
Melk 157, 160
Mercia 125, 146
Merida 51, 135
Mesolithic 15, 22, 231
Messina 237
Methodius, St 174, 267
Metternich, 158
Metz 58, 197
Meuse, river 168, 169, 192
Michael the Brave 282
Michael of Romania 264
Miesko (Polish king) 132
Milan 36, 241, 243
Miletus 92
Minoan culture 29, 109–10
Mitterand, François 200
Moesia 70, 174
Moldavia 146, 261, 262, 264
Moldova 263
Monaco 307
Mongolia 139, 268
Mongols 109, 111, 133, 139, 140, 166, 174, 267, 268, 290
Mont-Beuvray 66
Montenegro 303, 304
Morava, river 178, 179
Moravia 69, 108, 132, 178, 179, 181, 182, 204
Moriscos 52
Morken 79
Morocco 51, 260
Moscow 54, 111, 257, 258, 270

Moselle, river 245
Mount Badon 125
Munich Pact 181, 300
Muscovy 268
Muslims 51, 52, 103, 104, 150, 155, 276, 303, 304
Mussolini, Benito 243–4, 204
Mycenaean civilization 29, 30, 54, 91–2, 94, 110, 162, 213, 237

N

Namur 245
Nantes 59
Naples 237, 243
Napoleon 150, 158, 170, 186, 198, 207, 222, 254, 278, 286
Napoleon III 199
Narbonne 99
Naristi 86
Navarino 215
Naxos 93
Nazi regime 96, 181, 187, 208–9, 256, 278
Neanderthals 14, 19–20, 193, 273
Neisse, river 256
Nemenoe 59
Neolithic Age 15, 169, 218, 257
Netherlands 82, 168–72, 207, 218–22, 246, 277. See also Belgium; Holland
Neuwied 79
New Grange 101, 231
Nice 193
Niemen, river 165

Nocera Umbra 108
Noricum 156–7, 231
Normandy 112–3, 126, 143, 196, 249, 296
Normans 102, 112–3, 147, 154, 232, 241, 249, 296
Norrie's Law 116
Norse language 227
Norsemen see Vikings
North Africa 51, 52, 114, 118, 121, 122, 141, 243, 244, 260
North Sea 82, 87, 142, 168
Northumbria 125, 142
Norway 72, 105, 142, 143, 144, 145, 208, 227, 228, 248–52, 279
Norwegian language 183, 227, 248, 279
Nottingham 72, 142, 144
Novgorod 132, 143, 144, 267, 268

O

Oberflacht 49
Octavian 119
Odense 72
Oder, river 17, 131, 132, 202, 204, 253, 256
Odoacar 90
Offa of Mercia 146
Oghuz 139
Olaf I of Norway 228
Olaf II of Norway 249
Olaf Tryggvason 249
Öland 135, 280

Olbia 288
Olof Scotkonung 280
Olympia 93
Orange, House of 246
Orkney Islands 41
Orleans 97, 196, 197
Orvieto 73
Oscan language 44
Oseberg 144, 145
Oslo Fjord 249
Osman al-Ghazi 139
Ostrava 178
Ostrogoths 37, 38, 39, 49, 88, 90, 97, 240, 285
Otho I of Greece 215
Otto I, Holy Roman Emperor 148, 157
Otto I of Germany 109, 149, 240
Ottoman empire 61, 68, 104, 129, 139, 150, 158, 176, 270, See also Turks
Ovid 121
Oxfordshire 125

P

Palaeolithic 14, 193, 257, 266, 293
Palermo 112
Palestine 102, 103
Pamplona 55
Pannonia 106, 224
Panticapaeum 288
Paris 33, 196, 197, 201
Parisi 33
Paros 93
Pas-de-Calais 126
Patrick, St 102, 232
Pavia 241
Pechenegs 133
Peloponnese 91

Pepin the Short 80, 240
Perinthus 137
Perpetual League 285
Persian empire 114, 137
Perugia 75
Peter the Great 164, 270
Petrovic, George 129
Phaistos 109, 110
Pheidias 93
Philip II of Macedon 94, 137, 213
Philip II of Spain 170, 220
Philip Augustus of France 196
Philip the Good of Burgundy 219, 246
Phoenicians 30, 99, 113–4, 257, 274
Piacenza 75
Picts 38, 115–6, 127, 128, 294
Pindal 273
Pisa 241, 242
Plovdiv 173
Po, river 17, 30, 74, 107, 238
Poitiers 51, 80, 276
Poland 39, 62, 69, 88, 103, 111, 128, 130, 132, 141, 149, 150, 159, 162, 166, 181, 182, 208, 253–6, 268, 270, 290
Polanie 253
Polish language 45, 131, 178, 253
Polybius 64
Pombal, Marquis de 260
Pomerania 186, 204, 254

Pompeius Tragus 99
Pompidou, Georges 200
Portugal 28, 91, 98, 150, 257–60
Portuguese language 43, 257
Powys 297
Prague 69, 178, 179, 182
Protestantism 69, 150, 151, 158, 206, 235, 286, 298
Provence 80, 196, 197, 201
Prussia 96, 151, 158, 164, 166, 187, 198, 204, 207–8, 255, 256, 283
Ptolemy 124
Punic Wars 118
Pyrenees 16, 55, 80, 99, 192, 274, 275

Q
Quadi 179, 224
Quisling, Vidkun 252

R
Raeti 284
Ravenna 240
Reform Act (1832) 300
Reformation 235
Reims 58
Remus 116
Renaissance 40, 76, 242, 298
Rennes 59
Reykjavik 227
Rhine, river 17, 48, 50, 57, 77, 80, 85, 87, 121, 134, 141, 168, 169, 202, 219

Rhineland 78, 103
Rhodri the Great 147
Rhône, river 17, 62, 192
Richard II, Duke of Normandy 112
Riga 164
Riksmal 248
Ringerike 145
Risorgimento 243
Rolf (Rollo) 112, 196, 249
Roman Empire 15, 34–7, 70, 71, 74–5, 84, 88, 100, 103, 118–22, 148, 162, 203, 214, 219, 224, 262, 274, 284, 293–4
Romance languages 41–3, 192, 257, 261, 273
Romania 53, 70, 84, 88, 95, 96, 146, 177, 226, 261–5
Romanian language 43, 261
Romans 28, 48, 55, 75, 97, 116–22, 152, 169
Romansch 43, 284, 287
Rome 15, 24, 31, 34–7, 38, 64, 70, 74, 83, 95, 103, 116–8, 141, 238–40, 242, 243, 244
Romulus 34, 116
Roncesvalles 56, 80
Rothart 107
Rouen 112
Roxolani 123
Rugii 157, 224, 285
Runder Berg 49

Russia 16, 17, 18, 24, 39, 40, 50, 54, 61, 64, 67, 70, 72, 76, 77, 90, 96, 97, 103, 105, 111, 130–3, 140, 142, 143, 150, 151, 155, 158, 159, 162–7, 176, 182, 184, 190, 198, 199, 209, 226, 254, 256, 261, 262, 264, 265, 266–72, 280, 283, 290–1
Russian language 45, 131, 173, 266, 288
Ruthenes 180, 181, 264
Ruthenia 182

S
Saale, river 138
Sabines 118, 122
St Brieuc 58
St-Denis 79
St Malo 58
St Petersburg 170
St Pol-de-Leon 58
Salamis 93
Salazar, Antonio 260
Salic Law 80
Salonica 211
Samnites 123
Samo 69, 132
San Marino 308
Sanskrit 41, 91, 96
Sardinia 16, 114
Sarmatians 123–4, 128, 288
Sarmizegethusa 70
Savoy 197
Saxons 38, 39, 51, 80, 81, 104, 124–7, 194, 201, 203, 219, 222, 294
Saxony 80, 126, 203

Index 319

...a 16, 17,
1, 85, 88,
', 183, 184
ver 78, 168
187, 208
-Holstein
187
203, 210
35
04, 67, 101,
127–8, 143,
2, 293, 294,
-7, 298–9
234
7–8, 232,
04
s 32, 123,
39, 261, 267,

World War
1, 160, 163,
5, 172,
182, 187,
0, 216, 222,
6, 252, 256,
4, 271, 278,
6, 291, 300,

er 17, 78,
2
9, 131, 151,
3, 304, 306
bat 45, 131,
2
68, 129,
4, 265, 303,
06
Bishop 157
, 52, 135
7
56, 268, 271
0
0
26, 92, 95,
14, 118, 130,
41, 243, 244

Sidon 114
Siena 241
Silesia 69, 208, 254, 255
Simeon I of Bulgaria 61, 174
Sinn Fein 236
Skanderbeg 154
Slavic languages 44–5, 253, 266, 288, 302
Slavs 37, 39, 40, 53, 60, 61, 68, 80, 108, 130–3, 157, 174, 179, 182, 194, 204, 210, 214, 253, 254, 262, 267, 268, 272, 290, 303
Slovak language 131, 178, 253
Slovakia 132, 178, 182
Slovaks 69, 133, 179, 180, 182, 224, 226, 264
Slovene language 131, 156, 237, 302
Slovenes 129, 134, 303
Slovenia 129, 134, 159, 303–6, 309
Smolensk 132, 143
Smyrna 216
Snorri Sturluson 228
Sofia 173
Soissons 58, 78
Sophocles 93
Soviet Union 151, 271–2
Spain 16, 18, 28, 30, 37, 38, 39, 50, 52, 55, 63, 78, 80, 89, 90, 95, 96, 98, 99, 100, 103, 104, 113, 114, 118, 119, 121, 134–5, 141, 143,

150, 151, 158, 170, 220, 242, 246, 260, 273–8
Sparta 92, 93, 94
Spina 74
Spoleto 240
Stalin, Josef 155, 271, 272, 291
Stalingrad 209
Stamford 72, 142
Stefan Dusan 154
Stefan Nemanya 129
Stephen I of Hungary 109
Stockholm 280, 282
Stone Age 14–5, 20, 22–6, 101, 211, 261
Stonehenge 293
Stuttgart 207
Sudetenland 181, 182
Suevi 50, 55, 134–5, 141, 258, 275
Sumeria 26
Suomalaiset 77, 188
Sussex 59, 125
Sutton Hoo 125, 136
Svear 135
Sweden 71, 72, 77, 105, 135–6, 142, 144, 150, 184, 186, 188–90, 191, 249, 251, 268, 279–83
Swedes 135–6, 191, 283
Swedish language 44, 183
Switzerland 22, 33, 48, 207, 284–7
Syracuse 73, 237
Syria 139

T

Tacitus 38, 106, 121
Tallinn 162

Tannenberg 166
Tara 102
Tarquinii 72, 75, 76
Tarquinius Priscus 117
Tarquinius II 118
Tarragona 274
Tatars 291
Tavastians 77
Tencteri 86
Tervel (Bulgar leader) 61
Tesin 182
Teutones 85
Teutonic Knights 162, 164, 166, 204
Thebes 214
Theodoric the Great 90, 240
Thera 29, 110
Thermopylae 93
Theudelinda 108
Thirty Years War 69, 158, 186, 206, 286
Thrace 94, 137, 174, 176, 177
Thracians 177, 306
Thucydides 93
Thuringians 80, 138, 203
Tisza, river 123
Tito 129, 304, 306
Toledo 51, 52
Tomislav (Croatian king) 68
Torquemada 277
Tosks 155
Toul 197
Toulouse 89
Tournai 78
Trafalgar 198
Trajan, Emperor 70, 262
Transylvania 224, 226, 261, 264, 265
Trelleborg 72

Treveri 33
Trier 33, 58, 78
Trieste 304
Tripolitania 243
Trojan War 92
Troy 29, 116
Tunis 114
Turkey 16, 17, 91, 95, 138–9, 176, 198, 214–5, 216, 217, 262, 264
Turkic languages 98
Turks 53, 61, 68, 122, 129, 138–9, 150, 154, 157–8, 176, 177, 214–15, 224, 242, 262, 268, 303
Turku, Treaty of 190
Turnovo 174
Tuscany 30, 73, 241–
Tyre 114

U

Ukraine 39, 88, 97, 111, 130, 131, 140, 166, 254, 256, 264, 267, 270, 288–91
Ukrainian language 131, 140, 266, 288
Ulfila, Bishop 89
Ulster 231, 235, 236
Umbria 73
United Kingdom 292–301. *See also* England; Scotland; Wales
United Nations 287, 291
Unterwalden 285
Uppsala 136, 144, 280
Url 286
Urnes 145

V

Valsgärde 136, 280
Vandals 38, 50, 134, 141, 240, 253, 275
Varangian Guard 143
Varna 173
Vasco da Gama 260
Vascones 56
Vatican City 308
Veii 73, 75, 118
Vendel 136, 280
Veneti 58
Venice 154, 214, 241, 242, 243
Verdun 197, 199
Vergil 121
Versailles Treaty 208
Victor Emmanuel II of Italy 243
Victoria, Queen 300
Vienna 158, 224
Vienna, Congress of 246
Vikings 24, 40, 41, 54, 59, 82, 102, 112, 132, 142–5, 162, 184, 232, 233–4, 249, 267, 280, 290, 296
Vilnius 166, 167
Vindelici 284
Vis 303
Visconti family 241
Visigoths 37, 38–9, 51, 52, 55, 78, 88, 89–90, 97, 103, 135, 174, 194, 200, 240, 276
Vistula, river 17, 39, 85, 88, 130, 131, 143, 166, 253, 254
Vix 65
Vlachs 146, 177, 262, 265
Vlad the Impaler 267
Vladimir the Great 267
Vladislav II of Poland 166
Vlata, river 178
Volga, river 17, 108, 143, 266, 267, 268
Volsci 118
Voltaire 150
Vortigern 125
Vouille 78
Vulci 73, 75
Vyborg 190

W

Walachia 146, 262, 264
Wales 64, 67, 146–7, 292, 294, 296, 297
Walloons 168, 172
War of Spanish Succession 158, 278
Waterford 234
Waterloo 150, 198
Welsh language 43, 147, 292
Welsh people 146–7
Weser, river 85, 302
Wessex 125
West Indies, migrants from 151
Westphalia, Peace of 206
Wexford 235
Widukind 127
Wight, Isle of 104
Wilhelm I of Prussia 208
William the Silent 220
William I 113, 196, 296
William III 220, 299
William Nethe 246
William 297
Winches
Wollin 1
Worms 6

Y

Yeltsin, B
York 144
Yorkshire
Yugoslavi 68, 129, 150, 15 244, 30

Z

Zadar 30
Zakro 10
Zhivkov,
Zog of Al
Zurich 28
Zwingli, 286